S0-BZI-659

The unlimited POWER OF PRAYER

The unlimited POWER OF PRAYER

Doubleday & Company, Inc.
Garden City, New York
1982

The Unlimited Power of Prayer was originally published by Guideposts Associates in 1980.
Library of Congress Catalog Card Number: 81-43448
ISBN: 0-385-17235-4

Printed in the United States of America

Credits

"The Man from Ida Grove" excerpted from *The Man from Ida Grove* by Harold E. Hughes with Dick Schneider. Copyright © 1978 Harold E. Hughes. Published by Chosen Books, Lincoln, Virginia. Used by permission. "In the Morning of My Life" excerpted from *In the Morning of My Life* by Tom Netherton and Marie Chappian. Published by Tyndale House Publishers, Inc. Copyright © 1979. Used by permission. "Will You Take This Man?" excerpted from *A Walk Across America* by Peter Jenkins. Published by William Morrow & Company. Copyright © 1979. Used by permission. "Prayer for the Fourth of July" excerpted from *Hold Me Up a Little Longer, Lord* by Marjorie Holmes. Copyright © 1971, 1972, 1973, 1974, 1975, 1976, 1977. Published by Doubleday & Company, Inc. Used by permission. "The Way of Acceptance" by Arthur Gordon appeared in the May 1967 *Readers Digest*. "The Vacant Seat" by Don Mott. Reprinted by permission of Good News Publishers, Westchester, Illinois.

OUR FATHER,

which art in heaven,
Hallowed be thy name.
Thy kingdom come.
Thy will be done in earth,
as it is in heaven.
Give us this day our daily bread.
And forgive us our debts,
as we forgive our debtors.
And lead us
not into temptation,
but deliver us from evil:
For thine is
the kingdom, and the power,
and the glory, for ever.
Amen.

Matthew 6:9-13

ABOUT THIS BOOK

In this book you will find true stories about people—ordinary people like yourself—who have experienced the mysterious power of prayer. Some of their prayers are wordless whispers from the heart; some anguished cries of people in pain or danger. Others are thoughtful petitions, reverently offered. All demonstrate the reality of the unlimited power that is available to those who call upon God.

Do you sometimes feel that your own prayers are earthbound, ineffective, unanswered? If so, let this book show you how power-filled prayer led others to life-changing experiences. Remember, that power is available for your life, too.

To use this book effectively, read it through in its entirety. Then keep it close at hand. Consider it your personal storehouse of inspiration to dip into again and again for courage, comfort and guidance.

At the end of each chapter you will find *Spiritual Workshops* specifically designed to help the serious student of prayer experiment with step-by-step exercises in prayer power. Use these to strengthen any weak areas in your spiritual life and to broaden the scope of your prayer concerns.

Finally, all of us who have prepared this book offer this prayer:

Lord,
May these stories, lessons and prayers
serve to bring all who read them
into closer communion with You.
Grant that they may experience
Your kingdom,
Your power,
Your glory.
Amen

The Editors

CONTENTS

CHAPTER 1 LORD, HELP ME

CHAPTER 2 LORD, CHANGE ME

CHAPTER 3 LORD, HEAL ME

PAGE

CHAPTER 4 LORD, GUIDE ME

PAGE

CHAPTER 5 LORD, GIVE ME HOPE

PAGE

CHAPTER 6 LORD, GIVE ME GRATITUDE

PAGE

CHAPTER 7 LORD, GIVE ME COMPASSION

PAGE

The Unlimited Power of Prayer

LORD, HELP ME

Chapter 1

When danger strikes you have to respond quickly. You must rely on your reflexes. Some people fight; others flee. But some have another reflex grounded in faith. They pray.

That is exactly what the people in the following stories did. They prayed to God in their time of peril and He responded. He reached into the very heart of their own fear and danger and led them to safety. Their true tales are dramatic testimonies to the power of prayer as a reflex action. Did you know that power can be yours?

The Bible promises: "God is our refuge and strength, a very present help in trouble." (Psalms 46:1) When you face danger, when you are frightened, call out to God. He hears you as surely as He heard the ancient cry of the Psalmist . . . as surely as he hears the pleas of believers today. He is your *present* help.

When the accident occurred, she wanted to die. But she was given life instead.

A PROMISE MADE, A PROMISE KEPT

Diane Bringgold

Far up in Northern California, in the awesomely lovely wilderness of glacial lakes and towering granite pinnacles beneath Mount Shasta, there is a rocky height that is called Black Butte. Its slopes are steep and covered with boulders and loose gray shale. A few trees struggle to survive on its surface. To me Black Butte is the ugliest place in the world, and the most beautiful, for it is a place of terrible death, and vibrant life. On a December evening in 1975 I lay on its slope and asked to die, but I was given life instead, and faith to sustain it. It was a faith I didn't know I lacked.

The day after Thanksgiving that year Bruce and I and our three children flew up into the Shasta region from our home in Southern California. We had an invitation for the weekend from our across-the-street friends in Ventura, Bill and Edy LeFevre, who had a family compound of rustic cabins and a huge Victorian house near Dunsmuir. It was an easy trip for us to make, for we were a flying family. Both Bruce and I were licensed pilots and our kids were accustomed to being in the air.

On this Friday our own plane was down for its 100-hour checkup, but we managed to rent an identical aircraft which would accommodate the five of us as well as a couple we'd asked along, Jim and Virginia Dixon. Jim, like Bruce, was a successful attorney in Ventura.

The flight north was quick and easy, just like the weekend, which passed much too speedily. The mountain air was tingling cold, and the kids ran about and played at high speed. Proper Southern Californians, they were excited by the ice on the swimming pool, and when it snowed on Saturday, they flapped around in it like happy penguins.

On Sunday it snowed again, off and on. From time to time Bruce would put on his jacket and wander outside. He was like that wherever we went; his pilot's instinct kept him sniffing at the weather. We planned to fly home that afternoon, but the ceiling stayed too low.

On Sunday morning I went to a little Episcopal mission church in Dunsmuir where the priest, Father Torgerson, delivered a Thanksgiving sermon. Had it entered my mind, that quiet Thanksgiving weekend would have been a good time for me to have taken spiritual stock of myself, but when you have a multitude of blessings, you often fail to notice them.

My life was rich. I had Bruce, whom I loved, and our marriage of 14 years was good by any standard. Bruce had a fine law practice and was a leader in civic affairs. Our children were delights to us. They were all exactly two years and nine months apart in age, starting with Scott, who was 11, then Mary, who copied Scott in everything, and then our little Laura.

As for me, I was busy at home and in the community, and in our church especially. Shortly before my marriage to Bruce I'd made a commitment to Christ, and yet, in spite of all my conscious efforts to lead a Christian life, in spite of all my sincere work in church activities, my prayer life was not an active one; I had never really faced the fact that my faith was important to me, but not central to my life. There was always a hidden doubt, something left over from the intellectual probings of college days, I think, that stopped me from turning over my life to Him completely.

On Monday morning our hosts left for Ventura in their motor home while we waited, our eyes on the sky. Finally, in the afternoon, Bruce made another call to the weather station. "It's breaking to the north," he told me. "I think we can go."

A caretaker drove us out to the Dunsmuir airstrip. Bruce looked up at the sky. "The ceiling looks high enough for safety," he said. But still he hesitated. "Just to make sure, let's see what it's really like up north." We got in the car again and drove to Shasta, about half an hour away. True enough, it was clearing. "We'll fly north," he told me. "We'll take advantage of the wide valley up there. There'll be plenty of room to climb in."

The takeoff was simple. I felt relieved that it had all been so easy, and was just beginning to relax when the weather closed in around us. The clouds pushed lower and lower. We flew lower and lower to keep beneath them. Then they began breaking up into fog. Straining to follow the points on the ground, I tried to help Bruce navigate.

"I can't see, Bruce," I said, alarmed. My always calm husband now seemed to be getting nervous, too. "We've got to turn around," I shouted, and even as the words came out I knew that it would be more dangerous to do that than to go ahead. And then, in the most terrifying moment of my life, I saw the ground. "Bruce, the trees!" I screamed. Bruce saw them, too, and turned the plane to the left, but there wasn't time.

We hit. The plane slid, then jarred sharply. I was knocked unconscious.

We had come to Black Butte.

I don't know how long I was unconscious. A minute or two, I think. The next thing I remember, I felt the weight of Bruce's body against me. He was dead. I looked back. The Dixons were gone—the doors on either side had popped open—and the kids, the kids weren't moving. In the same flashing second that I knew they, too, were gone, orange fire burst out of the instrument panel. I threw my hands over my eyes and screamed as the flames seared my face. I squirmed, struggling to get free of the seatbelt that held me. The belt flipped open. I pulled myself out from under Bruce and through the door. There was no drop, for the plane was level with the ground as I crawled out the uphill side. Flames shot out from the engine to the gas tanks on the wings and everything exploded. The plane somersaulted into the air and came crashing down to lie on its back.

I lay on the slope of Black Butte in the darkness. I couldn't look at the plane. *Bruce,* my mind kept repeating, *Scott . . . Mary . . . Laura . . .* I lay there knowing that I was severely burned, one side of my face in shreds, my right hand causing me agony. *Dead, all my loved ones are dead . . .* I kept thinking.

"Diane! Diane!" My name. Called in the mist. Virginia's voice. "Are you there, Diane?"

I did not answer. I did not want to answer.

"Diane. Answer me if you can. Please."

I dragged myself over to some rocks where a tree had fallen. I tried to hide myself behind them. I did not want to live without Bruce and our children. I did not want to face the physical pain of my burned body, or its ugliness. "I can't handle it," I said to myself.

And at that moment, five feet away, a figure appeared in the fog, a figure robed in white. I cannot tell you the color of hair or eyes, but this obviously was a man, a large man, larger than most, and He stood suffused in light, not like the light of a flashbulb, not a beam, but a soft luminescence.

I knew without any doubt or surprise that this was Jesus Christ. He was too far away for me to touch, but close enough for me to hear Him perfectly. He stood majestically in front of me, yet His Presence was not overpowering. I had no sense of awe; a sense of amazement perhaps, but I didn't feel that He was some omnipotent being to whom I couldn't relate.

"It's not for you to decide whether to live or to die, Diane," He said. "That's My decision to make."

I still did not want to live, and I replied, "It's easy for You to say, Lord, but I can't handle being widowed, and childless, and being badly burned as well. Maybe two, but not all three." It sounded like a flip statement; I didn't mean it to be. "If You want me to live, I will give You my life. You will have to handle the grief, the pain and the loneliness; I can't."

Suddenly, He was gone. It wasn't as though He walked away. One moment He was there, the next He wasn't. But when He left, I knew that I could conquer the grief and the pain and the loneliness; I could handle whatever lay ahead, because He was going to be there, helping me. For me, that is the meaning of the gift of faith that I received on cold, mist-bound Black Butte. All doubt was abolished. What the Bible said about asking and receiving was all true. Jesus was real.

For two years now Jesus has been with me. Have I suffered? Yes. But He has made it bearable, for He was there when I found the will to call out to Jim and Virginia down the mountainside; they were seriously injured, too, but not critically. Jesus was there when the young hikers who saw the flash of fire arrived, and when the girl held my head in her lap while I kept telling her how brave she was to hold me, looking the way I did, and she kept saying, "No, *you're* the one who's brave." He was there in the emergency ward down in Shasta when my vital signs were so unstable that the doctors thought I'd not survive, but I knew I would, and that I'd recover fully. He was there on the three-hour ambulance drive in the fog to the hospital in Chico where a mass of people in green hats and masks rushed me into surgery. He has been there during all the months of these past two years, and He has kept His promise to handle the hurts that once caused me to prefer death to life.

How has He helped me?

For the first week or so in the hospital, it took all my resources, physical, emotional and otherwise, just to begin the healing process. I didn't have any energy left to grieve. Bruce and the children were always in the back of my mind, but by the time I was well enough to face life without them, the sharpest pain of loss had been blunted. Jesus did that for me.

That is not to say that there were not times in the middle of the night when I'd start to cry and ask the "Why me?" questions, but those depressions would only last a little while because I'd pray to Him, and He would help me cope.

"Lord, why did You take them?" I said out loud one night, but the words were no sooner out than I felt ashamed. *How selfish I am,* I thought. And I was. Knowing that Christ was real, knowing that I myself had seen Him, how could I begrudge my loved ones the life they now had with Him? To this day I miss them, and sometimes I ache to have them back, but I rejoice for them, and I'm always grateful that they didn't suffer or be crippled or live in pain.

As for my own pain, He has taken care of that, too. For anyone like me who once dreaded the tiny sting of a hot iron, who was a sissy about needles, I've felt astonishingly little pain. There were a few bad times, early on in the hospital during the four times a day when we changed dressings, but I've gone back to Chico five times for additional surgery in the last two years, and except for one pain pill, I remember no post-operative suffering.

Loneliness? Yes, from time to time I feel it. But the surprising thing is that when I tend to get depressed it isn't when I'm at home. I continue to live in the same house we lived in before the crash. There are pictures of Bruce and the children around me, just as before. But this house is full of good memories. I don't feel alone here. No, if ever I'm inclined to get sad, it's in the hospital, or as an out-patient in a motel room. At times like that I've learned to say, "Hey, Lord, I really need somebody to be here," and then the phone will ring and some friend will be calling. If it's late at night, too late for anyone to be phoning, I'll start to pray hard, and He will come to me. I don't see Him, not the way I did on the mountainside, but I can feel Him, and it's just as if someone were there holding me, saying, "It's okay, you're all right."

Often when I tell people about meeting the Living Christ on Black Butte, I can see by their expression that they think I dreamed the whole thing up out of my own need. I can understand this. I also know that a lot of people have been watching me, waiting for the full realization of loss to hit me, waiting for me to fall apart. But the longer it goes on, the longer I show my strength—the strength He has given me—the more these people themselves are going to start believing that the Lord is alive and working in the world, their world. I know that He presented Himself to me because He wanted me to have the faith I lacked, the faith I want everybody to know about, the faith that says you can go through fire and come out strong, and beautiful.

The violent wind shook the tree in which this family of five had taken refuge. The water rose higher...

HURRICANE!

Frank Eifert

Lucinda Sears stared out over Lake Okeechobee with a troubled light in her eye. The sky was darkening and the wind was whipping dust about the sides of her cabin.

It was a day in September that southern Florida will never forget. A monstrous storm was on its way, but people like Charles and Lucinda Sears and their three children—people who lived just off Florida's biggest lake—had no warning of its approach.

A tall, proud woman, Lucinda had worked hard with her husband to make a living and build their small home. When the storm came, she closed the windows. Then she and Charles watched the dust whipping around the cabin. The wind increased and soon their roof blew off as if it were a piece of cardboard.

The terrifying storm had boiled up out of the Caribbean, intent on destroying everything within its 500-mile range. The monster slashed its way through Miami, roared across the Everglades and up the peninsula, leaving behind destruction and death. The dead were everywhere: among the timbers and masonry of demolished homes, in city streets and on highways.

As soon as the roof had blown off their cabin, Lucinda grabbed her daughter, Effie Ann, not quite two years old, while her husband, Charles, reached for their two sons, Cleofus, almost five, and Charles Jr., three. They ran outside looking for shelter.

All they could see was an old bent tree which had withstood an earlier storm. The nine-foot mud dike around the lake had burst with the pressure of the flood. The rising water drenched them and made everything so slippery that Cleofus dropped from Charles' arms and disappeared for a moment. Charles, balancing the other boy in one arm, finally pulled Cleofus from the watery muck. Then carrying the children, Lucinda and her husband climbed into the tree's sheltering branches.

Silently they watched as their cabin broke into pieces. Parts of a chair, a dishpan, blankets, shoes, lamps—everything they owned—washed by them in one enormous wall of water.

Cleofus was limp; he had swallowed too much water. Was he gone? The father, his arms aching, worked on his small son. Soon he felt the child's breath faintly against his ear. Just the slightest breath, but it was enough to start him working more frantically to drain the water out of his son. Soon Cleofus was joining his little brother in whimpering: a blessed sound now.

The fury of the storm grew. As the water level rose, the frightened family climbed higher into the tree until they were clinging desperately to the top branches which were thrashing wildly in the mighty gusts of wind. The water slowly began to creep up around their bodies. They could climb no higher.

Night came. The enraged wind tore unabated at the family in the tree. Torrents of rain stung them. And the water inched relentlessly higher, slowly reaching muddy hands of death toward them.

Once Charles slipped and he and the two boys were nearly swept away. Lucinda made Effie Ann lock her little arms around her neck and then, legs wrapped around a branch, Lucinda reached down and one by one pulled the boys up with her. She held all three children until Charles could get back into the tree and again help her.

After a while even breathing became a struggle. Charles called through the screaming wind:

"Cindy, we're all gonna die."

Her voice rang back across the tempest.

"No, honey, we're not gonna die. God's right here with us!"

The water was almost up to her neck. She was straining to hold Effie Ann's head above the water. How could she believe they would live?

"Cindy, if I could just get closer to you. . . ."

"You just hold on to those boys!" she called back.

Praying for a little more strength in her almost paralyzed arms, she painfully lifted Effie Ann a fraction higher. Faintly she heard her husband's voice again.

"Not much more time."

She lifted her eyes to a stygian sky, to One Whose quiet command had stilled another tempest in Galilee. Then she began to sing, accompanied by the gurgling of water and roar of the wind:

Father, I stretch my hands to Thee,
No other help I know;
If Thou withdraw Thyself from me,
Ah, whither shall I go. . . .
Author of faith, to Thee I lift
My weary, longing eyes;
O may I now receive that gift;
My soul, without it, dies.

As Charles Wesley's old hymn was carried away on the wind, it seemed to Lucinda that she could hear a great chorus of angels singing with her. And as she reached higher for the everlasting arms of faith, she saw three flashes of light streak across the eastern sky in perfectly timed succession.

"Thank You, God. Thank You," she murmured. She knew without a doubt that the flashes of light had been a sign from God.

It was no surprise to her at all when the water began slowly, very slowly, to recede.

The wind slackened, spent, decreasing with the reluctance of an ebbing tide. The storm drifted back to the sea to hide its face. Then it was quiet once more.

The family in the tree, muscles aching, chilled to the bone, hungry and thirsty, clung to the branches, waiting through the long hours of the night.

The children whimpered low and then, too tired to even whine, they were silent, half-sleeping burdens to be held close. It was well into the next day before the waters were low enough for the parents to climb from the tree and wade to safety. They stumbled to an aid station in a state of shock. Tender hands ministered to them and put them to bed.

Their night of terror had passed. But that's not all the story. Not for tall, proud Lucinda who, within inches of death, sang a song of faith into the teeth of one of the worst hurricanes on record.

For, eight days after the storm, Lucinda bore her fourth child—a healthy girl.

KEEP ME SAFE, LORD

Lord, be Thou within me, to
strengthen me;
Without me, to keep me;
Above me, to protect me;
Beneath me, to uphold me;
Before me, to direct me;
Behind me, to keep me from straying;
Round about me, to defend me.
Blessed be Thou, our Father for ever
and ever.

Lancelot Andrewes

Empty—emotionally and spiritually—this actress recalls the day she gave up on life.

HAND ON MY SHOULDER

Virginia Graham

As a child there were many times when I went to bed fearful of the darkness because I was unable to touch and see the things that made my waking hours secure. Then my father would pillow my face in his palm and tell me stories about men and women of the Bible. He made these people come alive and the miracles of faith seem very real.

"God's love will always sustain you," he would say. "It sustains everyone who seeks Him."

One night I asked him, "Papa, you've been up in a plane and seen how small the houses and cars are? Well, how can God have eyes and ears which can see and hear everyone and everything in all those millions of houses and cars?" And then I got to the question that really bothered me: "How can I hear Him?"

And my father replied, "If you stop talking long enough, you can hear Him. God is inside you. He loves you and He is there to help you when things go wrong."

The wisdom of his faith grew in me, like an inner companion, and when Father passed on I felt that my faith was strong enough to help me over life's bumps. The first test came at age 19 when I was in an automobile accident. After surgery and prolonged treatment the doctors said that in all probability I would never be able to bear a child.

At first I refused to accept this verdict. Many prayers later I saw that we can hardly expect to have everything we want, even if we want it very much. Our way, our will, are not as important as God's will.

Some years later when I met and fell in love with Harry Gussenberg, I told him that we probably wouldn't be able to have children. Nine months and four days after we were married our daughter, Lynn, was born.

In the years which followed I began to get sudden temperatures and infections without any apparent reasons for them. Yet there was no loss of weight and certainly no loss of energy. I was active and busy, both as a mother and in radio work, and my energy seemed to come not so much from physical strength as from spiritual vitality. The doctors took dozens of tests and found nothing wrong.

One test, however, revealed something they hadn't even looked for in the first place: I was to have another baby. I was the happiest woman alive because the gift of life was going to be mine again.

One night three months later I suddenly felt a terrible pain and was rushed to the hospital. I was taken immediately into surgery. When I awoke the next morning the room was empty and gray, except for the sunlight filtering through the venetian blinds. When my doctor came in, his face told me that the news was not good.

"You lost the baby," he said. Then he added hesitantly, "There were other complications too."

Just then Harry entered. He looked pale and worn. Gently he took my hand. "I want you to go to sleep now," he said.

"I don't want to go to sleep," I said, miserably. "I want to go home."

"You've got to go to sleep," Harry insisted. He turned his face away and then left the room.

I turned to the doctor. "Why is he acting so peculiar? I'll be going home tomorrow, won't I?"

"No. We're going to have to do a little more surgery."

"What do you mean? What surgery?"

Then for a while time seemed to hang in suspension. When my heart and mind began working again, I looked imploringly at the doctor and asked, "Do I have cancer?"

He is one of the sweetest and gentlest and finest men in the world, but he couldn't erase the answer I saw in his eyes. In agony of spirit I clutched his sleeve, "I'm not going to die! You told me I had no cancer!"

"Virginia," he pleaded gently, "Virginia, that was a preliminary test. I thought you were intelligent enough to understand. . . ."

"Intelligent!" I shouted. "A woman of 36 with a child and a husband and the glorious experience of living. How do you ever get intelligent enough to accept cancer?"

Harry came back into the room and on his anguished face was the same knowledge that was now mine.

After a while they quieted me with sedatives.

A day later the parade of doctors and tests began. On the second day I told myself, "This is not going to be. I cannot inflict this pain on my husband and child too. I cannot kill them."

And my heart cried out, "I have tried to love where it was needed. God, why have You failed me? How could You betray me like this? You do not love me."

I was angry and for the first time in my life I knew the terrible emptiness of being alone.

My head was whirling. I picked up the phone and called Harry and said, "I am not going to put you and Lynn through this suffering. Thank you for all the wonderful years we've had. I want you to know that what I am going to do is best."

I hung up, got out of bed and walked to the window. The day was bleak, gray and sunless. Deliberately I raised the window and swung one leg over the sill. I turned to swing the other leg out. But suddenly there was a powerful grip on my shoulder. It was real, very real, as real as my breath. I knew who it was.

"Papa," I said. "Papa, you told me that God is in me. What happened?"

His voice was clear, as if he were talking to his small child: "Don't let anger and fear talk. Listen. Listen to His voice. God is in you. His love will sustain you."

The voice diminished to a whisper, then faded. "Don't go, Papa, don't go. . . ."

But the strong grip on my shoulder was gone. I looked up. The sun was beginning to probe through the gray overcast and light was pouring through the window. I put my hand to my face and realized it was wet with tears. I knew I could not take my life. Only the Giver of life could be the Taker. I could only accept His will, not mine.

I swung my leg back over the sill into the room. A flood of relief swept over me, as if cold water had been poured over a burning person.

The next morning I was taken to the operating room for ten hours of surgery. I was ready for it—and for the 35 radium treatments in the weeks that followed. The strength to go through this was given me as I needed it.

Many years have passed and my doctor still talks about that experience and says, "There was always something in you that made me feel you were going to make it. Your recovery was a kind of miracle."

And I tell him—and the world—that what he calls a miraculous recovery was only God in me—or me in Him. This is stated better in His Book: *For in Him we live, and move, and have our being.* *

*Acts 17:28

A PRAYER UNDER PRESSURE

Our Father, when we long for life without trials and work without difficulties, remind us that oaks grow strong in contrary winds and diamonds are made under pressure.

With stout hearts may we see in every calamity an opportunity and not give way to the pessimism that sees in every opportunity a calamity.

Peter Marshall

Our house spun like a top. How would I save my family?

THE DAM'S BROKEN

Dave Eby

The rain was coming down in torrents that night, as the wind howled and a terrific thunderstorm raged. Eventually the storm knocked out the electricity for the campus of Toccoa Falls College where I am the Dean of Men. We live on the campus, which nestles in the gentle foothills of Northeast Georgia. Our house is located across a street and a creek from the men's dormitory, Forrest Hall. When the lights went out around 9:30 p.m., several guys in the dorm took advantage of the darkness to play some practical jokes. The victims of these pranks were not amused and tempers flared. So for several hours I had to deal with those problems. It did not make my day any better.

November 5, 1977, had not been a good day for me at all. My wife, Barbara, had put some things on lay-away for the kids' Christmas gifts with money we simply did not have, and the kids had gotten on my nerves at supper.

I went to bed around 12:30 after watching a little TV to help me relax. But it would be a night I would never forget. For up on the mountain, above the 186-foot-high Toccoa Falls, a 55-acre man-made lake was relentlessly gnawing the old dam with the pressure of 176 million gallons of water. Finally, at 1:30 in the morning, with a tremendous roar, a wall of water burst through the dam, unleashing some 700,000 tons of irresistible fury. With unbelievable speed, this juggernaut raced down the mountains and through the forest, crushing trees like matchsticks. Faster and faster it rushed to the lip of Toccoa Falls where it plunged the 186 feet at an estimated 150 miles an hour.

Barb and I were awakened by what I thought at first was an earth tremor. But Barbara jumped out of bed and yelled, "The dam's broken!"

"You're crazy," I retorted as I pulled the curtains apart to look outside. The water looked higher, and as my eyes adjusted to a street light I suddenly realized the water was almost level with the house windows.

As Barb ran through the playroom to get the kids, the nightlight went out as a result of a transformer upstream being engulfed. However, she managed to grab Kim, our older daughter, age seven, and bring her back to me in the bedroom. Then she rushed back to get the other two children, Kevin, five and Kelly, two.

I decided to try and break out through a window in the bedroom so Kim and I could run up the mountain beside our house. In my anxiety I did not even notice the gash I inflicted on my arm at this time. To make things worse, there was plastic on the other side of the glass and punching through that was like hitting Jell-O.

Meanwhile, Barb had gotten the other two kids, whose room was on the corner of the house nearest the creek. They were in the hallway running back to our bedroom when a 30-foot wall of water swept over the house. Suddenly a slimy, brown liquid accompanied by a sickening stench was pouring through the windows.

The house groaned as it was ripped off of its foundation. Floor boards buckled, walls were torn out of place and even the carpet was peeled off its base. The tremendous force of the water twirled the house downstream like a merry-go-round. This violent circular motion prevented Barb and the kids from ever reaching our bedroom. They were forced out into the living room where they grabbed onto four spindles that connected a five-foot-high wall divider to the ceiling.

In the meantime, the water had pushed Kim and me through a bedroom door into a utility room that we had added to the house. Then the floor lifted up and shoved us against the ceiling by the back door of the room. Barb could hear us struggling as we tried to get out.

The whole utility room then broke off from the rest of the house. This kept Kim and me from being crushed and drowned. But now we were also thrown out into the water.

Somehow in the darkness we were washed up against the house and I caught hold of the roof.

The house continued spinning through the waters for about 50 yards until it wedged itself between the heating pipes of what had been an old warehouse.

Eventually I was able to put Kim on the roof and then climb up myself. Although we were safe, for the moment, I thought for sure that Barb and the other two kids were dead. I tried to prepare Kim for this: I told her I was afraid the others were lost. She nodded silently, as if she understood.

Sitting on the rough surface of the roof we watched the swirling waters shatter the music building across the street. A little while later I saw the roof of the utility room floating nearby. I thought that if we could leap onto it, maybe we could somehow paddle it over to safe ground. So I coaxed Kim to climb up on my back, paused for a second and then made a frantic leap. Unfortunately the roof went to pieces when I landed on it, and Kim fell off. The water closed over my head.

Then, in the next few moments, I experienced something I will never forget. I thought to myself, *My wife is gone, my kids are gone and I'm the only one left. Nobody knows I am under this cold, filthy water. Nobody knows my pain and sorrow.*

But suddenly, in that moment of the most awful loneliness I have ever experienced, I felt God's presence. *He* knew I was there and that was enough. If I died, I knew I would be with God and with my family.

At the same time, I felt two small arms grab my neck and a frightened little girl's voice say, "Don't let go of me again, Daddy!"

Somehow just hearing Kim's voice gave me new strength.

We bobbed to the surface and hung on to the awning that had been part of the door to the utility room. A wild hope came to me that maybe if we were still alive the others might be, too. I began shouting for Barb at the top of my lungs. To my amazement, through the roar of the water came a happy voice that sounded far away. And then two other little voices started yelling excitedly. Soon, the whole family was shouting in joy that we were all still alive.

But the danger was not over yet. The force of the water

was still powerful and we were getting weaker by the minute. Barb's arms were becoming numb from the strain of having to hold the kids and herself.

We then decided to pray that God would either allow the water to drop quickly or that He would bring death painlessly. We had to yell at the top of our lungs to be heard, and even little Kevin was praying with the rest of us.

Within seconds, it seemed there was a definite shift in our house and the water seemed to drop quickly to a safer level. There was also a quiet conviction that with God's help we had made it.

By now we could see people on the other side of the water, so we started yelling to them. Eventually several ambulances and fire trucks arrived. Someone shouted, "How many are there?"

I yelled back, "All of us!" A cheer went up from the other side that almost drowned out the subsiding roar of the water.

It was then I felt a warm trickling on my arm and looked down to see it was covered in blood. A paramedic yelled out to wrap it as tightly as possible. So, grabbing a sheet that had miraculously remained in the house, Barb and I bandaged it securely.

Suddenly I saw the beam of a flashlight that was coming down the hillside behind our house. As the figure came out of the woods, I recognized Greg Bandy, a university student who lived about 100 yards upstream. His house was on higher ground and had suffered little damage.

In a few minutes Greg was leading us through the woods, over briars and stones, back to his house. We were all barefoot and had little more than wet, dirty sheets to cover us, so the dry clothes and warm blankets awaiting us at the Bandys felt great.

When Barb and the children were dry and comfortable, Greg and I hiked downstream where the water had now dropped low enough to expose a fallen log. We crossed the stream. On the other side, I was greeted by Ken Sanders, the Dean of Students. After a joyful and emotional reunion, he said grimly, "We can't find three of the boys."

This was only the beginning of the bad news. As I sat in the emergency room of the county hospital getting nine stitches in my arm, ambulance drivers and rescue teams started to quietly carry in stretchers with bodies wrapped in white sheets. The flood waters had taken the lives of 39 people that night and injured 60 others. About half of those fatalities were children—some had played and gone to school with my kids.

Since that unforgettable night, I think I can honestly say that my life has changed. The little taste of the reality of God that I got during that moment of unbelievable loneliness has developed in me a thirst to really know God and stay close to Him, not just in moments of crisis, but in the quiet moments of everyday living.

To be quite honest, I was pretty bored with life before the flood. Now I realize what a marvelous privilege it is just to be alive and to love God and serve Him.

Several months after the flood, a minister was visiting the school and I was asked to give him a tour of the campus and the damage. Afterward, as he was getting out of the car he said something that I'll never forget. He said, "Remember, the same God Who was with you in those moments of peril will be with you in the doldrums of life."

I know He is—and I'm bored no longer.

When things became intolerable, her prayer became my . . .

PRESCRIPTION FOR PAIN

Marilyn Helleberg

The pain was excruciating. I'd had migraine headaches for years, but never one like this one. Fortunately, my husband, Rex, had been able to get Mrs. Graham, my neighbor, to come in and help with our little children while he was at work.

"Look here," she scolded as she straightened the covers on my bed, "you're not the first person to suffer this way and you're not going to be the last. Now you can either lie here and feel sorry for yourself or you can put that pain to work."

With that, she whisked off to get the children started on a finger-painting project. When she came back, she had a Bible and started to read to me.

I was used to Mrs. Graham's brusque ways, but this was a bit too much. I moaned and pulled the covers over my head. "If you prepare your heart, and stretch out your hands toward Him . . . " she read, "you shall forget your misery, and remember it as waters that pass away . . . ." (Job 11:13, 16)

When she finished, Mrs. Graham told me to think of this forced retreat from daily tasks as a gift of time. She said that I should use it to "prepare my heart" for Him.

"But I can't think about *God* when my head's splitting!"

"Well, *something's* got to be going through your head while you're lying here. It might as well be a prayer."

"All right," I said meekly, "what kind of prayer?"

"Well, for starters, Deuteronomy thirty-three twenty-seven—'God is my refuge, and underneath are the everlasting arms.' "

"That's a prayer?"

"Well, it's about as much of a prayer as people in pain can manage. Just say those words over and over in your mind."

"Will that get rid of my headache?"

"Who said anything about getting rid of your headache? Just do it."

What does she know about pain, anyway? I thought. *Here she is 65 years old and looking no more than 50. She's got more energy than I have and she's never sick. She doesn't know about migraines.*

Still, I was miserable enough to try anything, so I started in. "God is my refuge, and underneath are the everlasting arms. God is my refuge, and . . ." Before long, a stab of pain reminded me of my throbbing head; my mind had wandered away from my "prayer." So I started in again. "God is my refuge and . . ." Prayer, mind wandering, awareness of pain, prayer, mind wandering, awareness of pain . . . Gradually, that prayer became a lifeline, something to hold onto when the pain became intolerable. It didn't "get rid of the headache" but it made the pain bearable. And as the hours dragged on, those everlasting arms became very real. I could feel myself surrendering into them, releasing all kinds of pent-up tension. I could feel the reassurance of His Presence.

Ten years have passed since the day Mrs. Graham led me to that discovery about bearing pain. Though my wise and helpful neighbor is dead now, it was at her funeral that I made another discovery.

"She loved life so much," I said to one of her dearest friends.

"Yes, she did, in spite of the pain."

"In spite of what?"

"Didn't you know?" the friend said. "Well, I guess not many people did. Grace was never one to complain, but she suffered terribly from sciatica for the last fifteen years of her life. Not a day went by that she wasn't in pain. I don't know how she stood it."

"I do," I murmured. Because I did.

Have you ever had a sudden, startling urge to pray for someone else, though you had no special reason why?

OUT OF THE DEPTHS

Shirley-Jo Jessup

The day had started out so happily, for it was the day, six years ago, that we were heading for Los Angeles. There my husband, Bryce, was to go back to school for his master's degree in religion. We were sorry to leave the church in Oregon where he'd been minister for two years, but he wanted the extra education.

Our plan was to leave after supper that night, when we could put our two little girls to bed on a mattress in the back seat, and to drive straight through to Bryce's parents' home in San Jose, California. It was 700 miles of straight driving but easier, we thought, than dragging three-year-old Jerri and six-month-old Janni in and out of restaurants and motels. Besides, we told ourselves, it was July; driving at night would be cooler.

We didn't know, then, how fatigue can numb the brain and slow the muscles. All through that hot summer day we carried things from the parsonage to the big U-Haul trailer we had rented. It was happy work. Our belongings were like a résumé of our five wonderful years of marriage: my wedding dress, Bryce's theological library collected book by book, dishes, furniture, albums of precious photos. Many of our wedding gifts had never left their boxes, waiting for that dreamed-of day when we would have "a permanent home."

By 6 p.m., car and trailer were loaded. After supper at a friend's house and a dozen goodbyes, we tucked Jerri and

Janni into their back-seat bed and started out.

The heat and the hauling and the emotion of leaving good friends had taken their toll. From the start it was a struggle to stay awake. Because of the trailer, Bryce didn't want me to drive. It was my job to keep him alert. But as the miles passed my head would snap up with a jerk and I would know I had been asleep.

At 4 a.m. we pulled into a gas station in Klamath Falls, Oregon, and bought soft drinks, then walked back to check the trailer. In the gray, pre-dawn light the little red rocking chair looked strangely comforting strapped to the top of the load. It had been my mother's as a little girl and then mine, and now it was Jerri's.

Through the rear window we peeked in at our sleeping children. To find a motel at this time of night and get out bags and baby food and all the rest seemed almost harder than to keep going.

And yet we knew that just ahead lay the hardest driving on the trip: the treacherous straight stretch of road south of Klamath Falls, with a deep ditch running along the right-hand side and on the left a main irrigation canal 12 feet deep and 25 feet wide. But by now the cold drink was reviving us. We climbed back into the car. Fatefully, we made the decision to keep going. . . .

Ten minutes later and 400 miles farther south, Bryce's father sat up in bed.

"The children are here," he said to his wife.

Bryce's mother squinted at her watch. "They can't be," she said. "They weren't going to leave till after dark. They couldn't get here till mid-morning at the earliest."

But Bryce's father was already on his way to the front door. When his wife joined him he was standing outside, staring into the empty night. At last, reluctantly, he went back inside.

"You dreamed it," she said.

"It wasn't a dream," he insisted. "It was something much stronger."

Back in bed, they both offered silent prayers, not really knowing what they were praying for or why. But both felt a compulsion to pray.

At the moment that Bryce's father awoke, I, too, was startled from sleep. I must have dozed off almost the minute we left the gas station. Now I was wakened by a cry from Bryce:

"Hang on!"

He was wrestling with the wheel. The car was rocking sickeningly on the rim of the steep ditch at our right. For a horrid moment we swayed there. Then at last the headlights swung left and we felt pavement beneath the tires again.

Now Bryce spun the wheel the other way. But the car continued a slow, relentless arc to the left. We were heading straight for the deep water canal on the other side. Bryce threw all his strength against the wheel. But the heavily-loaded trailer, jackknifed behind us, was forcing us off the road. We were crossing the shoulder. And then we plunged down the incline into the canal.

For an unbelievable moment the car floated there in the early morning darkness, then sank. "Roll down your window!" Bryce yelled.

I heard the handle crank on his side as icy water gushed over us. Bryce was leaning into the back seat. I saw him drag Jerri forward and then, like figures in an underwater ballet, float out the window.

It had happened so fast that only then did I rouse myself from my stupor. I seized the window handle on my side, but it was jammed. I threw my shoulder against the door but the water outside pressed it shut.

The window's open on Bryce's side. That was the thought I held in my mind as I groped for Janni in a floating debris of diapers, bottles and blankets. The water was cold and thick with slimy moss. There was a pain in my back and my lungs were straining against my chest. The mattress had floated to the ceiling but I couldn't find our baby.

I found a tiny air pocket at the top of the car and pressed my face into it, but soon the oxygen grew short and my lungs seemed to be on fire. For the first time I realized I was screaming. All that seemed to matter was to keep the slimy water from touching my face.

"Dear God," I prayed, "let me faint first. Don't let me be alive when the water covers me."

I felt a hand take mine. It was Bryce. At least I would die holding his hand, I thought. But he was pulling at me, dragging me away from the roof. I struggled to get free. He was pulling me; I was swallowing the slimy water. He wouldn't let go.

And then suddenly, unbelievably, fresh air was in my face. My lungs were swelling, filling with it. My hand touched something solid and I held on.

"Janni!" Bryce was screaming at me. "Where's Janni?"

While I coughed, unable to speak, he dove back beneath the dark water. From somewhere I heard crying. Then in the gray light I saw Jerri standing on the bank, shivering in her drenched little nightie. I saw that my hand had closed on the rocking chair.

Bryce's head appeared a few feet away. He was treading water, gasping, too winded to speak. Then he disappeared again. This time he was gone a long, long time. When he came up he was holding Janni. I didn't want to look at that tiny limp form. His feet found the roof of our car and he stood on it, water up to his chest, our baby in his hands. Her head fell back and I knew she was dead.

From the bank came an anxious little cry. "Don't drop Janni, Daddy! Don't drop Janni!"

Bryce lifted Janni's face to his own and blew into her mouth. He took a breath, then blew again, and then again and again. At last, her chest shuddered and she let out a tiny wail.

"She's breathing!" Bryce shouted.

He splashed with her to the bank while I followed. Jerri threw herself into my arms, and a few minutes later an early motorist found us.

At the hospital in Klamath Falls doctors assured us there was no damage to Janni's brain. X-rays showed three crushed vertebrae in my spine which would quickly heal: the only injury to any of us.

From the admitting room Bryce put through a call to his parents. For the first time the wonder of our being alive and well swept over me. How had Bryce ever gotten us all from that car? How had a man who was exhausted, who was only a novice swimmer, who knew nothing about mouth-to-mouth breathing—how had he done all the right things at the right times?

"Hello, Pop," I heard him say into the telephone.

"What's wrong, Bryce? Are you all right?" his father interrupted.

"Don't be alarmed—we've had an accident but everyone's fine."

"Thank God," said his father. Then he asked, "Was it at four o'clock this morning?"

Bryce stared at the phone in surprise. "How did you know? Did somebody tell you?"

There was a little pause at the other end. "Yes, Somebody told me," said his father.

A PRAYER FOR STRENGTH

Oh Father, Whose voice I hear in the winds and Whose breath gives life to all the world, hear me. I am a man before You, one of Your many children. I am small and weak. I need Your strength and wisdom. Let me walk in beauty, and make my eyes ever behold the red and purple sunsets. Make my hands respect the things You have made, my ears sharp to hear Your voice. Make me wise so that I may know the things You have taught my people, the lessons You have hidden in every leaf and rock. I seek strength, Father, not to be superior to my brothers, but to be able to fight my greatest enemy, myself. Make me ever ready to come to You with clean hands and straight eye, so that when life fades as the setting sun, my spirit may come to You without shame.

Chief Tom White Cloud
Ojibway Indian

A storm. A battered ship. A prayer . . .

FOR THOSE IN PERIL ON THE SEA

Jack Ford

The doctor who conducted my post-operative checkup that day looked at me somberly. "You've asked me to be honest with you, Mr. Ford," he said. "And so I will be. As you know, we did everything we could for you surgically. But the cancer was too far advanced for us to get it all. So the outlook is not good. And I'm afraid you won't have much use of that right arm for the time you have left."

I heard myself asking, numbly, "How much time is that?"

"Perhaps six months," he replied.

Six months! Something in me seemed to freeze up tight. How would I break the news to my wife, Emma? How could I adjust to this death sentence myself? I had hoped that the radical surgery on my right shoulder and chest would give me many more years of life. But now this.

Leaving the doctor's office, I walked the long way home past docks where husky men hauled on ropes ("Not much use in that right arm"), past the yacht basin where mast sticks, rocked by the wind, clawed at the sky. I scarcely heard the gulls shriek as they dive-bombed the bay. I thought perhaps I should pray. But I had always regarded the Power that rules the universe as a vast, impersonal Force, mighty indeed, but beyond the reach of troubled or suffering people. So I walked on, fighting back despair.

Some of the iciness inside me seemed to melt as I noticed a sign, "Boats for Sale." I had always wanted a boat. If I had only six months, why not enjoy those 180 days? I went in and heard myself ask for a second-hand boat I could afford. "How about that half-submerged one beside the dock?"

"The *Hyding*? You don't want her; she's fifty years old and leaks like a sieve. Mortgaged to the hilt, too. Not worth salvaging, believe me."

But I wanted that boat. So even before I told my wife, Emma, about the doctor's verdict, I got on the phone and finally located the bank in Oregon that held the mortgage. They were willing to sell for the price I offered, and within a few days the boat, all 117 feet of her, was mine.

I hired an old half-Scottish, half-Indian sea salt to help recondition the *Hyding*. He had a world of experience with boats and skillet-sized hands that would make up for my limp, useless one.

"Call me Scotty," he ordered.

Fortunately there had been no leak in the engine room, and the motor was in excellent condition. But the decks were rotting and slimy and the cabins a mess. We had to replace the boards in the main deck, and as we were ready to toss them out, Scotty ran his hand over a plank.

"Teak," he said. "Wouldn't surprise me if this old girl was solid teak. That's why it lasted: nails won't rust in it; termites don't like it."

Sure enough, when we sanded the dull dark wood, the grain came to life with the luster of a midnight opal. It was hard work, but I was determined to use my right arm. I'd put the sandpaper in my fingers, and grasping my wrist with my left hand, force the right one to move back and forth against the woodwork. Or I'd try to pull myself up through a hatch with both arms. At first the pain was excruciating, but I had to find some muscles that would still work.

I couldn't hammer left-handed, so again I folded my fingers around the handle and held them there with my left hand, trying to pump some life into that jellyfish of a wrist. Each time I thought there was a little less pain. Or was it only because I yearned so to be able to use that arm? I still didn't know how to pray, but I did know that somewhere out there was The Source of all power and energy, and I visualized that power converging on my arm, healing and restoring it.

Emma helped me; we were down at the boat every day. Small as she was, Emma was strong, and her enthusiasm for the project matched mine.

When Scotty pronounced the boat ready, we cruised to

the Mexican coast. The sea was calm and the sun smiled down on us. We decided to head up to San Francisco and outfit for a cruise to Alaska, stopping in the Bay to pick up Emma's sister, her husband and four children. With Scotty, two crew members and a cook, we were an even dozen.

For the first few days all went well. But suddenly waves began to pile up and to crash across the bow. I saw a seagull, buffeted by the rising wind, shoved backward on frantic wings.

"What is this?" I yelled to Scotty. "No storm was predicted."

"Tidal wave," he hollered back. "Must have been an underwater earthquake somewhere. We could be in big trouble if there are aftershocks. Better get below and keep everyone in their cabins."

As I staggered to the hatchway, I looked up to see a mighty wave towering high above the deck. It came pounding down, slamming me to my knees, swirling around me. It poured through the open hatch and disappeared under cabin doors. I heard one of the children cry out.

In our cabin Emma lay on the bed, already seasick. She moaned as the ship rose and then plunged wildly into the trough of a wave. A shoe floated past as I lurched against the door.

"Stay right here," I shouted. "I'm going up to help Scotty."

"Be careful," Emma moaned. "Oh, Jack, be careful. Your arm . . . God help us."

"We'll manage. Don't be afraid. It can't last long."

I was dead wrong. Hour after hour the waves pummeled the ship with no respite. I was hungry, but there was no time to snatch a bite. It took both of us to keep the wheel from spinning crazily. With the violent motion of the ship, even Scotty and I were nauseated. It grew dark, and I thought with a sense of relief that now the seas would grow calmer.

But, if anything, the wind increased. All night long, Scotty and I clung to the wheel while avalanches of water poured over the rail. I tried to radio the Coast Guard, but the only reply was a crackling, garbled sound. I kept trying at intervals throughout the next day as the storm continued to toss us about.

I knew that if the storm kept up much longer, there was no way we could survive. As the bilge filled with water, we were sinking deeper and deeper into the canyons between the mountainous waves at least 50 feet high.

My eyes kept closing only to be jarred open as tons of water smashed onto the deck. We had now been 41 hours without food or sleep, with no sign of a rescuer. We had no equipment to pump out the bilge, no way of keeping the water from eventually inundating us completely. The last time I tried a quick check of the cabins, the water was knee deep and Emma's bed kept sliding from one side of the room to crash against the other wall.

The hours lengthened into the next night as the ship flung herself wildly about, buffeted by the lashing waves. Both Scotty and I were exhausted. I thought of the four children for whose safety I was responsible, and the waves of despair that washed over me were as devastating as the ones that swamped the ship.

Suddenly I caught a flash of light in the darkness. The next time we crested on the skyscraper top of the wave, the light appeared nearer. Finally, through the banshee wail of the wind we could detect a steady bass rumble, which materialized into a whirring helicopter just discernible against the dark horizon.

The radio crackled, giving our position. Then, as the helicopter hovered above us, the gray shadow of a ship appeared. At last, a coast guard rescue vessel. But she couldn't come too near; the heaving, sliding wall of water kept us apart.

It seemed incredible, but into those seething seas they launched a tiny boat with five extremely brave men and as many pumps. It was a toy bobbing up and down but coming nearer with every giant wave. Just when it seemed they must be dashed against the side of our ship and capsized, they were washed close enough to jump to our deck. They gave us a brief greeting and went below with their pumps.

I knew that even if they succeeded in pumping out the thousands of gallons of seawater in the bilge, our drenched engines would never be able to work to get us to safety. And the rescue ship standing by seemed helpless. The crew tried to shoot a line across the churning sea to us, but each time it either was bounced back by the waves or slid off the deck before our crewmen could grab it.

I yelled to one of them to lash me to a beam, thinking I could at least keep from sliding overboard while I reached for the rope, but the waves breaking over the very top of the boat kept my head under water for an eternity before I could breathe again. Once I touched the rope, but the sea pulled it out of my grasp.

"They won't keep trying much longer," Scotty shouted as the coiled rope slithered into the sea again. "Maybe they can pull us, one at a time, up to the helicopter."

I shook my head. "Couldn't possibly take all twelve."

Would I, as captain, have to make the choice? If the 'copter could manage eight, which three would be left besides me? The tradition of the sea would be honored. I probably didn't have much time left anyway, and I was too tired now to care. They'd take the children and their parents, of course. Would Emma decide to stay with me? Scotty?

Yet as thoughts raced through my mind, I knew I didn't really want to die, and I couldn't condemn the others without a last try. I heard my own lips echo Emma's swift prayer as the storm had begun, "Help me, Lord. Give me strength." And it was directed, not to some impersonal Force but to a loving, caring God Who could really reach me.

As the rope arched once more over the waves, I braced my feet against the anchor winch, reached out, caught the rope and hung on. I visualized the strength that I'd asked for pouring into my arms as the rope cut into my palms.

Then Scotty was beside me, adding his strength to mine until we could loop the rope around the winch.

"We did it, man! We finally did it," Scotty exulted.

I never thought I'd disagree with Scotty, but this time I had to. It had not been *my* skill that brought the helicopter to us, to an unknown spot in a vast, churning sea. It had not been *my* strength that let me clamp onto the rope on its final throw.

At last I knew that the unseen Power that could reach out to touch even me had always been there, had always cared, and I had not recognized it.

I looked up to see another wave rising, but now the towline grew taut, and I felt the deck move forward in the wake of the rescue ship. The great wave reached for us in all its fury. But we kept just ahead of it under a power not our own.

And from now on, so would I.

PRAYER IN TIME OF TROUBLE

How hard for unaccustomed feet
Which only knew the meadow
Is this hard road they now must
tread
Through valleys dark with shadow.
Until they learn how sure Thy love
That girds each day, each morrow,
O Father, gently lead all hearts
That newly come to sorrow!

Leslie Savage Clark

Held hostage by desperate men, we prayed . . .

THE PRAYER THAT BROUGHT US HOME

Faye King

Soft September rain was soaking into our good farm soil that Wednesday evening. I was sitting in my favorite recliner in the living room of our small frame home, my Bible in my lap. But the words were blurred. Across from me my husband, John, sat quietly in his green recliner, looking at one of our unexpected visitors. We'd relaxed in our chairs many evenings since my husband had retired. Now I wondered if we'd die in them.

Our nightmare had begun several minutes—an eternity—earlier, when my husband answered a knock on the door. A man of medium height stood there, rain drops glistening on his dark hair. His damp white tee shirt clung to his muscular body; his tight jeans were splashed with mud. His voice and his smile were warm and pleasant. "Our truck is in the ditch, could I come in and call a wrecker?"

"Sure, come on in," my husband replied. The man entered, and my husband led him to the hall telephone. As he was thumbing through the yellow pages, another man in a black tee shirt had come to the door. Wet brown hair framed a fragile face. "Could I use the bathroom while he uses your phone?"

Another "sure," another entry. And then, three more men were at the door. But this time, instead of smiles and polite inquiries, there were pistols and a sawed-off shotgun pushing their way into our home. A tall, blond man, his thick mustache hovering over a thin-lipped smile, pushed the barrel of the shotgun into my stomach. I backed into the far wall of the living room, my head tilted back, staring into glacier blue eyes. "Hello, there, lady, glad to make your acquaintance." He turned his head, but the shotgun never moved an inch. "Well, Larry, big man, you say you're in charge, what's next?"

Afraid to breathe, I inched my head around to look at the slight man in the black tee shirt, now sitting on the edge of the couch, his face contorted with pain. I couldn't see my husband. *Dear God, had they taken him into another room to kill him?*

"Bring them both over here," Larry said wearily. Relief washed over me as I heard the word "both." My captor removed the shotgun. "Get over there to the big man, honey." I turned and walked over to the couch. Before I got there, I felt the gun barrel nestle between my shoulder blades. A fourth man, thick-bodied and dark-skinned, pushed my husband to my side.

Larry stood and slowly pulled the tee shirt almost up to his chin. "Take a good look, both of you, and listen." I gazed at a small round hole that looked as though it had been drawn with a red pen, inches above his heart. "We've escaped from a prison in Tennessee, and we've already shot one man while escaping. We won't hesitate to shoot anyone who gets in our way. Now," he continued, "we're taking over your house for the night. If you do as we say, you won't be hurt. If you don't . . ."

He pulled his shirt back down and didn't finish his sentence. He knew it wasn't necessary.

"Now, I want all three of you to sit down somewhere." Larry's voice never lost its softness. "And don't get any funny ideas about escaping. We have some things we have to do." For the first time, my eyes focused on a young man, standing rigidly in front of the man who had first come to our door. When he walked to a chair I saw the reason for his stiffness—a pistol had been shoved into his back. I wondered where he had been kidnapped and what fate he would share with us.

"You heard the big man," my blond-haired guard barked, "now sit down!" He nudged me with the shotgun. I walked to my recliner and fell into its familiar softness. My husband walked slowly to his own chair. I was heartened by my husband's calmness.

From my seat in the living room, I could see a man in each of our three bedrooms, opening drawers, throwing clothing and personal items out into heaps. My mind screamed at them to stop. How dare they come into our home and throw our things about as casually as rags! Their presence had turned a love-filled home into a house loaded with their violence and hatred.

"Big man, we've checked out everything." It was the blond giant's now-familiar voice.

"Listen, Dude, I've had about enough of this big man talk, see?" Larry stood up. Lamplight glinted on his gun barrel.

"Yeah, well, why don't we decide who the *real* man of this outfit is?" "Dude" walked over to Larry and towered above him, his pistol pointed at Larry's stomach.

"Okay, why don't we?" Larry stood there, staring up at the bigger man.

I'm going to see a man die on my living room floor! I felt as though I were going to suffocate as I watched the two men staring at each other. I could see Larry's eyes, and I knew I was looking at death. He'd kill the big man as casually as I'd swat a fly.

The big man must have realized the same thing, because he put his gun down at his side and gave a small laugh. "Hey, man, don't get all up-tight—the strain is getting to us."

One of the men turned on the television set to check on news bulletins. Another turned out all the lights except for the lamp that was now shedding a soft light on my worn Bible.

But the light was doing no good—fear and anger had blinded me. Desperately, I tried to remember the 23rd Psalm, *The Lord is my Shepherd* . . . but fear was paralyzing my mind—I couldn't remember the Psalm! "Dear God," I prayed, "I can't read or remember Your word, and maybe I'm going to die. Show me what to do."

"Okay, you'd better go to bed now." Larry's words interrupted my frantic thoughts. "And, remember, there's a guard at your bedroom door and it won't bother him a bit to pull the trigger if you try anything." My husband and I were sent to the guest bedroom, the young hostage to another bedroom. One of the convicts pulled a chair to our doorway and sat with a shotgun.

In the dark bedroom, clinging to my husband, I listened to the grandfather clock chime away the hours—one o'clock, two o'clock . . . Suddenly, I felt a compelling urge to pray—aloud—as though God was instructing me to voice my fear and concern.

But I just *couldn't*. Praying aloud in church was one thing—praying aloud in front of four desperate criminals was quite another! I'd heard the newscaster's warning: "Remember, these men are armed and considered very dangerous." I'd looked at their taut faces; I didn't want to upset them any further. But the urging became stronger—it was as though God's gentle hands were giving me a nudge. I sat up on the bed, and the convict guarding the door straightened in his chair. My own voice startled me, "Do you mind if I pray?"

"What did she say?" I recognized Larry's voice.

"She wants to know if she can pray," our bedroom guard replied.

A long silence—then, "I guess it will be all right."

I knelt down by the bed and began pouring out my heart, and the sobs I'd been holding inside began tearing out of me. I prayed for my husband and myself and the young hostage. Then I prayed for my children, asking God to give them strength, no matter what happened to us. I paused a moment, but still felt a sense of urgency. *Pray for the four men*—more gentle nudging.

Pray for kidnappers and thieves? My mind balked. *I died for kidnappers and thieves, and you . . .*

"And Father," my sobbing voice sounded harsh and unreal, "bless these men; bless their folks and help them to see that You love them and will forgive them." I don't remember what else I said, but I remember how I felt. A warm blanket of divine love began covering my fear and hatred. After I finished, I got back on the bed with my husband, and a scripture softly slipped into my mind—"And, lo, I am with you always, even unto the end of the world." (Matthew 28:20) I clung to that scripture until morning finally came.

"Mrs. King, we're splitting up this morning; two men are going to take your truck, and Lyons and myself are going to take your car. We're taking you and Mr. King along as hostages." Larry's voice was gruff, but not unkind.

The tall blond man got the truck keys from my husband, and he and the shorter dark-skinned man hurried out the kitchen door. As I heard the truck motor start, I looked at Larry. But this time I did not see an escaped convict, I saw a human being. *This is some mother's son*, I thought.

"Don't you want me to fix all of us some breakfast?" My voice was calm.

"No, I don't want to take the time to eat." Larry looked at me and smiled. "You know, you remind me of my grandmother." His smile faded and the hard, set look came back on his face. "Come on, let's go—and remember, Mr. King, we're watching every move you make. You do the driving and I'll ride in the front seat. Mrs. King can get in the back with Lyons." We walked out to the car.

"My arthritis bothers me when I ride in the back seat. I should ride in the front seat with my husband." (Was that *my* voice that had said that?)

"Well, all right, Mrs. King, get in front. But just remember, there are guns pointed at both of you."

"Where's the young boy?" I held my breath, waiting for his answer.

"He's tied and gagged—now get in this car!" Larry and Lyons got in the back; my husband and I got in the front, and the nightmare continued.

We drove through the day, carefully avoiding all the main highways, stopping only once to get gas and use the bathroom, listening to the news bulletins all the way. The young hostage had managed to untie himself back at our house and alert the police. Now the news bulletins were changed—"An elderly couple, Mr. and Mrs. John King, have been kidnapped. Roadblocks are being set up through the area." Later, another news flash: "Two of the kidnappers have been captured; the search continues for the Kings."

About four o'clock that afternoon, Larry instructed my husband to pull over into a wooded area so that they could plan the best route. The rain had ended and the afternoon sun was filtering through the trees. I opened my purse, took out a small book of devotions and started reading. The gentle urging began once more . . . *Talk to them*. "What will I say, Father?" *Talk to them from your heart.*

"Why don't you boys give yourselves up?" I said. "Your mothers had rather see you in prison than dead."

"We'll die before we go back to prison," Larry said. Lyons nodded.

I asked Larry why he was in prison, and he explained that he had started using dope while in Vietnam. After going back to law school he was "into dope really heavy" and started selling it, which led to his arrest. Again I urged them to turn themselves in, but suddenly our talk was interrupted by the sound of a truck motor. Larry jumped from the car and watched the truck as it pulled into the wooded area. Lyons covered him as he sauntered over to the truck, a smile on his face. He started talking to the driver, then pulled his pistol out of his pocket.

"We're taking this truck; get out and leave the keys." His voice, so soft minutes earlier, had turned to flint.

But the driver rammed his foot on the accelerator and backed the truck out, slinging mud and gravel. With a curse, Larry ran to our car and told my husband to move over.

"I'm going to catch up with those guys and take that truck!" He gunned the motor and pulled out like a madman, pursuing the truck down the narrow road. Another prayer jounced in my head; "Lord, You said You'd be with us. Please don't leave us now!"

We soon caught up with the truck and forced it over to the side of the highway. Larry jumped out, made the driver move over, and spun out onto the highway. Lyons instructed my husband to pull out also. Suddenly I heard a siren, and when I looked back, I saw beautiful flashing blue lights. We were going to be rescued!

But we weren't. The police car sped by us, pursuing the truck!

On and on we drove, avoiding freeways and main highways, until we came to Covington, Kentucky. Lyons instructed my husband to drive to a certain street, then leaned toward me from the back seat. "Mrs. King, do you have two dollars?"

The news bulletins had said that Lyons was wanted for armed robbery and assault with a deadly weapon. He knew we had a lot of cash with us—we had paid for everything during the trip—yet he watched me thumb through the larger bills until I found the two dollars. I handed them to him. He looked at me a moment. "Thank you," he said softly, then opened the car door and melted into the night.

My husband and I looked at each other for a moment before reality finally dawned. The nightmare was over and we were safe. I did what I had done in my darkened bedroom earlier—cried and prayed—but this time all I said was "Thank You, God."

After we arrived home, we learned that Larry had been captured. I copied down some of my favorite scriptures and mailed them to him in prison.

A few days later, a letter came from him: "Mrs. King, you'll never know how much your prayer meant to me that night we forced our way into your home. I was reared in a Christian home, and you and Mr. King reminded me of my own parents. I went in the wrong direction when I started putting myself before God. Thank you for seeing some good in me—so many people see only the bad in others . . ."

"You'll never know how much your prayer meant . . ." Larry's wrong about that. I do know what the prayer meant—to my own life, too. When I was totally helpless—unable to read or even remember God's word—I still had access to Him, through prayer. When I prayed for those men, I felt the compassion of Christ reaching out toward them through me. That was why, the next morning, I was able to look at them as Christ looks at all of us—past human sin to human need.

What quiet force impelled this bus driver to step out into a raging blizzard?

LORD, DON'T LEAVE ME NOW!

Elwyn Mappes

I felt uneasy about the sky from the very beginning. It looked like a big slab of slate about to break loose somewhere and come down hard.

But so far I'd been lucky. Snow had started falling soon after I'd swung my big Greyhound bus out of the Iowa City bus terminal, but the traffic kept moving pretty well. All of my passengers were young people—college students from Grinnell and the State University, heading home for the weekend. "Well, God," I prayed quietly, "just get them home safely, and me safely into Omaha."

The snow was falling thicker by seven a.m. Worse, the wind was picking up. While many of my 25 passengers dozed, I could feel the big steering wheel pulling me into alertness with each gust.

I dropped south of Route 6, my usual route, onto Interstate 80. The road might be clearer there due to heavier traffic.

But by 7:30, the snow knifed across the highway horizontally. I told myself softly, "This is gonna be a regular blizzard."

Most of the hills around us were lost in the whiteness. In front of me, the cars and trucks brushed aside enough snow to keep a narrow dark stripe open on the Interstate. But the traffic moved slower as the snow continued to fall. About 20 miles before the Newton turnoff, it came to a halt. I eased the bus to the shoulder and prepared to wait.

In the lull, I could hear the dull rumble of my idling engine, the soft hiss of the blizzard whipping the side of the bus, and the low murmur of several passengers: "Wonder how long we'll be stuck here?" "I hope the driver gets going again soon."

In the swirling storm outside I could see little more than dim shapes of stalled autos and semi-trailer trucks ahead. I felt grateful for the heater humming at my feet. But something troubled me.

It was February 21st. My father, who had died several years before, would have celebrated his birthday today. Why did I think of that now? My eyes misted as I remembered my father. Dad was white-haired and balding. His face looked a lot like mine does now. He was a minister who could have had an affluent congregation. Instead, he chose to minister to the deaf, sacrificing himself in many ways to communicate God's love to those who could never hear His word preached.

I knew he would have liked me to follow in his footsteps. But as a young man I'd already set my heart on long-distance driving and the adventure of the open road. When I hesitantly told Dad of my calling, he chuckled and peered over his eyeglasses. "All of us minister to one another in different ways," he'd said.

A lot of miles—nearly two million—had gone by beneath the Greyhound buses I'd driven since that time. And I'd never really convinced myself that the words my father spoke weren't just his way of covering up his disappointment over my career choice. In that 25-year interval I'd been blessed with a good wife and four children. Sure, there'd be mornings when I'd have cranky passengers who'd had burnt toast for breakfast, but I always tried to smile them aboard my bus and treat them kindly. After a while, though, one face and one incident blended into another, and I wondered whether I was really *ministering* to anyone at all.

Minutes passed. It was quiet and peaceful in the bus. But as I looked out at the wild snowstorm, some odd feeling told me: *Go out*.

Of course I didn't want to. I'd get chilled to the bone out there in my short jacket. The passengers had been patient about the delay so far; why should I have to discover the cause of it?

All of us minister to one another in different ways.

I buttoned my jacket and stepped out into the drifts. Icy flakes stung my face, and my pants legs sank deep into the snow. I trudged up the road to where a truck driver sat comfortably in his cab. He rolled down his window.

"Anybody know anything?" I asked.

"Yeah. The county knows we're here. They'll get a wrecker."

I peered ahead. In the whiteness I saw the dark shape of a semi-trailer truck crossways over the highway. I walked back to the bus. Inside it was warm.

The passengers looked up. "Looks like we'll be here awhile," I said. "A truck is jackknifed across the road."

I settled back behind the wheel. Again that urgency to go outside. *How stupid,* I thought. Yet I couldn't quell the feeling. This time I pulled on an old stocking cap and a heavy overcoat. Then I trudged through the snow while drivers inside warm cars and trucks stared at me.

In about 300 feet I reached the jackknifed truck. I saw a man standing on the road. His back was to me, his light topcoat blowing in the shrieking wind. I called into his ear: "What's going on?"

He reeled slowly, and my breath grew short for a moment. Blood streamed down his face from gashes in his head.

I grabbed his arm. "Come with me," I said firmly, leading him back to the bus. As I started to help him up the steps, I thought of bus drivers who'd been sued for getting involved in similar situations. But I dismissed that thought and helped the man onto a front seat, praying, *Lord, send me some help.* "Is there a doctor or nurse here?" I called to the passengers.

"Yes," sounded a gentle Iowa voice in the rear. It was a girl about 24. "I—I'm a practical nurse," she said, brushing back her dark hair as she came up the aisle. I offered her the bus' little first-aid kit. It was only a little tin box with smelling salts and bandages, but she went to work.

"We need water," she whispered. "He's lost so much blood he's dehydrating."

I filled a cup in the restroom. When I brought it to the injured man his eyes seemed to clear for an instant. "I wonder how my buddy is?" he mumbled.

His *buddy*?

I pulled back on my cap and overcoat and scrambled back to the jackknifed truck. Then I saw it—a mass of twisted steel in a ditch. It had been a car. Near it stood another man, swaying in the storm gusts, coat soaked with blood. Shock glazed his eyes, and I half-carried him back to the bus.

Both were older, gray-haired men. And both appeared to be dying. Inwardly, I prayed, *Oh, dear God, keep them alive!*

Some passengers offered to help, but there was little they could do. No one could run for help in the blinding whiteness outside. I'd already asked a trucker with a CB to radio the police.

The young nurse looked up at me with fear in her eyes. She whispered, "I'm afraid we're going to lose them if they can't reach a hospital soon. You'd better start praying."

I touched her arm. "Honey, I'm way ahead of you," I said.

Suddenly yellow lights flurried outside the windshield. It was a state gravel truck. I leaped outside. A deputy sheriff was in the cab. He shouted down through the swirling snow, "There's an ambulance waiting at the exit three miles ahead, but he can't get here. We'll plow the way for you as you follow us." He handed me a large first-aid kit and I swung back into the bus. With it the nurse continued working on the two men. Both were ominously quiet now, their skin turning blue. I waited behind the wheel for the truck ahead to start. Its yellow lights dimmed. The driver leaped out and yelled into my windshield. "Batteries are dead!"

Lord, don't leave us now, I thought. The snow was blinding. But suddenly the white curtain parted to reveal a highway patrol car. The trooper said he had chains and would lead the way. I began following him. My drive wheels were slipping, but we moved.

"We're going to try to make it on our own, folks," I announced.

The calm voice didn't sound like mine. And I knew we were not on our own. "Lord, please be with us," I prayed.

I thought about the slipping drive wheels. A Greyhound bus has eight wheels in the rear on two axles. One set of four wheels is powered. Hydraulically lifting the unpowered axle's wheels off the ground would place the tremendous weight of the bus on the four drive wheels. That might give us the needed traction. I pulled the hydraulic lift lever, praying again that God would keep His hand on the bus as I slowly accelerated.

On the empty road ahead, snow was thick, but we kept moving. In a half hour I finally pulled off the Interstate onto the exit ramp. The ambulance was waiting. Two attendants climbed aboard with a respirator and other equipment. Then one turned to me.

"We can't move them," he said gravely. "They're too far gone."

"How far is the hospital?" I asked.

"In Newton. About six miles away."

"Well, if someone will lead the way, I'll follow."

A highway trooper guided us, and we started off. There was more drifting snow, more bad visibility, more treacherous winds. The Iowa nurse aided the ambulance attendant behind me as I drove. As the minutes passed, I felt their tension increase. Fifteen minutes. Twenty. Twenty-five. Finally, the outline of a building. It was Newton Hospital. I pulled up to the emergency entrance.

After the two men were rushed inside by an emergency room team, the hospital administrator came out and invited our passengers in for lunch. I headed to the emergency room where I asked a nurse about the two men.

Her face was grim. "We're afraid we're losing one of them."

I sank on one of the waiting-room benches and prayed for the men, and the doctors and nurses working on them. And something happened as I sat there.

I felt the closeness of my father, and with it an illuminating understanding of what he had tried to tell me so many years ago. Even his Bible verse came back to me: "As every man hath received the gift, even so minister the same one to another, as good stewards of the manifold grace of God." (I Peter 4:10)

It was clear to me now. No matter what we do—bus driver, doctor, policeman, office worker, store clerk—we can *all* be ministers unto another, whether it is through a friendly smile, a word of encouragement or . . . stepping out onto a snowy highway to see what's wrong.

A hand touching my shoulder interrupted my thoughts. I looked up into the face of the head nurse. "Mr. Mappes," she smiled, "I thought you'd like to know . . . the men you brought in, Mr. Hixon and the Reverend Root—they're out of danger. Both of them are going to be all right."

My heart leaped. One of them was a minister! I seemed to hear that familiar chuckle my Dad used to give when, after trying hard to fathom one of his lessons, I finally understood.

TWO HANDS

Two hands upstretched—
one yours, one mine—
Touch gently in the air.
And when we touch, I lose all fear.
Just knowing you are there.

Two hands entwined—
one God's, one mine—
We share a moment there.
His hand and mine become His church;
Our touching is a prayer.

M. Charles Rebert

Inside the cabin, the cold was claiming my baby. Outside, the blizzard howled. In my heart I prayed, "Lord, send help."

THE LESSON

Pauline McClellen

"Chechakos," they called us.

It's a word Alaskans use to describe outsiders—people experiencing their wild land for the first time. They say it takes tenderfoot "chechakos" a few years before we learn all the qualities necessary for survival in the north country.

Maybe so. This Alaska just wasn't woman's country, I told myself. My husband, Jim, was a sergeant stationed at Fort Richardson, a bleak Army outpost near Anchorage. At first we lived on the base. But when I became pregnant, we bought lumber, and on a small parcel of land several miles out in the woods we built a small house.

It seemed like Jim was always on duty. Tending a garden and the regular household chores kept me busy, but I felt awfully alone much of the time. And when I looked out the front window of our isolated home, my gaze met only the blank stare of the pine and aspen trees across the gravel road.

Late fall was full of gray, overcast days; soul-hurting, cheerless days. *Even my friends, the aspen leaves, are gone,* I brooded late one morning.

"Oh," I criticized myself, "you'd think you were alone in the world!" I decided to walk to the community pump where we, along with a dozen other families scattered in this still primitive area, fetched our water supply.

"Maybe I'll meet somebody there," I reflected.

Unfortunately, I did.

I'd been walking on the forest path. As I turned a little bend, I saw a large, bearded man coming my way. With his long matted hair, he looked like a lumbering grizzly bear, although he wore dirty trousers, knee socks and a plaid coat, and carried a great woodsman's axe on his shoulder. I shuddered as he passed, stepping aside to give him plenty of room. His gray-blue eyes glinted like gun metal. I felt them boring into my back as I walked on. A stupid sensation, but I couldn't shake it. So I spun around. Sure enough, the old man had stopped. He was watching me.

I hurried on.

Later, at a gathering of neighbors, I heard the stories.

"Old Otto," one serviceman mused. "We call him 'the Madman.' "

"I sure think he's looney," his wife chimed in. "Especially after living by himself forty years."

"He come up here prospectin' for gold," an old-timer put in. "They say he once killed a man in a bar room brawl. But now he just raises Malamute huskies and trains 'em for sled dogs."

He wasn't the kind of man I wanted to meet. Although he lived less than a mile away and was, in fact, our nearest neighbor, I never spoke to him, even when I passed by his yard as he went about his endless task of cutting firewood.

Then one day, shortly after Jim had taken the car for night duty on the post, a blizzard blew up. It seemed to come from nowhere. It frightened me, especially since I was now caring for our new-born daughter, Linda. But I knew what to do.

"Sit tight," Jim had told me once. "Never—*never*—venture out in a snowstorm. It's too easy to get lost. People have been found the morning after an Alaskan blizzard, frozen stiff a few yards from their front door."

The words had made their impression on me. I stayed in the cabin, even though huge drifts piled up against it and the temperature inside seemed to drop sharply.

I was especially concerned about the effect of the cold on Linda, only seven weeks old. Sighing, I wrapped another blanket around her. Then I became alarmed. I now was aware that I could see the frosty condensation of my breath.

Slightly panicked, I ran over to the oil stove. It wasn't working! No matter how hard I tried, I couldn't get it lighted again.

"No! No!" I cried aloud. And Linda started to cry. I picked her up and held her close to me. Her body was very cool. I pulled a heavy blanket off a bed and wrapped it around both of us. Then I sat down, wondering what to do. *If only we had a telephone*! I thought in despair.

Already, moisture from our breath had formed a white frost along the walls and ceiling. Outside the wind howled and whipped the snow higher. It would be many hours before Jim was due back—and he'd probably wait the storm out before returning.

Time, almost literally, had stopped: The wall clock had frozen in the cold. As the hours passed, I had no way of measuring them—except by gauging the steady, relentlessly increasing chill of the cabin. The cold wind was robbing it of warmth.

I unwrapped a layer of blankets from Linda's head to check her breathing. Her features had a definite blue tinge. Tears from her eyes had frozen on Linda's tiny face. I blew my breath against those eyes, then held my baby close, squeezing her tightly, willing the warmth from my body to hers. My heart pounded.

I knew there was no way Linda and I could survive until morning, when my husband was due to return. Still, my prayers said, "Please, God, don't let us die!" There seemed no way help could come. But, against reason, I prayed, "Please, Lord, send help."

As usual, after praying, I felt a certain calmness stealing over me. But this time even that held a sinister threat.

"This is how it is, when you freeze to death," I told myself. "You just . . . fall . . . asleep. . . ."

Fighting tiredness, I couldn't keep my eyes open. I had let the lantern burn low, afraid to lose the body heat I'd hoarded for Linda by disturbing our blankets. So I sat still in the darkness, waiting for the end.

Even on that wild night, there was no mistaking the distant barking of dogs. I heard them. They were coming closer. In a moment the snarls were loud and clear, right outside my door. I heard a shuffling of footsteps, and the sound of snow being scraped away.

An instant later a hulking figure burst in—Old Otto.

He looked fiercer than ever, with the snow clinging to his

hair and beard like some figure from Norse mythology. White breath billowed from his mouth like smoke. In my fear, I barely suppressed an urge to scream.

He looked at me. He saw me huddled on the couch, holding my baby, trying helplessly to keep warm. And suddenly, I saw for the first time that the fierce light in the old man's eyes was burning with warmth and compassion.

"I come vit' firewood. Oil stove no good," Otto said in his broken accent. "I make wood-burner from stove. Make house warm."

I watched speechlessly as he ripped parts from the oil stove, fashioned a makeshift grate from coat hangers, and put hunks of wood in his new apparatus. A few minutes later, Old Otto had a fire roaring in the stove, spreading warmth throughout the cabin.

He brought in snow, melting it in a pan on the stove. There would be warm milk for the baby, and coffee for us.

As I looked at the old man I'd been so frightened of—now caring for my baby's needs—I felt terribly ashamed. I had judged Old Otto wrongly, based only on the gossip of others. I had thought him ugly and menacing. I had avoided him. And now, in my hour of despair, he had cared enough to come and help me.

As I gulped his hot coffee, Otto explained, "I see no light, no smoke from your cabin. I come to look." He went on, explaining that he'd found the oil barrel tipped over by the wind outside—which is why the stove had stopped working. He said he didn't know what it was that had compelled him to leave his cabin, to harness up his dogs and go out into the blizzard; after all, our cabin might have been just empty.

"God vatching us," Otto commented. And I thought of my prayers.

Otto and our small family became good friends throughout the rest of Jim's tour of duty. He often came by to visit, delighting us all with stories of Alaska in the Gold Rush days. He loved Linda especially. I remember her tiny baby hands grasping one of the gnarled fingers he'd hold out to her so tenderly. The baby would laugh and gurgle as if she, too, had seen beyond the fierce madman of rumor and found Otto as he was—a lonely, gentle old man who'd known years of hard work in a brutal land.

A "chechako," I had learned a valuable lesson of survival in Alaska. And yet it wasn't any different from the lesson you needed to live anywhere.

Trust. In God, and *in His people.*

A PRAYER FOR STEADFASTNESS

O God, our Father, Thou searcher of men's hearts,
help us to draw nearer to Thee in sincerity
and truth . . .
Make us to choose the harder right instead of the
easier wrong,
and never to be content with a half truth when the
whole can be won.
Endow us with courage that is born of loyalty to all
that is noble
and worthy, that scorns to compromise with vice and
injustice,
and knows no fear when truth and right are in
jeopardy . . .
Kindle our hearts in fellowship with those of a cheerful
countenance,
and soften our hearts with sympathy for those who
sorrow and suffer . . . .
Help us, in our work and in our play, to keep ourselves
physically strong,
mentally awake and morally straight, that we may
better serve Thee and our Country.

An excerpt from the *West Point Cadet's Prayer*

YOUR SPIRITUAL WORKSHOP

ARE YOU AFRAID?

Norman Vincent Peale

An experiment to help you deal with your fears.

Is fear a constant companion in your life? If it is, something is wrong. Normal fear is a built-in preventative, for it keeps us from doing hazardous and foolish things, but abnormal fear is a mortal enemy which siphons off energy, destroys inner peace and makes people ineffective and powerless.

"How do I know if my fear is abnormal or not?" you ask. A businessman came to my office once with an unusual amount of fear. He told me:

"I think I am losing my mind. I cannot make the simplest decisions. Throughout my business career I have handled matters of large importance which have involved vast sums of money, but now the smallest decisions cause me no end of struggle. I am haunted by the possibility that I will make a mistake. Whether it's selecting a green or a brown tie in the morning, taking the bus or my car to work, eating in the office or out, I fear I will make the wrong choice. Often I have trouble making any decision at all."

Obviously, the businessman's fear was abnormal. But often the line of distinction is more finely drawn. If you are in doubt, test yourself on the following questions:

Is my sleep disturbed by one or more fears? . . . Do I stop in the middle of work because my mind is taken over by fear? . . . Does fear often make me listless and ineffective?

. . . Do I avoid social gatherings because of my fear? . . . Does fear keep me from enjoying the little things of life?

If you answer yes to any one of these questions, it is time for you to confront this fear openly and make an effort to rid yourself of it. I recommended the following procedure to a friend who found it helpful in dealing with his problem. See if the plan doesn't prove effective for you. Before you begin find a quiet place and a comfortable chair. You will need a Bible, paper, pencil and a pair of scissors for this Workshop.

Spelling It Out

Begin by drawing a line lengthwise through the center of your paper. On the left hand side write down in detail the fears that trouble you. "Why must I put them on paper?" comes the question.

There is a great therapy in trying to write out what it really is that bothers you. In the case of a deep fear, you need to see it laid out before you. Once you begin to describe it to yourself on paper, it may suddenly take on a different shape. A fear that may seem enormous bottled up in your mind can assume quite normal proportions when put in words on paper.

Body Relaxation

Psychologists report that fear produces tension which can block creativity. So it follows that you need a relaxed body before you can have a relaxed mind. And it will take a relaxed mind to enable you to rid yourself of fear.

Sit down in an armchair. Stretch your arms out as far as possible. Then allow them to fall limply on the arm rests. Relax your fingers. Stretch your legs out as far as they go and let them fall limp too. Take a series of deep breaths, slowly letting the air out of your lungs. Open and close your eyes by letting the eyelids drop laxly. Conceive of your entire body as being inert and totally yielded to the chair. Spend several minutes picturing in your mind some peaceful scenes: wheat waving in the wind, a lake full of soft ripples, green moss in the middle of a forest.

Continue this exercise until you are sure the tension has drained out of you.

3. Mind Relaxation

If your body is sick, you go to a physician and receive a prescription for medicine. Since abnormal fear creates an unhealthy condition in the mind, a prescription for another kind of medicine is needed. We suggest it can be found by searching your Bible. On the right hand side of your paper write down some of the verses that speak to your need. Passages like these:

For God hath not given us a spirit of fear; but of power, and of love, and of a sound mind. II Timothy 1:7

Be not afraid, neither be thou dismayed: for the Lord thy God is with thee withersoever thou goest. Joshua 1:9

Lo, I am with you alway. Matthew 28:20

The verses go on and on—all assurances that God can handle your fear, that He wants you to be free of it and to have a sound mind. He asks, yes implores, you to give Him your burden.

Read through the Psalms for further comfort, ending with the 23rd Psalm.

4. The Act Of Trust

All the steps taken so far will be inadequate to rid you of fear unless you can now do one important act. It is perfectly described in Proverbs 3:5:

Trust in the Lord with all thine heart; and lean not unto thine own understanding.

If you really do not think that God has your best interests at heart, then it is pointless to pray to Him for help. Your negative attitude will block the channel; prayer, Bible-reading and churchgoing thus become meaningless routines.

The key then is *trust*. You trust God. Regardless of all that goes wrong, you believe He loves you and cares about what happens to you.

How can a person full of doubts do this?

It takes an act of acceptance, of becoming childlike in your faith.

A pastor called on a young mother who was afraid for her husband who was traveling in a foreign country. She reached a state of near panic as she imagined the things that could happen to him. The pastor noted a child playing nearby. "How old is your daughter?" he asked.

"Carol's four."

"Is she upset and worried too?"

"Of course not."

"How do you explain Carol's lack of fear?"

The woman hesitated. "Carol's just a baby. Besides, I'm here with her. I suppose she puts her trust in me and that's that."

The pastor suggested to the mother that she take the child in her lap. "Now, just as Carol puts her trust in you, I suggest you transfer the picture and think of yourself as a child in relationship to God. Put your trust in Him. Believe that He is looking after Jack. Every time you feel a sense of panic sit in this chair and picture yourself, Carol and Jack all safe in God's hands."

Into The Wastebasket

One final action is needed. Go back to the sheet of paper on which you wrote out in detail the specifics about your fear. Offer up a prayer something like this:

"Lord, I have brought this matter to Your attention. I know now that while I am unable by myself to throw off this fear, You are totally adequate. I put my trust in You."

Now take a pair of scissors and cut your sheet of paper in two, leaving your fears on one side and the Scripture verses on the other. Take the half which lists your fears and tear it up and throw the pieces into the wastebasket. As you let them fall, say to yourself, "It is done." Then take the list of verses and place them in your Bible to reread whenever you need strength. A good spot to place the list is near Proverbs 16:20 which says:

He that handleth a matter wisely shall find good: and whoso trusteth in the Lord, happy is he.

The Unlimited Power of Prayer

LORD, CHANGE ME

Chapter 2

Are you troubled by a habit you can't seem to break? Are you worried about a flaw in your character? Do you wish you could be a better person, but lack the will power to change? Let God's transforming power into your life. He can change you as surely as He changed the people in the following stories.

Here is a bored housewife caught up in an illicit affair, a successful performer with a nasty temper problem, a tough-minded intellectual, a young thief . . . nine men and women who turned to God when they finally acknowledged they couldn't change themselves. Change came gradually for some. For others it was a dramatic and sudden transformation. All experienced a re-creation that can be yours when will power is turned into *prayer power*.

The Apostle Paul tells us, "If any man is in Christ, he is a new creature." (II Corinthians 5:17) This is the promise you can rely on when you give your life—your habits, your character—up to God with the prayer: "Lord, change me."

Sometimes, just when you think everything's under control, the bottom drops out.

TRYING TO BE A BETTER ME

B. J. Thomas

I was feeling great.

Looking out the jet airliner's window, I marveled at the sparkling emerald waters of the Mediterranean. It was August, 1978, and my family and I were on our way to a long-awaited two-week vacation in the Holy Land. I smiled at Gloria, my wife, who was engrossed in a book, and reached over and wrapped my arm around Paige, our eight-year-old daughter.

We had just completed a four-day crusade in Taiwan that had been successful beyond our wildest dreams. For me, the experience represented a spiritual milestone. More than 100,000 people had attended the four evening services where I performed as the guest singer, and thousands had given their lives to the Lord. I could still feel the joy that emanated from that hot, crowded stadium.

What a difference performing in a Christian concert had been! There were the same hassles, problems, foul-ups as in any other concert—but what a different spirit. There was a time I used to be in a constant state of anxiety and anger while on the road or performing. And my temper, which had been a life-long problem, could explode at any moment into violence. I had been known to wreck hotel rooms and start brawls; once I even pulled a knife on one of my best friends. Ironically, such stunts were really desperate cries for help; but when you're the boss, few people have the guts to grab you and say, "Stop." So the cries got louder, my behavior more bizarre, and soon I was on a downhill slide toward inevitable self-destruction.

Just three years ago I was living in darkness, hopelessly hooked on drugs. Once a top pop singer—a healthy guy with a great future—I had become a walking skeleton, a wasted addict. I had lost everything—my marriage, friends, career and money—to dope. It brought all the dark sides of my character to the surface: self-indulgence, anger, violence.

Then, thanks to Gloria and her Christian friends, I learned about the Lord, and asked Him into my life. He gave me a peace and purpose for living I had never known before. By His grace—that's the only way I can explain it—I quit drugs cold turkey, and never went back.

That crusade in Taiwan proved to me that I was a new person. I congratulated myself on my success at achieving self-control.

Yup, B.J., I thought, tightening my seat belt as the plane began its descent, *you've finally got yourself together*. For the first time in my life, everything seemed in order. Gloria and I had never enjoyed a better relationship, and Paige was a happy little girl. My records were topping the gospel music charts and I had a new book coming out in the fall. I was looking forward to this trip to the Holy Land—to the home of the Man Who had so dramatically changed my life. I wanted it to be perfect.

Our first morning in Tel Aviv, we breakfasted on the terrace of our hotel room, which overlooked the beach and sea. Gloria and I excitedly pored over the pile of travel brochures we had collected, planning the day's activities. Paige, I noticed, was rather quiet—a little bit sulky. Figuring she was still tired out from the trip, I didn't say anything. There was no sense in starting the first day of our vacation with a fuss.

But as the day went on, Paige's behavior didn't get any better. She remained moody the entire morning, and by lunchtime, she was downright ornery. Still, I didn't say anything. It was so rare that we ever enjoyed full days together as a family—I didn't want to spoil this one.

That evening, we returned to the hotel hot, tired, hungry, and loaded down with souvenirs. Fumbling for the key to the door, I asked Paige to hold a package. She looked the other way.

"Paige," I said severely.

She turned to regard me with mischievous brown eyes, testing me, trying my patience.

"Paige," I repeated, "I'm not in the mood."

She giggled—and I could feel my temper rising.

Then Gloria spoke up. "Honey," she said, "if you'd straightened Paige out this morning, this wouldn't be happening."

That did it. Gloria's words added fuel to my already hot temper, which shot up like a skyrocket.

"Don't," I bellowed, kicking the door open with my foot, *"tell me what to do!"*

My face was red with rage, and for the next 10 minutes I ranted and raved around the hotel room like some tyrant. Unable to control myself, I couldn't believe my behavior. Paige started crying. Gloria fell strangely silent.

I glanced over at her, and my heart sank when I saw the expression on her face. I hadn't seen that look in years; a horrible combination of disappointment and pity.

Suddenly, a million nightmarish memories came flooding back. More than once in the past I'd wake up in the hospital after some drunken brawl. Gloria would always be there, wearing the same sad expression she had now.

I tried to say something, tried to break the tension-filled silence, but no words came out. I felt confused, bewildered, as if a rug had been pulled out from under me. True, my outbursts weren't public anymore, but this was worse; I had hurt my family, the ones I loved the most. Besides, if I planned to spend the rest of my life "praising the Lord" in one breath, then losing my temper in the next, what kind of example was that?

How can this be? I thought. *I'm different now; I've changed. I am, supposedly, a new man.*

But, it was painfully clear, I was a new man face-to-face with an old problem. My temper, like an old demon in hiding, had surfaced again with a roar.

Finally, I couldn't stand the silence.

"Gloria?" I said. She was sitting at the desk writing a postcard. Paige was at her feet, flipping through a comic book. Both looked up at me warily.

"I'm sorry," I said.

"It's okay," Gloria said, resting her hand on Paige's shoulder.

"I don't know what to do," I said.

Again, the room was quiet.

"Well," said Gloria thoughtfully, "we could try praying. I mean, that's never failed to help us before, no matter what the problem."

I had to agree.

"Let's do that," I said.

The three of us sat cross-legged on the big king-size bed. And a beautiful peace settled over our once-turbulent little family as we joined hands in prayer.

"Lord," I said, "I confess I've got a bad problem here with my temper. I'm sorry, and I want to be rid of it. Please give me the right attitude; give me Your patience, tolerance and love. And please bless this vacation and make it a special time for all of us to get closer to You, just as we originally planned. Thank You. In Jesus' name—Amen."

We all felt better. I slept like a log that night, secure in knowing that, now I'd turned the problem over to the Lord, He would somehow take care of it.

I have to admit the next morning wasn't easy. Little things still annoyed me. We overslept, missed breakfast, and had to rush to get ready to meet our car and tour guide, which we had hired for the day. But each time I felt myself losing my cool, I'd quickly say a short prayer. It worked. For the remainder of our vacation I never lost my temper, and each night we returned to our hotel a happy, tight-knit little family.

We did a lot of walking during our days in the Holy Land and with each step—from the dusty path lined with ancient olive trees leading to the Garden of Gethsemane, to the crowded city streets of Nazareth—we felt ourselves growing closer to the Lord. And, by the time our two weeks were nearly over and we were packing to go home, I felt I had come to a full understanding of what had happened that first night in our hotel room.

It's probably the most important lesson I'll ever learn. And that is: Once you welcome the Lord into your life, you embark on a journey of Christian growth that never ends. It is a constant step-by-step refining process that works to transform you into the kind of person He wants you to be.

Like a spotlight, He shines His healing love on the dark troubled areas of your life and asks that you release them—one by one—to Him.

Looking back, it's exciting to see how lovingly and patiently the Lord has worked His will in my life. Once I had a problem with drugs; He took care of it. Then Gloria and I had a broken marriage to contend with; He mended it. I've still got this problem with temper; He's working with me on that one, and won't let me be satisfied until the job's done. And, when that time comes, you can be sure there will be something else.

That's fine with me—I'll be ready and willing.

A PRAYER FOR JOY

Lord, I am a fool. I sought joy and fulfillment in worldly things and have become increasingly empty. I see now that all along You have been waiting to give more joy, yet I have been unwilling to receive it from You. So now I make this act of holding out empty hands, a waiting heart, an unfilled life for You to fill. May the power of Your love and gladness drive gloom and drabness from me. And help me become the kind of person who can radiate Your joy to others. Amen.

Catherine Marshall

A hasty marriage, an illicit romance and the "Hound of Heaven" are the ingredients of this dramatic story.

I CAN'T FIGHT YOU ANYMORE!

Roberta Lee

As I look back now I wonder how differently things would have turned out if I had gone ahead and dropped the letter from my pen pal, Rebecca Ward,* into the wastebasket. But I didn't and therein lies the story.

It began with a too-hasty marriage. My husband and I went in different directions from the beginning. We tried to put on a good front for the sake of our two children, but behind the facade was boredom and indifference.

My ideas of marriage, I know now, were gleaned from romantic movies and magazines. When my husband did not measure up to these juvenile fancies, I felt full of self-pity. In this mood, I suppose it was inevitable that I be tempted into an extra-marital affair. The man turned out to be our next door neighbor, Ralph Carlson.

My husband and I spent occasional evenings with the Carlsons. Betty Carlson was a critical, discontented person, constantly holding her husband up to ridicule, while Ralph and I got along beautifully. His compliments were music to my ears.

Soon the liaison started, with all the lies and furtive meetings and whispered phone calls that go with this messy sort of thing. My conscience bothered me at first, but I rationalized my actions. Betty had made it clear she did not like her husband, and it was quite obvious that my husband did not care for me or he would have been more attentive and romantic.

*All names in this story, including the author's, have been changed.

Caught up in this new "love," my interest in all else waned, including my hobby of writing letters to pen pals all over the world. Thus, when I received a letter from Rebecca Ward, one of my correspondents, I considered dropping it into the wastebasket.

With the letter poised over the basket, I for some reason did not let go. I put it back on my desk, thinking, "It's only polite to answer her." And I did.

Our correspondence increased and soon I looked forward to hearing from her. I liked her sense of humor and her enthusiasm for life. What I didn't like were the prayers and tracts that she often enclosed. She knew nothing of my infatuation for Ralph: how was it that these enclosures were often uncannily apropos?

Meanwhile, I was being an attentive and loving mother, salving my conscience by throwing myself into activities with my children during the day. It was the nights I began to dread. My husband worked the late shift and I slept alone. Only I wasn't doing much sleeping.

For, increasingly, I was consumed by a restlessness, a sense of Something hounding me and leaving me no peace. I tried reading a novel at bedtime but couldn't concentrate on it. I'd turn out the light determined to sleep, only to toss and turn all night.

One lonely night in sheer desperation for something to read, I picked up a Bible and idly leafed through it. I read a verse here, part of a Psalm there . . . then the first verse of the 51st Psalm caught my interest when it spoke of God's mercies blotting out our transgressions. I could use some of that, I thought.

As I read the fourth verse I felt a sudden pain in my heart! I read it again: *Against Thee, Thee only, have I sinned, and done this evil in Thy sight. . . .*

For the first time I was filled with a sense of shame. Always before I had thought that sin was wrong because it hurt other people. That I could have hurt God, Himself, by my sin was a horrible shock!

I remembered how I felt when somebody hurt me; then I realized how much greater God was than I, and so how much greater His hurt. Stunned, I slid to my knees beside the bed. I couldn't pray. All I could do was moan "Oh God" over and over as He opened my eyes to my shallowness and selfishness.

This was the beginning of an all-out battle, with my bed the battleground. I didn't surrender easily. Night after torturous night, I argued with the Hound of Heaven. I would go to bed and the only book I *could* read was the Bible. I was afraid to read it, yet I couldn't leave it alone.

Sometimes the struggle lasted till dawn and I'd have to drag myself out of bed to attend to the children. I avoided people as much as possible. Days would go by without my ever combing my hair because I couldn't stand the sight of myself in the mirror!

The truth was I did not want to change. I liked the way I lived, or told myself I did. All I really wanted was to get rid of the overpowering guilt connected with my affair. And so I worked through the Psalms, sticking up for my rights, arguing my case. After weary hours of battle, I'd cry, "I am weary with my groaning . . . I water my couch with my tears."*

One evening, after tucking the children in bed, I sat at the dining room table in no hurry to go upstairs to bed where I knew I would be in for another tussle with the Lord. My eye caught sight of the last booklet Rebecca had sent to me. Leafing through it, I saw the words *born again*. Instantly the old red flag was up, but I read on, just to prove to myself that it made no sense. Satisfied that it didn't, I tossed the booklet down and went upstairs.

There I opened my Bible again. "Bet it doesn't say a word in here about being 'born again,' " I muttered. But there, in the third chapter of John, mentioned in the pamphlet, were Jesus' own words: "Ye must be born again."

Feeling a little betrayed, I switched out the light and tried to go to sleep.

Then God was there again! It was not an audible voice, but sort of a voice in my mind. Yet I knew that it wasn't my own voice or even my own mind forming the words.

On this particular night my "conversation" started with Him explaining that this second birth, with me cleansed and free from my former sins, is what He gives to those who give themselves to Him. I recalled the awful things I'd done and offered the excuse that I was not "good enough."

He reminded me that no one is "good enough." It is a free gift.

*Psalm 6:6

I balked at this. It couldn't be that simple!

He informed me it was.

I wanted what He had to offer but I was afraid of all it might involve. He agreed that it wouldn't be easy, but He reminded me of His promise to be there always and to help me along the way.

I was torn in two, part of me wanting desperately to surrender my will to Him and the other part fighting tooth and nail to live as I pleased. Why did I have to go through all of this? If God wanted me changed why didn't He just change me? He was more powerful than I!

The answer came that He wanted me of my own free accord. I could refuse Him if I wanted.

I pleaded for Him to help me, to make it easy for me, but no answer to this came.

He was waiting.

I couldn't stand it any longer. I knew I couldn't go back to what I had been, and without Him there would be nothingness.

I cried, "I can't fight You anymore! Do with me as You will!"

Almost immediately peace came to me and soon I fell asleep. It was then I had the dream.

I was running down a lonely road in a dense fog. I was afraid. Then I came upon a beautiful staircase leading up into a thick mist. After a short pause, I started up the stairs. They were wide and not steep; there were bowers of flowers on either side giving off sweet fragrance.

After I had climbed some distance, I noticed that the flowers were gone and the stairs were narrower. I thought about going back, but there was only the fog below.

I continued climbing. The stairs were now curving. But the stairs seemed endless. Although now desperately tired, I somehow felt that life would not be worth living if I did not gain what lay at the top.

I was crawling now, one step at a time. The stairs were only as wide as my body and making sharper curves. Finally, completely exhausted, I could go no further.

In utter despair I cried out, "Jesus, help me!" My head was in my arms and I lay sobbing on the stairs. So it was that I sensed a Presence rather than saw it. I lifted my head and saw bare feet several steps above me. There was a large scar on the instep of each foot.

I reached up for His hand and rose to my feet, all exhaustion leaving me. His face was gloriously beautiful to behold. Joy beyond understanding flooded over me and I awakened to find myself sitting upright in bed.

I sat unmoving a long time, savoring the memory of the love that shone from that face. I was loathe to go back to sleep for fear it would fade as dreams most often do.

Yet, morning came and the dream remained fresh in my mind. Also a resolution of things to do.

First of all, I had to make a clean and final break with Ralph, although for some months I had been avoiding him.

Then the children and I began going to church regularly every Sunday. They enthusiastically helped me set up a family devotional center, using my cedar chest as an altar.

Surprisingly, one day my husband brought home a lovely wooden cross. He mounted it on a mahogany base, and as I watched him working I knew that this relentless love of heaven was pursuing him as tirelessly as it had me, down the avenues of his particular resistances and defenses. We set the cross on our altar, along with candles and the Bible, and here the children and I kneel for evening prayers.

The wonderful, exuberant glow of conversion when I felt washed and free lasted only several weeks. Then came a series of tests, doubts and difficulties. And it was then that I saw the significance of my dream.

The pleasant, flower-strewn first stage of my climb was like the exhilaration of those first weeks after my rebirth. But then the stairs got steeper and narrower. Trying to heal bruised and broken relationships is a painfully slow process. But it is when the Christian walk seems too difficult that we can lift up our eyes and catch a glimpse of the One who has gone this way before.

What happened to a tough-minded intellectual when he encountered the Holy Spirit?

THE SKEPTICAL LAWYER

Yager Cantwell

Beatrice, one of the most beautiful blondes I had ever seen, was looking at me intently. Soft Hawaiian music drifted through the fish net decorations of an exotic Cantonese restaurant. I had only known her a short time, but from the first moment I was more serious about this girl than any other girl I'd ever met.

I had just told her a little of my family background. Then she made the statement that couldn't have shattered my romantic mood any more completely than if she had kicked me in the shins.

"My father is a minister," she said.

I was rocked. As a member of a tough-minded family of lawyers, I had always prided myself on being a scientific humanist, a bit of an intellectual and a militant agnostic. All through college and law school, I had been ready to attack religion as a mish-mash of wish projection, distorted fact, ignorance and irrationality. During my early years of law practice I maintained this same hostile attitude.

In a way, the practice of law had made me even more cynical, because quite often I was thrown into contact with more people who called themselves Christians, yet whose private lives were radically different from the pious masks they wore in church on Sundays. I was not even willing to concede that such hypocrites were a small minority: to me they were an epidemic—and the ease with which they were able to use religion as a cloak of respectability hardly enhanced my opinion of the church.

Not that this antagonism deterred me from finding an occasional use for religion. For instance, while still at college and while riding the crest of my arrogant agnosticism, I took a course in the teachings of Jesus. Why? Because I knew that juries are often swayed by pleadings and arguments based on religion. I wanted to be able to outperform any opposing lawyer by Biblically outquoting him. So I figured I had better be prepared.

The teachings of the Man of Nazareth had enormous impact on me—intellectually. No lawyer concerned with communication or persuasion could study what He said and not be impressed by His brilliance of mind, His dialectical thrust, the powers of argument, His use of parables, His astounding narrative ability, His poetic imagery, His magnificent denunciation, even—it seemed to me—His occasional bright patches of humor.

The intellectual "discovery" of Jesus only increased my contempt for the distorted, watered-down image of Him presented by some churches. When anyone asked me for my opinion of theology, I continued to reply that it was the height of concentrated nonsense.

This went on for about 10 years until I met Beatrice. Through most of these bachelor years I had lived by a playboy philosophy in which any pretty girl was fair game and what two consenting adults did in private was no concern of anyone else—as long as no one was hurt. Beatrice had vastly different ideas, however.

Although jolted by the information that her father was a minister, I cared enough about her to take a vacation and follow her all the way across the country to her home. There I met her father, the Reverend Harry O. Nash, of Coronado, California. He was the first man to say to me, "God loves you."

I looked at him in disbelief. I said, "I don't know what you mean by the word 'God,' and I've been trying to define 'love' for over 15 years, and still trying to find out what this 'me' is."

The next day the confirmed agnostic sprained an ankle playing tennis, sprained it so badly that he was laid up for a week with nothing to do but talk to this calm, patient man who burned like a pure blue flame with the love of God. A man who had the guts to lay *his* alleged relationship with the Holy Spirit out on the dissecting table—under the searching scalpel of agnostic cross-examination.

I had known dedicated scientists, doctors, artists, lawyers and tradesmen, I had known what they were dedicated to; but here was a man passionately dedicated to something I didn't understand. From my omniscient viewpoint he was either psychopathic, intellectually debauched or phony, and I intended to find out precisely which.

Meanwhile, an interesting push-me-pull-you developed in my courtship of his daughter: she was beautiful—but Christian; I was vitally attracted to her, but intellectually repelled by her reactions. She was contaminated, I thought, by the bacilli of a long dead and rotting tradition. When I learned that she actually took this Christian stuff seriously, I determined to convert her to the cold, clear beauties of agnosticism. I told her that it "takes stamina to live with truth; it's easy to live with illusion."

When my subtle and extensive campaign finally ran aground, I attempted to enlist the aid of my closest friend, Ernest L. Badenoch, who for years had shared my revulsion for organized Christianity. However, when he met Rev. Nash, within five days he became converted himself, dumped his promising teaching career and went into the ministry.

This was a severe psychic shock: it put me in a most uncomfortable position. Either Nash was not the phony I had presupposed, or Badenoch was—and I knew this last was impossible. Soon I, the agnostic, found myself wondering if somehow, just possibly, I was missing out on something terribly important, experientially; something that for years I had been too intellectually arrogant to attempt to understand.

Did boy get girl? Did boy marry girl? No, as a matter of fact, Beatrice married somebody else. But a process had been started in me, a process that ended months later with a decision to abandon my god of reason, let go of my common sense and rely on God's. Then, like a frightened child going off a high diving board with eyes shut, I took the final plunge, gave up the faculty I prized more than anything else in the world: my sovereign right to decide for myself—and asked God to come into my life and take charge.

My petition was heard and answered. Very slowly, but unmistakably, I changed. Or rather, I *was* changed. I *experienced* that change. After the leap of faith came personal experience. I found out that the girl's father was right: trying to love God wasn't simply a question of knowing about God, it was knowing God, personally and intimately.

After I made this leap, many areas of spiritual difficulty remained. "Intercessory" prayer, for example, still seemed a wild violation of all the laws of logic. Why should I pray for somebody else? Surely the Power that ruled the universe knew far more about other people's problems than I did, and if He were omnipotent, He could take any necessary action. Why should my words or thoughts affect such actions? In fact, how could they? My verbal and logical approach prohibited experiment with this ridiculous sort of prayer.

Two years later my father became dangerously ill. Not believing in them, intercessory prayers were out of the question for me, but at a church service one morning I was startled to hear the minister pray for my father. Involuntarily, something inside me cried out, "Lord, please help him." And instantly, as if it were written across my mind in letters of fire, an answer came from outside of my own consciousness: *He will be saved.* And he *did* recover.

From that moment on, all argument or verbalizations about intercessory prayer went out the window; I began to experiment in earnest. I found that, with or without verbal logic, intercessory prayer *works*—for me and for others. Things happen that simply cannot be explained by coincidence or accident or fantasy or illusion or any known law of predictability. Again, the proof is the experience, and no one will admit more quickly than I that until you've had the experience it is hard to believe.

I have much to learn and a long way to grow. But I have discovered that the Holy Spirit can *do* things in loving ways through me, for me and for others which I can't do for myself. He can plan events beyond my imagination and carry out projects beyond my strength. I find that spectacular and unbelievable results occur when I pray as if my life depends on it—as, of course, it does:

"I want only Your will in this situation now, Lord, regardless of consequences—even if it costs me my life. . . ."

This is when things start to happen, when the lid blows off, the roof falls in, life, love and joy begin. This is where the action is, where the excitement starts, where freedom reigns and Power enters.

A PRAYER FOR HUMILITY

Take me and break me and make me, dear God,
Just what you want me to be—
Give me the strength to accept what you send
And eyes with the vision to see
All the small arrogant ways that I have
And the vain little things that I do,
Make me aware that I'm often concerned
More *with* Myself *than with* You,
Uncover before me my weakness and greed
And help me to search deep inside
So I may discover how easy it is
To be selfishly lost in my pride—
And then in Thy goodness and mercy
Look down on this weak, erring one
And tell me that I am forgiven
For all I've so willfully done,
And teach me to humbly start following
The path that the dear Saviour trod
So I'll find at the end of life's journey
"A Home in the City of God."

Helen Steiner Rice

This singer shares a personal discovery that "lights up her life."

THE WEAKNESS I'M GLAD I HAVE

Debby Boone

Something happened in my life with the recording of *You Light Up My Life*. My career, like the song, took off like a rocket. But something else also happened: I discovered a weakness in myself.

Since childhood I had known that I would be a singer. It was never an egotistical feeling that I was great or destined to be a star. It was just a sense that this was what my life held for me. As I grew older, various people began pressuring me to make some recordings and get started on a career, but my parents always held me back. The important thing was to make the right spiritual commitment and not think in terms of the "right" career moves.

Then last year, when I was 20, a producer friend came by our house and left a tape of *You Light Up My Life*. When I came home, I listened to it. I adored it! I immediately associated the lyric with my deep spiritual relationship with God.

I wanted to record the song. And suddenly my parents, who had been discouraging me from branching out on my own for years, said: "Wonderful! Do it!"

I flew to New York, with my mother. I recorded the song almost on a trial basis. When we cut the record, my mother prayed the whole time that I sang. When it was over, we looked at each other almost fearfully. We felt strange, like something was about to happen.

Two months later, the record was released, and things did start happening. The record just kept building and building and became a smash hit.

Wonderful things happened from my record. People wrote to say that it helped them through some difficult times in their lives, that the words gave them strength and hope. And good things happened to me professionally as well—concert tours, TV appearances, a Grammy award (Best New Artist of the Year), and a new record, *God Knows*.

But there's been a lot of stress, strain and pressure. And that's how I discovered my special weakness: nervousness.

I may be Pat Boone's daughter, but I'm still a very nervous type. I don't take things like my dad does. He can walk on stage, cool as a cucumber, and never feel any strain. But I'm not that way. Every time I have to face doing a show I keep wondering: "How am I going to get through this?" I hate my nervousness, because it destroys the things that I try to do—my voice quivers, my face begins to twitch, and I can't sing the way I want to sing, or look the way I want to look.

Too much imagination is part of the problem. When I started to think, as I did preparing for the Grammys, "Wow, Barbra Streisand's going to be sitting in the audience right below me when I sing!", or when I thought about the audience, or the millions of viewers, it sent a surge of fear through my body.

I knew I had to sort things out. I asked my parents to help me, and they did. Gradually they made me see that I was focusing on the wrong things: I was concerned with pleasing audiences when I should have been concerned with pleasing God. I finally said to myself, "I'm not singing so that Barbra Streisand will go away thinking, 'Wow! That girl's great!' That's not the reason I'm up there on that stage. When I'm up there I have a chance to stand up on national TV and sing a song that to me is really a prayer."

When I started thinking of the situation in those terms, everything seemed different. That's what I kept concentrating on when I got up on stage at the Grammys. I took my eyes off the faces in the audience and sang the song as I had sung it originally. The words took on deep meaning, a calm came over me—a warmth and a calm and an emotion—and I sang the song and I found tears coming into my eyes. No longer was I thinking about the reactions of people, or what this could do for my career, or whether I would win this award or that. I only was thinking: "Whom am I pleasing now? What counts now? God and my relationship to Him, and that's it!"

I keep thinking that as time goes on and I get more used to this business, I'll be more relaxed. But I hope now that I will never come to the point where I can handle any situation on my own. I hope I'll always have to look to God and say, "I can't do this. It's up to You now, not me."

I still dread being nervous. But I see now how God uses this. I rely constantly on the passage in Scripture where the Lord says to the Apostle Paul, "My strength is made perfect in weakness." (II Corinthians 12:9) I kept thinking about this over and over again, as I faced that moment at the Grammys.

I thought: "I couldn't be weaker than I am right now. I couldn't feel more inadequate than I do right now. It's His ball game, not mine."

Now I know that my worst weakness is what God uses to draw me to Him. And I thank Him for it.

THE HARD WAY

For every hill I've had to climb,
For every stone that bruised my feet,
For all the blood and sweat and grime,
For blinding storms and burning heat,
My heart sings but a grateful song—
These were the things that made me strong!

Anonymous

How a loser from the slums became the world's number one salesman.

SOMEDAY YOU'LL BE SOMEBODY, JOEY

Joe Girard

I hurried across the back yard, the knot of shame and frustration tightening in my chest. The shoes I had shined that morning were caked with mud, and I had torn my pants climbing over the back fence.

I tiptoed up the stairs and opened the back door. In the brightly lighted kitchen, my wife, June, was at the sink. I came up behind her and kissed her lightly on the neck. "Hi, honey." Without acknowledging my greeting, June turned to me, her face expressionless.

"Joey, there's nothing to eat in the house." Her voice was flat.

"But, honey . . . I couldn't get anything today. I don't have any money." I felt humiliated and angry.

"Joey, the kids are hungry. What am I going to give them?"

"How would I know!" I shouted, turning away.

A lot had happened to me in the past year, but this was the worst—to hear that my kids were hungry. I was deep in debt. The bank was threatening to repossess my car, my home—everything. I had taken to sneaking in the back way to avoid process servers and bill collectors.

I had tried to make a killing in the construction business and had been swindled instead. Now, eight months later, I had reached rock bottom.

As if on cue, the doorbell rang. Apprehensively I tiptoed into the darkened living room and looked through the curtained window. Another bill collector.

I sank to my knees, my hands covering my face. There in the dark living room, with the bill collector standing just outside the door, I prayed from my heart: "God, is it true what my dad said about me—that I'll never be any good? Is that what You want for me, God? Lord, if You will help me, I promise I'll try to help other people. I swear I will! Please, God . . . I can't take any more!"

Tears squeezed from my eyes and my throat ached with the need to cry away the pent-up anguish I felt, but I couldn't. I just remained there, on my knees, in the dark, until I heard footsteps descending the porch steps. Then I stumbled up to the bedroom.

I was 35 and a total failure. Maybe my dad had been right—I never would amount to anything. I remembered when I was a kid, growing up in an Italian neighborhood on Detroit's tough East Side, how I used to defy him. He was hot-tempered and sometimes when I'd push him too far he'd take me to the cellar and tie me to a post and beat me with a razor strap. "You're no good!" he'd shout. *"You'll never be nothin'!"*

Thank God for my mother. Afterward she'd comfort me and say, "You will be good, Joey. You'll show your father someday. Don't cry, Joey . . . you're going to be somebody!"

When I was nine years old I got a shoeshine box and used to go around to neighborhood bars. And if I didn't earn enough, I'd get a beating when I got home. So I used to stay out until I did.

Later on I began to get into trouble. I stole tires and car radios and finally broke into a bar and wound up in a juvenile detention center. After that, I had a series of menial jobs. Nothing seemed to go right.

I know now that a lot of it was my own fault. Even after I was married and had gotten into the real-estate business, I was sometimes dishonest; I often misled people.

Now, lying there in the dark, I felt that even God had had enough of Joe Girard.

But that desperate prayer of mine must have been heard, because the next morning I woke up with a renewed determination to get a job.

I went down to a local Chevrolet agency where I knew the manager. It was the first week in January and no showroom manager in his right mind would hire anyone after the holidays; there's simply no business. But I was desperate, and I talked him into giving me a chance—as a salesman.

That day, from a beat-up desk way in the back of the showroom, I called everybody I knew, trying to sell them a car—relatives, neighbors, friends, guys I had worked with. I dialed until my finger was numb. All the time I kept thinking of June and the kids with no food at home, and me with nobody I could borrow from.

Finally, after hours of trying, I gave up. As I was about to leave, I saw this guy come into the showroom—just 15 minutes before closing time. I tried to act nonchalant, but I grabbed him by the arm. I practically begged him to buy a car from me. And all the while I was trying to sell him, I was hearing June's voice in my head: *"Joey, the kids are hungry . . ."*

"You know," he said finally, "I've never met anyone who *asks* the way you do—you really mean it. I'll take the car."

After he left, I rushed to the manager's office and told him that I had made my first sale. Then I borrowed ten dollars from him. I went out and bought a big bag of groceries for June and the kids. I told them all about it over a nice big dinner.

From that point on things began to turn around, and I knew why. I had asked God for a break and He had given me one—a job I loved. Soon I was selling more cars than anyone in the showroom.

I didn't have any plan; I worked by instinct—harder and longer than any other salesman. I was driven by my needs—my need to provide for my family, my need to get out of debt and, above all, my need to prove to my dad that I could be somebody.

For a few years I made a comfortable living. Then my mother died. It was one of the saddest yet most mysterious events of my life, because from that time on, my sales production literally doubled, tripled and then quadrupled. I have no explanation for it, except maybe Mom was up there, pulling strings with the Lord, still insisting that her Joey was "a good boy."

Ideas came pouring into my head. I remember one night lying in bed, thinking about a mailing. And a voice seemed to whisper, "Joe, that mailing piece you've been using is the same old stuff that everybody is sending out. St. Patrick's

Day is coming up; why not send your customers St. Patrick's Day cards?" I honestly believe it was God giving me a little hint. We all get them from Him, but most people keep their ears closed to the message. This time I didn't. I sent those cards out—no hard sell, just a card with "Happy St. Patty's Day—I like you."

At Easter and Passover I sent another batch of cards out with a similar message. Soon I had a program of sending 12 mailings a year, geared to holidays. Sales went up and up.

On another occasion, I was selling a car to a funeral director and that little voice inside prompted me to ask him, "Mr. Brown, how do you know how many of those little prayer cards to print up—you know, the gold-edged cards with the holy picture and the name of the deceased person?"

"We've discovered through experience," he replied, "that the average person knows 250 people."

A short time later I asked a wedding caterer the same question and got the same answer: The bride will have 250 guests and the groom will have 250 guests. I hit upon what I have since come to call "Girard's Law," and it's simply this: If everybody knows about 250 people and you treat one customer with indifference or rudeness, or cheat him, the word will get around to 250 people—"Don't buy from Girard." Pretty soon you'll have a whole stadium-sized crowd not buying from Girard, because each of those 250 people know 250 people.

With this in mind, I'm always careful about the way I talk to my customers. When they tell me about their families or their problems, I really pay attention—not only with my ears, but with my eyes, my hands, my smile, my whole attitude. But it takes a genuine interest in people, a real caring, because they can spot a phony a mile off.

Over the years I listened to my inner voice and came up with many other sales techniques that really work. But the basic secret is having respect for people. As the Golden Rule says, you have to treat people the way you would like to be treated. It's a law of life that you get back what you give.

By applying this age-old principle, I was named the world's number one salesman for 12 years running.

But no matter how successful I was, I still hadn't won the

respect of my father. Then one December day in 1974 my dad stopped by the showroom. I was busy with a customer.

"Joe, I'm going over to your sister, Tina's," he said, shuffling toward the door.

"Wait a minute, Pop," I said, excusing myself for a minute. "I've got something I want to show you." I took a book out of my desk and handed it to him. It was *The Guinness Book of World Records*. "Look, Pop," I said, showing him the entry naming me the world's greatest salesman.

He said nothing. "Pa . . . there are four billion people in the world, but I'm the only salesman they've got in the book."

My dad turned to me and, putting a strong, gnarled hand on my shoulder, said the six words I had been waiting all my life to hear: "I am proud of you, Joey." And he meant it: I could see it in his eyes. It was the greatest thing that ever happened to me.

I gave him the book and he left. Two days later he died.

Thinking back on it, I realized that although sometimes my dad had been very harsh with me, I owed a lot of my success to him. He gave me the challenge, the need to prove myself. And to succeed in life you have to have a need—you have to say *I want*. And if you say it often enough, and ask for God's help, *you will.*

I proved to myself that it's in overcoming obstacles and learning from his mistakes that a man really finds himself and learns to get ahead. St. Paul said it best, almost two thousand years ago: "All things work together for good to them that love God. . . ." (Romans 8:28)

When you're in love with the wrong person, what can you do?

QUIET TEARS

Karen Barber

The tears were hot on my cheeks as I entered the courtyard behind the University of Maryland chapel. White street lights shone through the dark oaks as I passed the well-trimmed boxwoods. The campus was calm, peaceful, beautiful. Yet my throat was aching and the tears came.

Why was I crying? Pent-up confusion and frustration seemed to be boiling inside. Why could Allen upset me so? It wasn't just the hurtful things he had said tonight, I thought. No, things had never been right. We had met in geology class. He was a senior, I a sophomore. I had been attracted to him because I imagined he possessed a sensitivity in addition to his good looks.

But something was missing. Something that drove a wedge between us. Although he was a true nature-lover, Allen did not believe in God. Each time he belittled my faith, the gap widened.

It had been so easy to believe at home, secure in my own church. I knew that God existed because of the love and care of those around me. Now here I was, standing in the cool white moonlight, crying and wondering if God really could see me, alone in the midst of strangers.

I opened the heavy chapel door, still sobbing. The front of the church was bathed in soft light. Then to my embarrassment I saw a dark-haired boy kneeling in front and praying quietly. He paused when he saw me enter, but after a moment's hesitation he returned to his prayers.

I felt awkward. I had expected to find the chapel empty.

But I decided to slip into a back pew. Even the embarrassment I felt did not quell my tears, and I sat trying to rein in my churning emotions.

My whole day had gone wrong, starting with the phone call home. Mom had put Grandma on the line. I had casually asked her, "How's Barney?" Barney was the family dog, just a mutt, but full of personality.

Grandma paused and then said, "Didn't your mother tell you? We had him put to sleep this morning."

I was stunned. Surely Grandma was mistaken. But Mom confirmed the story. Barney had been in a fight and had had to be put to sleep.

Tears welled in my eyes. Suddenly home seemed very distant. No friendly welcome-home bark would greet me on weekends. No more companionable walks in the woods with Barney prancing ahead of me, tail wagging, nose to the ground.

How unsophisticated of me, I thought bleakly. I knew what Allen would say if he could see me crying now. A college student crying about a dog!

The chapel was quiet and peaceful. I wanted to pray a long, eloquent prayer that would restore my faith, make it seem real again. I longed, too, for something that would change Allen so that I wouldn't feel hurt or confused any more. But the only words my numbed spirit could manage were "Oh, God, help me."

At last my tears were spent, but I felt unchanged. My eyes wandered to the front of the church where the tranquil indirect light illuminated the altar. The stranger in front continued murmuring, head bent over a little black book.

He must have real faith, I decided. *Maybe he comes here every night for a quiet time of prayer. Some quiet time he's having tonight,* I thought, *with me back here sniffling!*

I was more composed now. Maybe my roommate wouldn't even know I'd been crying. I wanted to slip out unnoticed, but somehow I felt I should apologize to the boy up front. I summoned my courage and went quietly forward.

"Hi," I said.

The boy looked up. He had very dark curly hair and dark eyes. "Hi," he said.

"Listen, I hope I didn't disturb you."

"No." He hesitated. "Are you okay?"

"Yes, I feel better," I replied. How could I tell a total stranger about the crazy mix of emotions and doubts I felt? "Just boyfriend problems," I murmured.

An awkward pause followed. "What are you reading?" I asked finally, pointing to the book he held open in his hands.

He looked a little sheepish. "This is a book of prayers the church back home gave me when I left for college. I've been repeating the prayers for the sick."

"Is someone you know sick?"

"You may think I'm crazy," he said slowly, "but I was praying for my dog."

Praying for a dog? Did God really care about dogs? I wondered. Yet here, I felt, was another groping for faith, perhaps not too different from my own.

"What's wrong with your dog?" I asked.

"I had a call from my folks back in New York. Missy is a little terrier. She's been in labor for two days. She's getting weaker. If she doesn't have those puppies soon, she won't make it. I thought these prayers might help."

"I know how you're feeling. You won't believe this, but my dog died today." I wanted to help him, somehow. I remembered our youth group back home and how, if someone had a problem, we would pray about it. "Why don't we pray together?" I suggested hesitantly.

"Sure," he replied.

I said a short prayer, and he thanked me. We got up to leave, a bit more at ease now.

"You were pretty upset when you came in, weren't you?" he said.

"Yes, I guess so."

"I felt sorry for you. I prayed that God would help you."

"Thanks," I said. *If we could ask God to save the life of a terrier,* I thought confusedly, *couldn't I ask Him to straighten my tangled emotions?* Was Allen really right for me? If I kept on seeing him would I continue to have my beliefs shaken, one by one, until all that was left was this frightening, frustrating loneliness that seemed to be creeping into my soul?

"I wish you and your boyfriend all the best," the stranger was saying. "You're lucky he lives nearby. My fiancée lives back in New York. Boy, it's tough being so far away from her."

His dark eyes softened. "Last weekend we were in a wedding together. I wish it had been ours. I just can't wait until that day. Look, here's her picture." He pulled a snapshot out of his wallet.

I looked at the photo. It was a picture of a brown-haired girl dressed in a long gown. Just a pretty, smiling girl. But suddenly I knew I was seeing something that the photographer could not reproduce. It was the love and pride with which the dark-haired stranger had shown the picture. Here was something special and precious. Something I had almost ceased to believe in. This was a love that enhanced each partner's faith and self-worth, instead of tearing them down.

And suddenly I knew where that kind of love came from. It came from God, Who was love Himself. He was the Author of it, and He cared about all of us. He cared about me in all facets of my life, from the companionship of a beloved pet to the ultimate decision I would face in choosing a life partner. Somewhere God must have for me someone who would love me as this stranger loved his fiancée.

I doubt that the dark-haired boy ever knew what he sparked that night in my soul. He said, "Listen, this is a big campus and I'll probably never run into you again. I tell you what. Give me your name and I'll leave a note on the chapel bulletin board to let you know how Missy does."

The next day I scanned the chapel board. There was a folded paper with my name in bold letters. I opened it and read. "Missy is doing fine. She's the proud mother of three puppies! Thanks for the prayers. May God bless you."

That was the last contact I ever had with him. Our paths never crossed again. But I'm sure it was more than chance that led me to the chapel that night.

Allen and I went our separate ways. Later that semester I met my future husband at a Methodist church near the campus. We're married now and have a baby. I'm so grateful to God—and to the stranger He sent to give me renewed courage and faith when I needed them most.

I thought my life would be completely transformed. Then I discovered conversion was only the beginning.

HOW TO LET GO OF A HABIT

John Sherrill

For a short while after I became a Christian, I thought my life was going to be completely changed. The Bible itself encouraged me in this. *If any man be in Christ*, wrote Paul, *he is a new creature: old things are passed away; behold, all things are become new.**

Yet as time passed I found many old and destructive patterns still with me. And all around me I saw that this is too often the case with Christians. I knew one faithful churchgoer who had a bitter distrust of Jews. Another had an overweening pride. A minister I knew had a deep antipathy for his own son. Even those closest to Christ felt the sting of the enigma: James and John vied for honors in heaven; the Christians at Corinth slid from glorifying God into debauchery.

Are we all hypocrites, then, who say we are Christians and lead imperfect lives? Don't we know from experience that we are much the same after conversion as before?

Shortly after I began grappling with this problem in Christian living, I met a dynamic minister who supplied what, for me at any rate, has been the key to the answer. This young man, a Southerner by the inheritance of generations, felt that as a Christian he must take a positive stand in the current civil rights struggle. He, therefore, continued to send his son to his newly integrated school, although it was being boycotted by most of the white community.

He acted this way, as I say, because of his Christian

**II Corinthians 5:17*

convictions. But ironically, some of the angriest criticism of him came from members of his own church. These were the people I wanted to know about: What did he think about their Christianity? I asked. His answer always has stuck with me.

"It is my feeling," he said, "that we are converted in different areas at different times in our lives. Many of my parishioners are simply not yet converted to Christ's view of brotherhood. But I do not question the genuineness of their conversion on other levels."

Now, I don't know what the theological status of this idea is; I only know it describes something that I see. It is as though Christ converts those areas of our lives which we surrender to Him, but will not force from us what we do not freely give.

It has been so in my own life. I did experience a conversion to the knowledge that God came down to earth in the form of a human being. In this area—the beginning point—I am truly *in Christ*, as Paul says, and here it is clear to me that I am a new creature.

But if I expected to find the habits and attitudes of a lifetime swept away and a new and Christ-like character substituted for the one I had been feeding through the years, I was due to be sadly disappointed. And I believe now that Christ rarely works in this way. Conversion seems to be more of a process than a status.

Well, how do we get on with this growth process, we partially-converted Christians? I decided to pick some recalcitrant area of my own behavior for an experiment in pinpoint conversion.

Before choosing, I set up some ground rules. I would select, I decided, some attitude or habit or preoccupation which consumed time and energy that properly belonged to God or to other people.

Next, I'd face up to my helplessness in the grip of this sin. By myself I could not beat it. I could only confess that this was so, and pray the prayer of every man who is asking for a healing: *I believe; help thou mine unbelief.**

Then from what I knew of the pattern of most conversion, I would have to take some public steps, parallel to going forward to the altar at a Billy Graham revival or going to the bishop for confirmation. Some step which would serve to

**Mark 9:24*

commit me publicly to the new pattern.

And after that I felt I should relax. My effort would no longer be the negative one of trying to combat a failing; it would be the positive one of keeping my attention centered on Him.

The area that I finally settled on for my own experiment was a destructive and time-consuming concern for money. For some people this is a minor vice. Not for me. It was as much of a preoccupation as hatred or the thirst for revenge can be for other men. It got in the way of relations with other people by occupying the front of my mind even when I was away from my checkbook. And, of course, every minute that we spend being anxious about money or anything else is a moment spent in isolation, separated from God.

Serious as these preoccupations were, however, I soon began to see that they were only symptoms of a far more pervasive disease. I once heard a psychiatrist say that he was surprised how many of his patients' troubles were traceable to the traditional "root sins": pride, gluttony, sloth, covetousness, anger, lust and envy. Behind my symptoms as I defined them, I saw very clearly the evil figure not of covetousness, which I might have expected, but of gluttony.

It came as a surprise. Me, a glutton? But as soon as the suggestion was there I began to see the sprouts of this root sin everywhere. I tended to overdo in a dozen areas, not to taste life but to gulp it. In some areas, such as work, I even tried to make gluttony a virtue. To ask for the conversion of this one trouble area might be biting off more than I had counted on.

But eventually, on a certain afternoon, in the presence of two friends, I did take the step of confessing that I believed Christ to be Lord over this area of my life too. One year has passed since that afternoon. What at first I believed to be a simple weakness has continued to show new faces. Almost daily now I recognize some varied growth of the hungry, insatiable root below. It will take many more months, perhaps years, to recognize all the damage done in my life by this single sin.

Yet this is not the whole story. For along with horror at its size and destructiveness, I also sense a healing going on deep in my being. Like most healing, it is slow. I still have moments of gluttony. But they are rarer. More frequent are days and even weeks together when to sip, taste and enjoy is my pleasure.

I don't know why it has taken me so long to see that this new creature the Bible promises, like all creatures, has a growth process. If a man is *in Christ* all things are indeed new. But the observable fact is that we do not join Christ all at once. We hold on to areas of ourselves that seem too dear, too dangerous or even too trivial to give up. The process of letting them go is a slow and often painful one.

But once they are truly surrendered, a new and mysterious element enters: Christ steps in between our weakness and our enemy, just as He did at Gethsemane when He intervened with the Roman soldiers on behalf of His followers: . . . *let these go their way,* Jesus said, surrendering Himself, *that the word might be fulfilled which He spake, of those whom Thou hast given Me I lost not one.**

**John 18:9, New English Bible*

Depressed? Bored? Listless? Try walking with God. I did, and it changed my life.

WALKING THE BLUES AWAY

Marjorie Van Ouwerkerk

After your children have left the nest and you're looking forward to some leisure time, watch out! You just might fall into the trap I did. Depression!

I don't mean one blue day or several blue days. I mean months of unexplainable sadness, a terrible sense of loss and pain when you can't even cry because you don't know what you'd cry about.

Unfortunately I quit teaching when my youngest daughter left for college. I didn't recuperate from an operation in time for the start of the school term. From being a person with many hobbies and one who was never bored, I now found myself inert, uncaring and disinterested. I withdrew from life and wallowed in self-pity. I'm sure my husband got tired of coming home to a wife as mute as a statue and about as interesting. My sense of humor deserted me and with it the joy of living.

Finally I realized I had a problem I couldn't solve. Knowing God has many channels He uses to heal, I sought medical aid. The doctor said he could help me; but, most important, he told me I had to help myself. He advised me to exercise. I promised, but I was dubious.

In desperation, I gathered my self-control about me like a cloak, silently asked God to help, and began my program. It wasn't easy, but at least it didn't take talent. I am not naturally athletic but I love walking, so I started there.

I bought a pedometer, pinned it to my slacks to check the

distance, put a leash on my dog, Muffin, and started out right after breakfast. I was so afraid I'd change my mind about the whole thing that I left beds unmade, dishes on the table and literally forced myself out the door. Soon I took pride in the fact that I was walking every morning, rain, shine or snow, and Muffin's tail wagged all the way. By the time I had covered five blocks I could feel the tension slip away and relaxation take its place. I hit upon the wonderful idea of saying silently to myself as I started out, "This is the day that God has made, rejoice and be glad in it!" Every time a sad thought crept in I'd replace it with my magic formula, "This is the day . . ." I also discovered that this was an excellent time for prayer. I prayed for my family, for myself, for the sick and the lonely. I also silently blessed everyone I met. And as I began to stop focusing on myself, things began to change.

Soon I began to thank God for my health and the beauty of the morning. All around me there was so much that was beautiful. In the spring there was the fragrance of budding fruit trees, open barn doors that emitted a fresh, earthy smell and the sweet arrival of chirping birds. In summer I walked early to avoid the heat and I had the feeling that I was the only one awake in a slumbering town. In fall I trod on fallen leaves, crimson and gold, and watched honking geese flying in perfect V formation on their way south. In winter I gloried in the burst of a pink dawn and felt sorry for everyone who missed this promise of a new day.

Before long I was walking three miles a day. It was wonderful to reach home feeling exhilarated. I began to feel happy for the first time in a year. Gone was the feeling that there was no reason to get out of bed in the morning. My prayer life deepened my awareness that God was leading me back to peace of mind.

I began to write again. I resumed my bowling. I got out my oils and put my walk scenes on canvas. I forced myself to play golf again and one day it dawned on me that I was having fun. I was reaching out to people again. It was a moment of deep thankfulness.

Out of this experience came a simple course of action that I shall follow all my life. Before I get out of bed in the morning I put myself in God's hands, literally, with unshakable faith. Then I thank Him for the gift of physical and mental health. I dress, have breakfast, call Muffin to me and away we go down the driveway. Then I begin my magic words, "This is the day God has made, rejoice and be glad in it!" I feel my spirits lift and try to make this the best day of my life. It works. Try it!

A WIFE'S MORNING PRAYER

I need someone to talk with, Lord. Do You have a minute?

I feel awful, a failure, sitting here and crying tears of self-pity.

When I shouted those nasty things last night, blaming him for being late, and adding all the other grievances of the past, the insignificant hurts, I thought I was right. But now, oh, now . . .

I should have said, "I love you. Have a hard day, darling? I'm glad you're home."

He looked so wretched this morning. Disappointed, miserable. The light gone from his eyes.

Oh, Lord—I did that! I snuffed out the light. We were going to be the happiest couple in the world, and I spoiled it. So . . .

Give me the courage to say, "I'm sorry. Please forgive me. I love you. I need you." Because I am truly sorry, Lord. And You'll forgive me, too? Now? Help me to be more like You.

Mary Lane Anderson

I was a thief. I wanted it. I took it. But God wouldn't leave it there.

THE CHALICE

Michael Bresciani

The heavy oak door of the church groaned as I drew it open. With thumping heart I stepped into the shadowy interior. The door closed behind me, hushing the afternoon traffic on a main avenue of Bridgewater, Massachusetts.

In the quiet darkness, a dim light glowed above the altar. As I scanned the empty pews I was relieved to see that I was alone. For I had come here to steal.

Nerves tingling, I crept down the carpeted aisle toward the altar where candles flickered. As a little boy I had attended this church of Saint Thomas Aquinas. But years had passed. Now I was 15 years old and no longer believed in God represented by that figure silently suffering on the cross in the shadows above the altar.

My parents' marriage had long since broken up and my stepmother abused me verbally and physically. Dad never seemed to be around, and I clung to my older brother, Bruce. He was big and got away with telling my stepmother he'd kill her if she ever touched him.

"Look, Mike," he whispered in our bedroom one night. "They tell us to believe in God just to keep us in line. But when you get older you'll find out there ain't no such thing."

He seemed to make sense. And I wondered: Why be good? Especially when I learned that I could get almost anything I wanted by stealing. It earned me terms in two local reformatories. And then I went to live with my natural mother in a little cottage outside of town. Here I became shrewd and streetwise.

Now, as I stood before the guttering candles at the altar rail, I grinned. Taking a candle, I touched it to ten more tapers. In the glow, I noticed currency stuck in the money slot of the depository. After fishing it out, I swore under my breath. It was only a dollar. My eyes wandered about. The altar adornments were brass and wouldn't bring much. But there was a door open to the side of the altar. Tiptoeing through it, I found myself in the priest's vestibule.

I ransacked the drawers; nothing but vestments. Straightening up, I saw a large gray floor safe in a corner. The door was ajar. Hoping for collection receipts, I pulled open the heavy steel door. No money. But on a shelf stood a gleaming silver chalice. I dimly remembered being served communion wine in one like it. Light from a window glinted off its graceful form.

Picking up the heavy cup, I studied the bottom. "Sterling!" There was also an inscription engraved in the base: "To the Reverend John A. Wilcox from his loving mother and father." The name meant nothing to me.

A velvet-lined case for the chalice stood on the shelf. I put the silver cup into it and carried it from the vestibule. As I passed the altar, I felt a tremor of fear. But God didn't exist, I knew. I slipped out of the church into the cold winter air.

Hurriedly I pedaled home on my bicycle, the chalice case in the basket under an old newspaper. I was thinking of a newspaper ad I had seen, placed by a jeweler in Taunton, a nearby town, who bought gold and silver.

At home I rushed down to the cellar and took out the chalice, shoving the case under some floor boards. With a spike I scratched out the inscription. Then, I laid the silver cup on the floor. With a large rock I pounded it into a shapeless mass.

The next morning I pedaled into Taunton with the chunk of metal under my coat. The jeweler took it into a back room for testing and weighing. He returned and, without comment, handed me nine dollars and 65 cents.

Back home, I glanced at the newspaper on our kitchen table. A front-page story told about the loss of a valuable chalice. The entire archdiocese was alerted, and church members had begun a prayer vigil for the one who had taken it. Somehow in my imagination I could feel those prayers beginning to surround me. I shuddered and attributed it to my concern about being found out.

The next day I was questioned by the local police in a routine check on local people with police records. I denied knowing anything about the theft. But that evening I panicked. What if they talked to the jeweler? I took 15 dollars from my mother's purse and bicycled to the railroad station, where I caught a train for Philadelphia. There I began hitchhiking west on Route 30.

Two o'clock in the morning found me trudging down a wind-swept highway and shivering in my lightweight jacket, ignored by drivers of diesel trucks roaring by. Finally I saw a little country church down a slope. I broke in and stretched out on one of the pews, but it was so icy I couldn't sleep. On the altar table I saw a heavy velvet cloth with embroidered words: "This do in remembrance of Me." That cloth kept me warm that night. The next morning I hitchhiked on into West Virginia. In Parkersburg I shuffled along a downtown street, tired and hungry. There the police picked me up and called my father.

He came, and the trip back to Massachusetts was the longest time I'd ever spent with him. But the news awaiting us was disastrous. The police, deciding to search our house, had found the chalice case under the basement floorboards.

In a few days I was arraigned before a Plymouth County judge, who looked at me grimly. "An atrocious act of sacrilege," he snapped. I felt the contempt of others in the courtroom and shriveled inside.

This time I was sentenced to the Institution of Juvenile Guidance. Formerly a state prison, it was unlike the previous reformatories. Here crime-toughened youths fought with sharpened bed springs and broken glass. I saw one boy beaten senseless for stealing another's pack of cigarettes.

A few days after I entered this prison, its chaplain stopped by my cot in the dormitory for a visit. He was a young man with shoulders like a fullback. His broad face and curly black hair looked familiar to me, and then I remembered seeing him in the courtroom at my arraignment. But I wasn't prepared for what happened next.

"Hello, Michael," he said, extending his hand. "I'm Father John Wilcox."

I stared at him in shock. John Wilcox—the name on the chalice! He had been in court that day. He *knew* who I was. I shrank back on my cot. But nothing happened. I looked up into his deep-set brown eyes. There was no condemnation in them.

He sat down on my cot, gave me some pointers about getting along in the prison, then touched my shoulder and walked out of the dormitory. Stunned, I watched his broad back going down the hall.

For days I tried to understand John Wilcox. He was like no other person I had ever known. My world had always been filled with rage and pain and hate. I remembered the boy beaten for taking the cigarettes. I thought about all the hate I had seen, people screaming in rage, taking, hurting, wanting. But Father John Wilcox was different.

As I pondered one day in the dormitory, I dimly remembered the stories about Jesus that I had heard as a little boy. They said He forgave sinners. I remembered how He never condemned anyone, even those who tortured Him on the cross.

Deep within me something suddenly seemed to burst, and I fell on my cot in tears. The next morning I asked to see Father Wilcox. After being ushered into his office, at first I couldn't bring myself to say anything.

"What is it, Mike?" he asked gently.

I looked up at him through misting eyes. "I'm sorry, Father," I choked. "I'd like to ask you to forgive me." I broke down sobbing. Then I felt his big hand resting on my head. As I lifted my face up to him, his eyes were shining with a kind of inner light.

"Mike," he said, "I already have."

That's when I think I first saw Jesus. In the eyes of Father Wilcox.

YOUR SPIRITUAL WORKSHOP

ONE DAY CAN CHANGE YOUR LIFE

An exercise in practicing the presence of God.

Will you make an experiment and try to spend one complete day with God?

"Impractical," you say. "Unless I try to find some Sunday."

No—not a Sunday. The idea is to take a regular working day, with all your usual routines, and *live it through with God*.

This may sound difficult to do. But it's certainly worth a try.

How To Begin

Decide on a certain day of the week for the experiment—maybe tomorrow. When you wake up, (at least half an hour earlier than usual) begin with a short, simple prayer. "Lord, I will try to stay close to You all day long. Please help me." Then think of yourself as being like a violin in the hands of the greatest artist of all time, producing your best music only when it is the Master who plays music which will also be in harmony with all the rest of the orchestra.

Take a few minutes to read a favorite selection from the Bible. The 23rd Psalm, for example. Give yourself at least 15 minutes to absorb God's word into your mind.

ok Ahead

Living a normal day with God certainly does not mean neglecting all other things. It means bringing God into every situation you encounter.

Summarize on paper what you expect the day ahead to bring. Perhaps lunch with an old friend . . . a session at the dentist . . . a report to the boss . . . club meetings . . . a hospital visit . . . shopping. Jot down the events as they come to mind. Then invite God to be a part of each activity. "Be with me, Lord, on the drive to Mother's house. Guide my hand as I write this letter. Be on my lips during this conversation." If you have such a fear, admit it to God. Ask Him to help you be bolder *for this one day*.

Activities Start

A day with God doesn't mean going about with a dreamy look on your face. God doesn't want to distract you from being friendly, smiling, warm and interested in what is taking place. A breakfast table conversation might be no different than usual . . . except you no longer react alone to what is said. If there is any gossip, or negative statements, however, you (and God) will somehow find a way to turn things in a more constructive direction.

The day continues. You are about to make a call. As you place your hand on the telephone, ask God to speak through you.

But God keeps slipping away, you say? Not surprising. Nobody said it wouldn't be difficult. The trick is, no matter how often He keeps slipping away, you've got to keep bringing Him back.

lk To A Stranger

To prevent this experiment from becoming too introspective, strike up a conversation or make contact with at least one stranger during the day. It should be more than a perfunctory talk, for God will be in on it, too, and He always is sensitive to need. You will be too.

The world famous teacher, author and linguist Frank Laubach once described a memorable encounter: "I was on the boat from Manila to Cebu (Philippines) and saw across from me a woman, whose face was heavily made-up. I spoke to her because she looked lonesome. Three of the ship's officers nearby tittered . . . so I talked loud enough for them to hear too. In our conversation, I told the woman that I was a seeker for God. As naturally as a preacher she replied, 'God is all around us if we only would open our eyes. All the world is beautiful if we would but see the beauty.' "

Then the woman told Dr. Laubach about her act in show business and how wonderfully people had treated her. Her tired eyes were full of life now as she said, "Oh, the world is full of such good people."

When Dr. Laubach rose to leave, he said to her, "I am going about the world trying to find wonderful hours, and I shall remember this as one of them."

Look For Beauty

God loves and enjoys beauty. Therefore, a day with Him will be incomplete without some time spent being aware of what He created. This does not mean a special trip to some scenic spot. It does mean a new, more concentrated awareness of the beauty around us.

For it does exist, if you but look for it.

An Evaluation

The normal person who attempts this experiment conscientiously, may feel some sense of discouragement at the end of the day. The total time of association with God may seem much less than 100 percent. We suggest that you not evaluate the experiment this way. Ask yourself instead, "Was the day any different? If so, how? Was it a better day than the average?"

If you feel any increase of love, faith, or just well-being, you will want to continue the experiment further. Try it for a week, a month.

The concentration upon God is strenuous, but we believe you will think more clearly and forget less frequently. Things which you did with a strain before, you will do more easily. You'll have less worry and hurry. God will always slip away from you from time to time, but after this experiment you will know that He is there to be found again.

A NEW YEAR'S PRAYER

Father, there is a longing in my heart for the new year to be better than the old one, with a clean, bright beginning.

I have a new perspective now. That new horizon was my brother's last legacy to me as he died without warning of heart failure last year on a sunshiny August afternoon.

That brought it home so sharply, Lord: Our mortality is very real; Bob was so much younger than I.

I see it now more clearly than ever before . . . we are but strangers passing through this life on earth. Like Bob, we, too—all of us—have another destination. Our arrival there is but a continuation of our journey here. So what we are, how we use our brief days, what we do with our mortal lives is of eternal significance.

And so, Father, I come in special need. In the new year let the fresh perspective be as a searchlight and a giant sifter to help me make the right choices. Help me to turn my back on the negative and the unlovely. Give me the grace to drop the trivial. Fortify me with the courage and the stamina to face difficult tasks with Your sense of humor and with the sustaining power of Your love.

I give You gratitude that the fresh beginning of the new year has no ending, but stretches on to all eternity in Your presence.

In Thy Name, amen.

Catherine Marshall

The Unlimited Power of Prayer

LORD, HEAL ME

Chapter 3

Can you really expect the Lord to heal you as He did others 2,000 years ago? Read the following stories.

"You only have to believe," says Millie Gordon. Through her prayers she was healed of cancer. When her story first appeared in *Guideposts* magazine, a terminally ill reader was so inspired by her faith-filled attitude he decided to adopt it himself. Eight months later he was given a clean bill of health! Amazing? Not really, if you believe "with God nothing shall be impossible." (Luke 1:37)

God's way of healing is His own. Sometimes He touches you physically; other times, spiritually. But the true stories in this chapter should convince you that healing *does* come—that God wills your wholeness—if you will only seek it through Him.

This former Senator struggled with a problem that threatened his marriage, his ability to earn a living and even his life.

THE MAN FROM IDA GROVE

Harold E. Hughes

For some time I sat in the car in our driveway not wanting to get out. A cold January night wind moaned through the bare trees. The house looming before me was dark. And I sensed it was as empty as my soul.

I felt sure my wife and little daughters were gone. Eva had often left when she thought I'd be coming home drunk. Finally, I climbed out of the car and carefully made my way to the house.

Dimly, I remembered kissing Eva good-bye this morning. She had reminded me of tonight's dinner invitation. We had a limited social life because of my drinking and this evening was very important to her.

It had been a busy day. I ran a small association of motor-truck drivers in Iowa and that afternoon had met with some shippers over a knotty problem. Finally, when all was settled, one of the men suggested that we retire to a bar and confirm our decision.

I hesitated. I had not taken a drink for the past two weeks. Something told me to go straight home. But then, why not just sit at the bar for a moment? Besides, hadn't I learned control?

Just one drink, I thought. That would be it. One drink and I'd say good-bye. I glanced at my watch; I still had time.

The bourbon tasted good and I relaxed in the pleasant warmth of it.

Later, through a murky maroon fog I heard someone say something about it being 11 o'clock.

Eleven o'clock!

I hurried to my car in the parking lot, where the cold night air cleared my head, and drove home.

"Eva?" I called hoarsely as I pushed open the front door. But my voice echoed hollowly in the hall. I was sure she had taken Connie and Carol to her mother's.

I stumbled and fell to a couch, breathing heavily. Cold sweat beaded my forehead as hopelessness overwhelmed me. I remembered how long Eva had sewn material to make a new dress for the dinner tonight.

Again, I had hurt the ones I loved so much.

Ever since my high-school days I had done this. It had started so easily. I remembered standing on the sagging steps of the country dance hall in a cricket-chirping night and feeling shy about asking a girl to dance. But after sharing a bottle of whiskey with my buddies, I found the courage to take part in the festivities.

Once I started drinking I couldn't stop. I left college in my first year and returned to Ida Grove to marry Eva. She tried to help but couldn't.

I was able to control my drinking at work, which was important since I became a truck driver hauling everything from livestock to grain elevators. And by now I couldn't see where my drinking was hurting anybody.

"After all," I argued when my parents and other relatives tried to advise me. "I bring home my paycheck every week. Besides," I added, "I can stop drinking whenever I want to."

Now as I lay on the couch in my empty house my head pounded with guilt and nausea. How many times had I sworn off drinking, promising Eva that I wouldn't touch another drop? How many times had I failed?

The sense of shame sank deeper into me as I lay there. I felt helpless. A father in his 30s who was worthless, a sot. What was the point in going on any longer? I thought of how Eva's once lively brown eyes had dulled and worry lines etched her face. Though I never struck her, I'd come home belligerent and foulmouthed and she would cringe like a beaten kitten.

A drumbeat of doom seemed to fill my days and nights. I cringed at knowing winks by other people, at seeing the flush in my face in the mirror, at the deepening fatigue that racked my body. Yet I was powerless to stop doing the one thing that caused it all.

Trying to escape the horrible self-loathing, I struggled up from the couch and wandered about the empty house. In our bedroom, I slumped onto the bed. I sat there, sunk in an awful despair.

What was the point of living? I'd failed everyone who had meant anything to me; I was a disgrace to my town. I was a hypocrite in everything I did; I couldn't even tell the truth anymore.

I couldn't do anything right. Why not just end it?

The thought hung there, like the echo of a tolling bell.

A cold feeling of logic overcame me. Why not? I had thought about this before but had brushed it away. Yet the more I now considered the alternative, the more sense it made. Why go on doing the things I hated? The more I thought about the disorder in my life and the inability to control it, the more I wanted to end it. I was just an evil rotten drunk, a liar. And what should happen to evil men? They deserve to die.

I remembered enough Scripture to know that suicide was not God's way. But as I weighed the balance, I felt it better to be eternally lost than to bring eternal hell to those I loved.

No, my mind was clear now. I hated what I did, but I still did it. When I promised loved ones I wouldn't drink and even prayed to God that I wouldn't drink and did it again and again, I realized in my heart that there was no way on earth I could ever control it.

I got up from the bed and went to the closet where I kept my rifle and shotgun. I opened the door and considered both, then reached for the shotgun. It would be most certain. It was a single barrel Remington pump gun, 12-gauge.

I considered what I was going to do to Mother, Dad, Eva and the children. Eva was still young and beautiful. She would easily find someone else and have a decent life. The thought hurt me. The girls would eventually forget me. As I was now, they could never forget, suffering only disgrace and sorrow.

I slid three shells into the magazine and pumped one into

the chamber. Tears streaming down my face, I lay down on the bed, rested the shotgun on my chest and put the muzzle into my mouth. The cold steel rasped my teeth and tasted of oil. Reaching down, I found I could push the trigger with my thumb. This way everything was certain: I did not want to botch it and spend the rest of my life as a vegetable.

Then I thought of the awful mess this would leave in the bedroom. I remembered the men I had seen shot overseas. I was leaving Eva and the girls with enough bad memories. Getting up, I walked through the hall and into the bathroom. It could be cleaned easier. Carefully holding the Remington, I climbed into the old-fashioned claw-footed tub, my shoe soles squeaking on the bottom. In it, I lay down, feeling strange to be there with my clothes on. With the shotgun resting on my stomach, I positioned it with the muzzle in my mouth toward my brain. Reaching down, my thumb found the trigger and I was about to push it.

A terrible sadness filled me. I knew what I was doing was wrong in God's eyes. Yet, my whole life had been wrong. And God had always been very remote. In a few years my family would get over it, I reasoned. They would have an opportunity to rebuild their lives. But if I remained here, I would never change and only hurt them more. The thought came that I should explain all this to God before pushing the trigger. Then if He could not forgive this sin, at least He would know exactly why I was committing it.

Climbing out of the tub, I knelt on the tile floor and laid my head on my arms, resting on the cool tub rim.

"Oh, God," I groaned, "I'm a failure, a drunk, a liar and a cheat. I'm lost and hopeless and want to die. Forgive me for doing this . . ." I broke into sobs, "Oh, Father, please take care of Eva and the girls. Please help them forget me . . ." I slid to the floor, convulsing in heavy sobbing. As I lay face down on the tiles, crying and trying to talk to God, my throat swelled until I couldn't utter a sound. Totally exhausted, I lay silent, drained and still.

I do not know how long I lay there. But in the quiet bathroom, a strange peace gently settled over me. Something that I had never experienced before was happening, something far beyond my senseless struggles. A warm peace seemed to settle deep within me, filling the terrible emptiness, driving out the self-hate and condemnation.

My sins seemed to evaporate like moisture spots under a hot, bright sun.

God was reaching down and touching me. A God Who cared, a God Who loved me, Who was concerned for me despite my sins. Like a stricken child lost in a storm, I had suddenly stumbled into the warm arms of my Father. Joy filled me, so intense it seemed to burst my breast. Slowly I rose to my knees and looked up to Him in awe and gratitude.

Kneeling on that bathroom floor, I gave myself to Him totally. "Whatever You ask me to do, Father," I cried through hot tears, "I will do it."

For a long time I knelt there. Then I stood up, breathing heavily as if I had just climbed a long hill. Reaching into the tub, I picked up the shotgun. I shuddered as I thought how close I had come to using it. Taking it to our bedroom, I unloaded the shells and placed the gun back in the closet. As I closed the closet door, a faint accusatory echo sounded: "Coward . . . afraid to pull the trigger."

Doubt chilled me. Had my experience in the bathroom been another of the many illusions I had gone through before? I was so deceitful to myself and others. But something far stronger kept saying: "Stay with God, follow Him, *believe.*"

I knelt at the bed: "Father," I prayed, "I don't understand this or know why I deserve it. For You know how weak I am. But I put myself back in Your hands. Please give my family back to me . . . and give me the strength never to run again. Father, I put myself in Your hands."

I finally climbed into bed, resting my head on the pillow, and for the first time in months slipped into a deep, peaceful sleep.

Bright sunshine streaming through the window awakened me. An exuberance filled me, and then I remembered the night before. I got up and made coffee thinking how close I had come to killing myself. I knew that if I drank again I would put myself under the control of dark forces that would lead me to the same horrible pit.

But I also knew I had Someone with me, a personal Being Who had reached down in my desperation and comforted me. As I thought of Him, again that strange joy filled me.

Eva! I wanted to call her but I could not summon the

courage to pick up the phone. Finally, as it neared nine o'clock, I dialed the number hoping that Eva's mother wouldn't answer. Eva answered and I sighed inwardly in relief.

But what could I say to her? Again I thought of my Help.

"Eva, I'm sorry. I don't blame you for never wanting to see me again. But Eva, I want you home more than anything else. I'm going to try . . . really try not to fail you again. Please bring the kids and come home."

For a moment the phone was silent. It seemed both our lives hung in the balance and I found myself praying silently. Then Eva answered. "You had better go on to work, Harold. Then the girls and I will come home."

That evening as I drove into our driveway and saw the house lights glowing, I suffered mixed emotions, as I did when I came home from the war, both a joy and an embarrassment about seeing my loved ones. It seemed as if I had been gone a long time.

Though I wasn't able to tell Eva what had happened in the bathroom, I felt she saw something different in me. After the girls had gone to bed, we sat up late in the living room talking in the light of a glowing fire, something we had not done for a long time.

I looked at her across the dim room, firelight flickering across her pale heart-shaped face. "Eva," I said huskily, "I believe I have changed. But I don't think people will accept me as changed."

My wife was silent for a moment, then said: "You mean run away from the problems?"

I looked down at the floor. She was right; that's exactly what I wanted to do. But I knew that wherever I'd go I would take my problems with me.

As I leaned back and watched an ember flare into a bright flame, I thought, *Wouldn't God be with me right here in Ida Grove where I could work my problems out?*

The next evening after dinner I found our Bible in the bookcase, took it into the living room and sat down with it under a lamp. I wanted to know God. I had made a commitment to Him for the first time in my life and I meant to keep it. To keep it I had to know what He wanted me to do. As I looked at the black leather-bound book in my hands, I sensed an expectancy as I opened the pages.

There was a movement at my elbow.

I looked up. Connie and Carol were standing there in their nightgowns. Connie was approaching her tenth birthday. And Carol—where did she get those large brown eyes?

"Daddy," said Carol, "we've come to kiss you good night."

My eyes blurred. It had been so long since the girls had done this. Either I had not been home or had been in such a dark mood that they had shied away from me.

Their kisses felt like angel wings brushing my cheeks and I remembered words I had heard as a youngster: "I will restore to you the years which the swarming locust has eaten." (Joel 2:25 RSV)

I thought back to when I was a child standing out on the hillside at night, before the locusts came, looking up and feeling the nearness of God, feeling He had something important for me to do.

What of the wasted years in between? What had happened to the boy who had memorized the Twenty-third Psalm in Sunday school? I leaned my head back and found I could still say some of the words . . . "Yea, though I walk through the valley of the shadow of death, I will fear no evil: for Thou art with me . . . "

Excitement surged through me. I *had* walked through the valley that night in the bathroom and He *had* been with me! Eagerly I opened the Bible and turned to the Psalms, found the twenty-third and read. This time instead of dry printed words it was as if that same Being Who had comforted me in the bathroom was speaking to me. I *would* be restored. He *would* be beside me, guarding and guiding me all the way.

Surely His goodness and mercy would follow me the rest of my life. I found myself being lifted as I read His powerful promises, and when I finished the Psalm I rested the book on my lap and shut my eyes, flooded with that wonderful assurance.

True to His Word, the Lord did restore the years the locusts had eaten.

Six years later I won an election to the state commerce commission and a year later was named its Director. Many were now suggesting that I run for governor.

By this time I had long been a member of Alcoholics

Anonymous. One evening the family, which now included a third daughter, Phyllis, age seven, and I were preparing to go to one of the AA fellowship's family get-togethers.

Little Phyllis and I were waiting inside the front door for the others to come downstairs. As I stood, impatiently jingling car keys, Phyllis looked up through innocent brown eyes and asked: "Daddy, why do we go to these meetings? You never drank."

Tears filled my eyes and my heart swelled in gratitude. I sat down on the steps and pulled her to me. "Honey," I said, looking into her cherubic face, "I did drink once. Much of it happened before you were born and I stopped drinking before you were old enough to remember.

"Yes, honey," I added, "your daddy did have a very sad drinking problem."

She threw her little arms around my neck. "But you don't now," she said, "and that's all that matters."

I hugged her tight and savored the wisdom of an innocent. *Yes,* I thought, *what we are today is all that matters, to a child . . . and to God.*

MORNING PRAYER

Give me the strength to meet each day
With quiet will.
Give me the faith to know Thou art
My Shepherd still.
Give me the light to find my way
When shadows fall.
Be Thou my steady, guiding star,
Father of all.

Hebrew Union Home Prayer Book

"Hopeless," the doctors told Milly Gordon. But this well-known writer refused to accept their diagnosis.

YOU ONLY HAVE TO BELIEVE

Charlotte Hutchison

Recently I came across a remarkable story—Mildred Gordon's story. It's a real-life experience that in some ways rivals the best-selling novels that Milly and her husband, Gordon Gordon, have been writing for years. In other ways, it's a quiet testimony to the power of prayer. Well, you'll see . . .

The Gordons live on a hilltop overlooking the San Fernando Valley in California. Beyond the nearest mountain is Hollywood, the rainbow's end for those who seek fame or wealth in the film industry. Eight of the Gordon's 19 published novels have been bought for films. Altogether, their adventure-suspense books have sold more than 14 million copies. A sign on their gate informs visitors that this is a home that was built and endowed by a cat: *That Darn Cat*, a Disney movie that propelled the Gordons, who wrote the story and script, to the summit of success.

But in the fall of 1974, a shadow hovered over the Gordons' mountaintop Shangri-La.

The trouble began after a strenuous tour of the East Coast where the Gordons were promoting their latest book *Catnapped*. Although they are accustomed to hectic schedules, Milly said that this tour seemed to exhaust her. In the autumn months following the tour, Milly was unable to work because of pressure in her chest and shortness of breath. Gordon insisted on taking her for a checkup. After an examination, the doctor gave Milly the bad news: She was suffering from a serious cardiac condition. She was rushed immediately to a hospital.

Milly spent most of 1975 in the hospital coronary care unit. Slowly her heart condition improved, but she was unable to understand her lack of energy. Late in 1975, she learned why: A bone scan revealed a suspicious spot on her lower spine; further tests indicated it was a malignant tumor.

Milly and Gordon have no secrets from each other. Both were orphaned young; they have no children and no relatives. For all of their married lives, they have been close companions, a working team, and best friends. Deeply religious, they talked the situation over and resolved they would not panic, would trust God, and would get further medical opinions.

After many tests, Milly was told that her cancer had spread so extensively that additional treatment would be futile. Because of her heart problem, radiation or chemotherapy would be impossible. She was sent home to await the inevitable with the aid of pain-killing drugs.

But Milly never for a moment accepted the verdict of the doctors. "A strange feeling of peace and tranquility came over me," she recalled. "I remembered that my mother, a devout Quaker, used to tell me as a child that fear causes the greatest hurt. And I've always believed in God's miracles. Just because Jesus doesn't walk the earth today doesn't mean that healing, in the twentieth century, can't be undertaken in His name. I used to read, over and over, the passage in the fifth chapter of Mark that tells about the woman who touched Jesus and was healed—and later in that chapter there's the account of Jairus' daughter who was brought back to life. Jesus says: 'Be not afraid, only *believe*.' God knows what you need, and the only requirement is trust. You wouldn't ask your best friend for a favor and doubt that it would be granted, would you? Then why is it so difficult to rely on God to answer prayer?

"Most of the time, we knock on the door so timidly and open it just a little crack. I think prayer is empty and meaningless if we really don't *expect* God to reply. So—once I accepted the fact that with God anything is possible, I didn't have to waste energy in being afraid."

Milly's chief concern was for Gordon. But faith was also

his strength. They agreed that they wouldn't allow fear to rule their lives; they would live each day with courage and hope and follow their usual routine of intimate sharing.

In the beginning, Milly was confined to her bed, unable to turn to either side because of the pain. Every evening, Gordon would bring their TV dinners to her room, put their favorite records on the stereo and light the candles while they ate. They laughed over the antics of their cat, D.C. (Dear Cat or Darn Cat, depending on his current activities.) And they discussed the progress of the latest book, which for the first time, Gordon was writing alone.

Milly refused to take any medication for pain, with the exception of two daily aspirins. She would lie in bed watching the birds and squirrels in the treetops outside her window and thank God for the beauty and variety of the world. ("It's important to concentrate on the obvious blessings—praise!") This must have been the low point in her ordeal; her blood count was almost fatally low at this period, and her doctor injected her with massive amounts of iron.

"But during this time," Milly emphasized, "I was really getting massive doses of faith, hope and love from another source." Three years previously, the Gordons had joined an ecumenical prayer group, with Jewish, Catholic and Protestant participants, who meet each week at the Sherman Oaks Methodist Church where the Gordons worship.

The group follows the Biblical formula prescribed by James, Chapter 5: "Is any sick among you? Let him call for the elders of the church; and let them pray over him, anointing him with oil in the name of the Lord: And the prayer of faith shall save the sick."

Although the members of the prayer group do use the ceremony of anointing the head of a sick person, laying on their hands and concentrating in earnest prayer, Milly believes that the formula itself is not so important.

"People worship in different ways," she says. "I just think that it's the faith that has the positive effect. I'm convinced that you can actually *feel* the power of prayer. Gordon felt it, too, I know. He always seemed to be optimistic. Every morning he would bound into my room and shout, 'This is the day which the Lord hath made!' And he would tell me jokes to make me laugh."

I said at the beginning that Milly Gordon's story was a

great testimony to the power of prayer, and that is what it is. There were no instantaneous cures or sensational developments, but gradually, against all the predictions, all the odds, she began to feel better.

"Eventually," she told me, "I found I was able to sit up a few minutes a day and rest on the edge of the bed. Presently, when my pain subsided, I could take a few steps and sit on the stairs every morning while we opened our mail. In the early spring, I felt so much better that Gordon took me out in the car. We stopped to see our pharmacist, a kind Jewish man who had been our friend for years. He told me he was praying for me. People I met in the market said I was on their prayer list—and I know that literally dozens of people I've never met were praying for my recovery."

Early in May, when Milly was examined by the local specialist, she heard the most unbelievable news that her cancer was in remission. In August, just six months after her condition was pronounced incurable, she paid a visit to her old friend, the cardiologist in Beverly Hills.

"When he saw me, he hardly recognized me," she said. "His mouth dropped open and he just stared. Finally he gave me a bear hug and lifted me onto the examination table. 'I can't believe it,' he kept repeating. He got out his stethoscope, listened to my heart, which he said sounded great, checked my blood pressure, which was normal. He was astonished. He said, 'It's like a miracle. It's fantastic! You've made me the happiest doctor in town!' "

Two months later, in the fall of 1976, the Gordons once again resumed their lecture tours, sometimes speaking twice a day to large audiences.

"When I started mending," Milly said, "my recovery was rapid. One month recently we gave twenty-seven talks, speaking from San Diego to San Francisco. We miss meals and work against deadlines, but I seem to get stronger all the time. I certainly believe in medical science. I know it helped me. But I also know that my cure was made possible in part by loving people who interceded in my behalf with their prayers.

"So I have an obligation to explain to my audiences the enormous power of prayer—practical power—that most of us never fully use, either for our own good or for the benefit of others we know to be in doubt or despair or pain.

"If I can help anybody by telling of my experience, that's what I want to do. So I just tell it like it is: Miracles *are* possible. And the only requirement is to cast out fear—and believe."

PRAYER OF ONE IN PAIN

O God, I'm weak and weary
I do not understand.
There are some times when I can do
All things—at Your command.
And then there are these other times
And why? I cannot see
When anything that I would do
Is much too much for me.
You know the weariness that fills
This pain-wracked frame of mine.
Be merciful to me, O God,
And grant the strength that's Thine.
I know the privilege that's mine
To care for those I love.
Grant me, O God, for this one day
Thine own strength from above.

Helen Miller

A father's loving story of his daughter's unbelievable recovery.

MY KATHY'S ALMOST HOME

Larry Miller

As the ambulance threaded its way through the rush-hour traffic, many worried thoughts flooded my mind. In the front seat, my wife, Barbara, sat with the driver, glancing nervously toward me now and then. In the back, I crouched beside our daughter, Kathy, clasping her small, limp hand.

Just minutes before, Kathy had been a bubbly teen-ager on her way home from junior high school. Crossing a busy thoroughfare near our home, she had been blindsided by a passing car, struck so hard that she had been jolted out of her shoes.

As I stared at her broken, unconscious body, I could only think the worst . Knowing her condition was grave, I urged the ambulance driver to go faster, to reach help at the hospital quicker.

Kathy was what all parents dream their child might be: bright, motivated, energetic, athletic. She had been inducted into the National Junior Honor Society just a few weeks earlier. She was also pretty, talented and popular. Most of all, though, Kathy was active. She was a cheerleader and one of the star distance runners on her school's track team. She loved running and she seemed always on the go.

I had been a professional athlete myself, a major-league pitcher. I knew the joy of being a disciplined competitor.

Kathy was always in a hurry to catch the school bus, and she always kissed us good-bye hurriedly. This morning I had had an overwhelming urge to hug her tightly. She was in a terrible rush and said, "Dad, let me go, I'm going to miss the bus." I said, "Kath, just give me some extra lovin' this morning." Her reply was "Okay." We embraced each other and I said, "Do you realize how much your mother and I love you?" She said, "Yeah, Dad, you tell me all the time." She then hurried off to catch the bus.

At Scottsdale Memorial Hospital, a team of doctors met us. After a time, which seemed like hours, a neurosurgeon came back to where Barbara and I sat anxiously waiting.

"Your daughter has extensive brain damage and an extremely bad break of her right leg," he told us quietly. "She's in a coma." I gripped Barbara's arm. He said the next 24 hours would be critical and Kathy might not make it through the night.

In a few minutes our other child, Larry Jr., arrived at the hospital to learn the awful news. Then a nurse escorted us to Intensive Care to see Kathy. There we learned her breathing was erratic and her temperature was rising perilously. Tears burned my eyes as my heart sank within me.

I simply couldn't bear the thought of leaving her. So Barbara and I began a bedside vigil. I would stay until exhaustion overwhelmed me, then Barbara would take over.

The long hours lengthened into days, with still no sign of consciousness from Kathy. The days stretched into weeks—two, three, four. The doctors told us the longer Kathy remained in a coma, the less her chances were of leading a normal life should she regain consciousness.

One night when we got back from the hospital, exhausted from tension and anxiety, I spilled out my feelings to Barbara, who seemed so calm and strong, though I knew her heart ached as much as mine. We had been married 17 years, and I had seen many times how she had made a habit of praying when facing some difficulty. I had seen her at the scene of the accident, placing her hands on Kathy's forehead and bowing her head in prayer.

"Why can't I handle this the way you are?" I asked her.

She thought for a moment. "Maybe," she said, her voice very gentle, "you're trying to do everything yourself, Larry. You need to turn Kathy over to God."

Later, unable to sleep, I got out of bed and restlessly

roamed our dark, silent house. Passing Kathy's empty bedroom, I turned on the light and looked in. A cheerful poster hung on the wall. The room was immaculate. Remembering how I always used to get after Kathy to clean up, I felt my eyes begin to water, and I thought, *I'd give anything to have this room messy again. Anything.*

I stopped myself. Barbara's words were coming back to me. Maybe I *was* trying to do it all myself.

I stood there in Kathy's room and said something like, "Lord, I'm going about this all wrong. Kathy needs You, and I need You. Help Kathy get better, please. And help me, too." It was a prayer I was to repeat many times in the weeks to come.

In the tenth week of Kathy's coma, I watched three hospital nurses prepare to change Kathy's bed linen. Picking Kathy up, the nurses placed her in a nearby chair.

"Is that better?" one nurse asked. Ever so slightly, Kathy nodded.

"Did you see that?" I shouted wildly from the doorway. All three nurses looked at me excitedly. Yes, they'd seen it.

The next day I brought a root beer popsicle to Kathy's room. Very timidly and slowly, Kathy pulled the popsicle to her mouth. Suddenly, with a tremendous sensation of release, I felt a strange power there in the room with us—a Presence, very real and close.

Over the next couple of days, Kathy began to sit up. We placed her in a high chair to feed her. She spilled her food over everything, but I didn't care, because I knew something was happening.

In the twelfth week after the accident we were allowed to take Kathy home. Her doctors weren't optimistic, however. Kathy had made progress, they admitted, but she still was little more than a vegetable. And her damaged right leg, they said, might forever keep her from walking. They also warned us that she could level off in her progress at any time.

When I carried Kathy into our house that day, she weighed only 55 pounds, half of her once vigorous 110. She couldn't talk, couldn't crawl, couldn't read, couldn't chew. I placed her on the living-room floor and watched her wriggle about like an infant, my beautiful, vivacious 13-year-old daughter. The Presence I had felt in the hospital room seemed so far away. Frustration began to rise in me. As earnestly as I could, I began to pray—for Kathy and for myself. We had come so far, I knew, I must not lose faith.

One hot day, Barbara and I noticed Kathy looking out toward the swimming pool in our back yard. "That's it!" I cried. "If Kathy can't walk, maybe at least she can swim."

At first Kathy was deathly afraid of the water. Slowly, though, we got her to go in. Wearing a life jacket and bobbing between Barbara and me, Kathy would gingerly poke at the water. "Float to me, Kathy," I challenged, holding out my hands.

Kathy froze, her big blue eyes filled with fear, her sticklike body trembling. "Float to me, Kathy," I urged.

Studying her motionless body, I thought of Kathy in her coma and how I had begged for some movement. All my pleading had seemed for naught until the day I had let go and let God take charge. That gave me an idea.

"Kathy," I said, "with God's help, you can do anything you really want."

She stared at me curiously, as if considering the truth of what I had said. Then, dipping her head slightly, she relaxed in the water. She began floating.

Soon it became obvious that Kathy would attempt anything in the pool if first she heard some words from Barbara and me. The words, "With God's help you can do anything you really want," were the words I needed to hear as much as Kathy. Within a few weeks she was swimming the width of the pool, another small miracle.

Kathy's speech progressed, although for a long time she would merely parrot our words. Remembering the doctors' warning that she might level off at any point, I thought that would be all she might ever do. One evening as we were sitting out on the back patio (Kathy was still in a wheelchair), I had been talking to her, but with no response. Suddenly she spoke clearly and distinctly, "All I need is time." I felt then that God was speaking to me through Kathy because up to that point, she could barely speak one word at a time.

Then one day when I knew she was feeling down about the slowness of her recovery, I phoned her from my office. "Kathy, honey," I said, "I love you."

Sweetly, softly, from the other end of the line, she replied, "I love you, too, Daddy."

By the end of August, four months after the accident, Kathy had begun to put weight back on. She had mastered swimming. Her speech was returning. And I wondered, *What shall we pray for now?*

Kathy came up with the answer. "I want to run," she told me one day. Her energy and joy of activity were returning, too.

There was a six-mile mini-marathon that was to be run in nearby Phoenix in about two months, and when I told Kathy about it, she quickly warmed up to the idea. To encourage her, Barbara said, "We'll run with you, Kath," and we started our preparation together.

Once a girl who ran with the ease and grace of a thoroughbred, Kathy now found that even the shortest jog was sheer torture. She looked like a newborn colt the first few times she tried it, legs and arms moving awkwardly in competing directions. The third time out, she fell and broke her nose. I could only stand by and fight the tears and the hurt I felt for her.

As the weeks went by, Kathy determinedly built up her distance—from a shaky few feet to a quarter of a mile, an almost incredible amount of progress. I still had doubts about her ability to endure six miles, though. After all, it had been only six months since the accident. Deep down I questioned whether Kathy ought to try it.

On the night before the race, I stopped by Kathy's bedroom to say good night, still wondering what would be best for her. Kathy was lying on her bed, saying her prayers. Above her bed was a poster that said, "Miracles happen only to those who believe in them." I paused to listen. "I can do anything I really want," she said in a voice that betrayed only the slightest hint of a slur, "with God's help."

The next day Barbara, Kathy and I nervously took our places at the starting line, along with about 4,000 other runners. Then the starting gun cracked, and we were off. Barbara and I stayed within a few yards of Kathy, close enough to be at her side quickly if she should need help.

After the first hundred yards or so, Kathy gained a fairly even stride. We were in the thick of the race, with other runners all around us. As the course lengthened out, most of the other runners put distance between us. Into the second mile, we began to feel the real challenge of completing the race. We already had exceeded any distance we had run before and we still had more than four miles remaining. Now we had begun to lag near the back of the pack.

At the midway point, everything seemed to go uphill. My legs began to feel heavy; my lungs ached. I could hear Barbara breathing alongside me. Then I looked over at Kathy. She was running a bit awkwardly, but moving right along. She turned to me when she caught me watching her. Her face was crimson, and her blond hair was soaked with sweat. But she was smiling.

That smile was all the assurance I needed. We kept running.

We finished the race far in the rear. *Where* we finished wasn't important, though. What *was* important was that our child, who had been little more than a 13-year-old infant just three months ago, who had been within a hair's breadth of death six months ago, had not merely walked again on that shattered leg but had finished a six-mile run.

When a reporter came over to interview Kathy after the race, she asked Kathy if she thought she would ever recover completely from the accident. "All I need," she said, smiling, "is time." Clearly, there was no doubt in her pretty head.

Gone were doubts in my own mind, too. The days of anguished frustration and helplessness, of trying and failing to handle things by myself, were ended. Not just Kathy, but her Dad, too, had discovered the amazing things a person can do—with God's help.

The story of a most remarkable comeback in baseball.

GIVE HIM 3 FAST ONES, TOMMY

Tommy John
Pitcher, New York Yankees

It was the fourth inning of a game with Montreal, when I threw a sinker—a ball that drops low through the strike zone—to Hal Breeden. As the ball left my hand, I got this crazy sensation, as if my left elbow were flying out somewhere into right field. And then it snapped back, just like one of those coiled Slinky toys.

That was five years ago, July 17, 1974, when I was pitching for the Los Angeles Dodgers; but to this day, I can't describe the feeling. It wasn't the kind of pain that drags you to your knees. I shook my arm, thinking it was a passing cramp. A big-league pitcher has to learn to pitch with pain, because if he doesn't, he'll never go out to the mound. But this was something I hadn't experienced before.

I wound up and threw another pitch. Again my elbow did a Slinky number out to right field and back.

I knew then that something was drastically wrong. I called "time" and walked off the mound. Soon the trainers' room was a madhouse, with players and reporters milling around and asking questions that couldn't be answered.

Our team doctor iced my arm down and suggested I come in the next day, when things had calmed down a bit. I thought I had torn a muscle, but special stress X-rays revealed that the ligament was torn; just how badly was not immediately clear. The doctor suggested we wait three weeks or so to see if it would heal. He said they wouldn't operate until I gave the okay. It would be serious, he said, and he wanted me to be sure in my own mind.

I had undergone a successful bone-chip operation on my pitching arm (my left) in 1972. To a professional pitcher, however, having arm operations is a little like gambling—you may win once, but each time you take a chance, you're coming closer to losing everything.

The timing of the injury was incredibly bad. My wife, Sally, was pregnant with our first child, due in September. Then, too, for the first time there was a possibility that I'd be in on a pennant race. Now it looked as though it could be all down the drain.

After another conference with the doctor, I went home to discuss my options with Sally. "They say that if I don't have the operation I'll never pitch again." "Then why don't they operate?" she asked, her voice strained with anxiety.

"Because if they do operate, even though my arm will be good enough for everyday activities, the chances are I *still* won't be able to pitch—that's what the doctors said." I tacked the last words on to disavow the terrible possibility. I was a condemned man talking about his own execution.

She began to cry. "Sally, please, don't!" I said, putting my arm around her. "It'll be all right, you'll see. If God doesn't want me to play baseball anymore, then I'm sure He has something else for me. We've got to believe that."

"Tommy, baseball's your life! Why should this happen to you? You're a good man—a good Christian! It's just not fair! And now, with the baby coming . . ."

Taking her face in my hands I said calmly but forcefully, "Sally, honey, God never promised us easy times. We can't always have what we want in life. We've got to give thanks in *all* things. That means the bad things as well as the good."

We prayed. There are prayers that are filled with peace and joy, but ours was a hard prayer, like the agonized prayer of Jesus in Gethsemane. We confessed we didn't understand why this had happened, but we asked for God's peace. We asked Him to let us know His will.

The following week we reached a decision: I would have the surgery. It was a slim chance, but it was our *only* chance.

The operation was performed in late September. The surgeons' worst fears were confirmed. Not only was the ligament torn from the inside of the elbow, but the muscles were separated and the nerve was bruised and traumatized.

It was necessary to remove a six-inch tendon from my right arm and fashion a new ligament from it for my pitching arm. It was a procedure never before performed on a professional athlete.

Sally was by my side in the recovery room and all the next day, driving with her mother the 45 miles from our home in Yorba Linda and back, in spite of her pregnant condition.

Two days after the operation she called me at seven a.m. "If you'd like to see your baby being born," she said in a breathy voice, "you'd better ask quick if you can leave your hospital and come to mine, because I'm in labor."

That afternoon I watched my daughter, Tamara, being born. My eyes filled with tears as I gazed at the tiny pink face and hands that I longed to hold but couldn't. "Thank You, God!" I whispered. In that moment I knew in my heart that His loving care encompasses all of life. This new little life, with its promise and possibility, filled me with hope.

A few days later, the doctor told me he had never seen an arm as badly damaged as mine. He said it was "highly unlikely" that I would ever pitch again.

I refused to accept his verdict; my whole being cried out against it. But as the weeks passed, instead of healing, I felt a growing numbness in my fingers; my left hand always felt cold. When I scalded myself and didn't feel it, I became alarmed and went back to the doctor. After examining me, he gave me the grim news: Scar tissue had grown over the nerve, resulting in paralysis. In December I entered the hospital for a third operation.

They removed the cast in January 1975, and I began the grueling work of rehabilitation: hot-water therapy, whirlpool baths, squeezing Silly Putty.

Nothing was happening. My pitching hand was lifeless; it looked like a monkey's paw. When I went to spring training at Dodgertown in Vero Beach, Florida, I found it impossible to grasp a baseball. I would pick the ball up with my right hand, place it in my lifeless left hand, then forcibly curl the fingers around it. I would have to tape them to the ball so it wouldn't drop.

The doctors had told me that nerves regenerate at the rate of an inch a month. I calculated the distance from my elbow to the middle of my hand—18 inches. That meant I wouldn't be playing for at least a year-and-a-half! Patient though the Dodgers management had been, I knew my career would be ended long before then.

Doggedly I continued working every day with our trainers in a regimen of hot water, massage, exercise and throwing. I knew it was my only hope.

One Sunday our minister preached a sermon based on the text, "For with God nothing shall be impossible." (Luke 1:37) He talked about God's sovereign power, which could give men victory over sin and sickness. He said God could give a man a miracle when nothing else could help him.

I reread the verse slowly, then looked up to see the minister looking directly at me with a strange intensity. I quickly lowered my head and underscored the verse. I felt that God was talking to me through the preacher—He was telling me that total healing was possible. What I really needed was a bigger faith—a faith that could believe the impossible was possible with God.

As I sat there listening with a growing sense of excitement, I felt Sally's hand pressing mine, letting me know that she had got the message, too.

I grabbed onto that verse and claimed it for my own. And as the summer wore on, I needed it. I could cope with the physical stress—exercise, running, punishing my body—but the mental strain of sitting and watching the other guys play, of being on the outside looking in, that was hard to bear. I clung to that special promise from God's word. Without it I'd have gone out of my mind.

Then one day in July 1975, I was driving to Dodger Stadium for my usual workout, when I had a sudden urge to straighten my little finger. Why I should have got the idea I don't know, because my hand was still totally paralyzed. I stared at the frozen fingers, lying curled and useless along the steering wheel. . . .

The little finger moved!

Hardly able to believe what I had seen, I tried it again. Once more the finger moved, then slowly straightened. *It's coming back!* I thought. *That little movement means my hand is coming back!* I knew then that somewhere down the road it was going to be completely restored. What the doctors told me would take 18 months was happening in six! I thanked

God for doing the impossible.

When I got home that night, Sally was ecstatic with joy. Then she cried. All this excitement over an insignificant little thing like bending a finger. Such a small thing—until you can't do it.

Then, little by little, there was more movement as the feeling came back to the other fingers. It was like water flowing over a dam, faster and faster, although it wasn't until the following season that I could really grip the ball and pitch with anything approaching my former skill.

The big test came in the second game of the 1976 season at Houston. The Dodgers management had been more than patient during my long rehabilitation, but at this point they were asking, "Can we afford to let John learn to pitch all over again? We've got the team to consider." I went into the game with foreboding.

The first two men up got base hits. I was in serious trouble: My entire comeback was at stake. *If you give up two or three more base hits,* I thought, *you're done for*. I steeled myself against a rising tide of anxiety. Cesar Cedeno was at bat, a strong hitter. Dodger catcher Joe Ferguson trotted out onto the mound and said, "Okay, Tommy, this is it. If you're going to go down, let's go down fighting."

I pitched a fast ball. Cedeno hit into a double play. I was still sweating. Bob Watson was up next, another dangerous hitter. I pitched him three balls.

Ferguson came out again, his face serious. "Tommy, let's give him three of the best fast balls you've got. Throw them as hard as you can—let 'em rip!"

I stood there for a long moment, eyeing Watson. *I can't do it . . . it's impossible!* I thought. *I'm going to walk him or he's going to get a hit. God . . . help me!*

I took a deep breath, wound up and let go.

Fast ball . . . strike one.

Fast ball . . . strike two.

Fast ball . . . and struck Watson out!

From that point on, I became more and more sure of myself, pitching seven innings of shutout ball. Now I knew I could pitch, and management knew I could pitch. First God had healed my crippled arm, and now He had healed my crippled confidence. *For with God nothing shall be impossible.*

A pioneer in Christian psychiatry, this dedicated doctor finds prayer his most effective tool.

THE THERAPY OF PRAYER

Dr. William Wilson

"Bill? Got a minute?"

I looked up from my desk to see an old school colleague standing in the doorway of my office at Duke University's Medical Center. He was an internist. I was a psychiatrist.

"Sure," I said, pushing aside the patient reports I'd been working on. "Come in."

It was late, nearly seven, and the cold fluorescent lighting cast thin blue shadows across his usually warm and animated features. He looked tired. He sat down in the chair facing me.

"What's up?" I asked.

"Well," he said, with a tight little smile, "my life is a drag." He hesitated. "I don't understand it.

"I mean, you'd think I had everything. Like you, I've just been appointed as a full professor here at the University. I have unlimited access to a huge laboratory, research facilities and library. Journals publish my papers, the government awards me grants. I've got a great wife and nice kids.

"So why," he asked, leaning back with a wry grin, "do I feel so empty inside?"

I wished I could give him an answer that would offer real help. But all I could say was, "The way you're feeling isn't unusual. If it's any consolation, I often feel the same way."

My friend grinned ruefully.

"Don't let it get you down," I said.

"Yes," he agreed, rising from the chair to go. "Guess you're right."

The interlude had left me feeling vaguely depressed. Why, I wondered, did I feel like my friend more often than I cared to admit? "Fatigue," I told myself. "You've been working too hard."

It *had* been an unusually long day. I was anxious to get home to my wife, Elizabeth, and the kids. In two weeks I'd be joining my oldest son and his friends on an eight-day Scouting trip deep in the wilds of northern Minnesota's Quetico Superior Wilderness Area. The trip, a canoe expedition, would take us close to the Canadian border via a 169-mile circular route, culminating with a 24-hour nonstop "survival paddle." Tonight, therefore, I was beginning a self-prescribed emergency program of jogging and sit-ups to get in shape.

"You know, Dad," commented my son a week later during one of these workouts, "I think you're looking forward to this trip as much as I am."

He was right.

As a boy, I'd spent most of my childhood hunting, fishing and exploring the wonders of North Carolina's woods. I'd never been a religious person, not even as a kid, but there was something about those quiet times in the forest that was, well—special.

Yes, I was looking forward to the trip. The change, I knew, would do me good.

The moment I shook hands with our expedition leader, Ray Mattson, I liked him. A tall, lean-muscled college student with copper-colored hair and beard, he took a liking to us, too. With unflagging enthusiasm, Ray led us on an unforgettable journey that challenged the strength and skills of the hardiest troop member.

The seventh day fell on a Sunday. That morning, according to Scout rules, Ray gathered us together for a brief outdoor worship service. Standing atop a craggy boulder, he gave a little talk based on the 23rd chapter of Matthew.

"Blind Pharisee!" he recalled the words of Jesus. "First cleanse the inside of the cup and of the plate, that the outside also may be clean." (Matthew 23:26 RSV) He went on to compare the wilderness, in all its splendor and untouched beauty, to the way the inside of our lives should be. Then he led us in a sing-a-long of simple religious songs that rang out pure and clear in the cool morning air. Listening to that sound, I felt something—some untapped emotion— stir deep inside me.

It had been a long time, I realized, since I had thought about God.

That evening, as the sun was setting, I walked to the edge of Basswood Lake, immense and sparkling beneath a pastel-painted sky.

I kicked off my moccasins and let my bare feet play along the pebbly shore. My thoughts wandered back to the morning worship service and the strange effect it had had on me. As a man of science in a field where religion was often viewed with skepticism, the idea of a living God had always seemed remote and archaic. But there was nothing outdated about the morning's message—God wanted us clean and healthy, *inside* as well as out, in order to be the kind of human beings He had designed us to be. Inherent in that concept, pure and simple, was the essence of modern psychiatry.

It suddenly became apparent that the only true way to clean up your life and be completely fulfilled wasn't through science, wasn't through medicine, and wasn't even through psychiatry—it was through God. And, looking out over those placid waters, I knew that was what I needed and wanted more than anything in the world—for God to come into my life and make me whole.

Before I knew it, tears were streaming down my face. As the sunset melted into a golden blur, I was overwhelmed, flooded, with God's love. He was truly with me. His Presence filled me with a peace and reassurance I'd never known. I savored the experience as long as I could, but soon it was time to go.

That night, as we paddled in the moon-lit darkness, I remained silent—lost in thought about what had happened. I knew I had changed. When I got home, it seemed that I loved my wife more deeply, and was more tolerant and kind with the kids. And I found myself going back to church. I actually *wanted* to go. This, in turn, led to new friends and fellowship that further nurtured my newfound faith.

But at work, it was a different story. The prevailing attitude of the hospital staff was generally negative where religion was concerned, and I chose not to "rock the boat." After all, all of us doctors were familiar with the deranged old character who thought that he was the prophet Jeremiah. And all of us had treated patients—pathetic cases—who suffered under self-imposed burdens of hate or guilt that they insisted on "justifying" by Scripture. In fact, we had a rule that incoming psychiatric patients were not allowed to have Bibles.

Once these long-held professional attitudes had seemed logical enough to me. But now it became increasingly difficult to resolve a growing inner conflict: I knew without a doubt that God was helping my personal life. *Why*, I wondered, *couldn't He do the same for our patients*? Still, I didn't have the nerve to speak out. "Lord," I prayed, "give me the courage to do something about this."

He did.

The changes in my work were subtle at first. But soon I found myself ignoring the no-Bible policy. And if a patient wanted to talk about religion, I would encourage him. The Lord led me slowly, no faster than I could handle, to the appropriate people and situations.

I remember one case in particular. In the late '60s there was at Duke's Medical Center a young man named John whom I had been treating with traditional psychiatric therapy and techniques. John was a drug-addicted physician. When he was first admitted, he was taking up to 40 tranquilizers a day—that's a paper cupfull of pills.

After two months of treatment with no discernible progress, there was really nothing more I could do. I told him so.

"Please," he begged. "Please don't say that. I'm standing here craving drugs just as badly as the day I checked in here.

"Please," he said, to himself as much as to me, "there's got to be something else."

"John," I said, "there's nothing else I can do . . . but maybe there's something God can do."

"God?" whispered John, a glimmer of hope in his voice.

"Yes," I said. "God." And I recalled that day in my office when my good friend had needed help—and I had nothing to offer. Never, I vowed, would that happen again.

Since returning from the Scouting trip, I had never spoken much about my experience to anyone. But now, I told John everything. He listened intently. My advice, when I left him, was simple.

"Pray," I said. "Just get down on your knees and pray. And don't get up until you've felt God in your life. He's waiting for you. And He wants to help."

The next morning when I looked in on John, he returned my gaze with eyes as clear and untroubled as the waters of Basswood Lake.

"You can send me home now," he said. "Everything's going to be all right."

So remarkable was John's recovery, I felt it best that he remain in the hospital for a short period of observation. For three days he stayed. Then he went home.

Prayer, to this day, remains my most effective tool in psychiatric treatment and counseling. Now, I pray regularly for every person in my care before and after sessions. I often pray silently during our conversations together. The power of prayer never ceases to amaze me. And its power has not gone unnoticed by others.

News of my success with heretofore hopeless cases like John's spread rapidly. Soon, associates were dropping by my office to chat about this "new" technique. Professional organizations began asking me to speak on the subject of Christian psychiatry at their meetings. Perhaps the most exciting development was the growing interest in the subject expressed by my students. As a result, I began offering a course called Christianity in Medicine and Psychiatry that proved to be extremely popular and is now being taken by students from all over the country.

But this is just the first step toward our ultimate goal. We are working now to establish at Duke University a formal Program of Christianity in Medicine, which will eventually offer complete curriculum, research, and regular counseling in this new and exciting frontier.

I do not consider myself an innovator in this field; other dedicated and farseeing men were pioneers long before I entered it. But it's exciting to share with them a wonderful discovery and a wonderful conviction: that religion and psychiatry really can work together to mend broken lives.

I was willing to pray for others. But what about my own needs?

FATHER, I NEED A HEALING

William Deerfield

"Looks like we've got some real trouble," the dentist said testily, peering inside my open mouth. "Haven't you been brushing the way I told you before I went on vacation?"

"But I did, doctor," I protested.

"Then you must have let the brush wear down. You brush too hard. Look, I'm supposed to operate on your gums next Monday. Your mouth is in such bad shape now, I might not be able to do anything."

Under the glare of the overhead light my forehead and palms broke into new waves of clammy sweat. I had been coming to the New York University School of Dentistry for over two months now and had patiently endured weeks of painful preparatory work to bring my peridontal condition to a point where an operation could be performed. Now it seemed as if all the work had been undone, and I'd have to begin the ordeal again.

My dental problems were just one more cloud on the darkening horizon. I was employed at the time as senior editor of an entertainment magazine that was in the process of folding. Since we had ceased actual publication, my unenviable job consisted mainly of fending off an army of irate creditors and handing out pink slips to staff members.

Doctor Shapiro was poking at my gums with a by now familiar steel pick, which I was convinced was a relic from the Spanish Inquisition.

After five minutes of probing, he stepped back with a

sigh. "Maybe Monday I'll be able to operate anyway—if you get a new brush today and get to work on it. But your mouth is in terrible shape."

Ten minutes later I was trudging up First Avenue to catch a bus back to the office. I felt discouraged and apprehensive, thinking about the ordeal that lay before me. "Oh, God," I prayed, "give me the strength to get through this."

I stood on the corner and waited, hands thrust deep into my pockets. My own situation caused my thoughts to turn to my prayer group and the elderly and sick who came each week for physical and spiritual healing, through "the laying on of hands," in accordance with the New Testament.

I had never asked for prayers for my own physical healing. I felt that my dental problems were a minor ailment compared to the really serious illness all around us. It never occurred to me that perhaps there was a deeper reason: I lacked the faith that God could or would heal me.

For whatever reason, I avoided putting God and my own faith to the test. But after my visit with Doctor Shapiro, I brooded about it. Should I ask the group to pray over me? My "minor" ailment was suddenly looming very large. I tried praying about it, but in a nervous, sporadic way, which was almost worse than no prayer at all.

And all the while a little voice kept nagging me, "You'd better start praying for a job instead of a healing."

It was true. I felt that the Lord would eventually come through somehow. But day after day I scanned the want ads and checked the agencies with no results. Leads that seemed promising would suddenly evaporate. I waited for some sign that things would improve, but there was no sign.

Thursday night came, and although I was feeling down, I forced myself to attend the prayer meeting. When it came time for requests for healing, I kept silent. I hung back as our pastor and others moved among the sick, laying their hands upon them, although I did join in the prayers. As I prayed for others, I was aware of my own problem, but I was unable to voice the petition.

I felt no peace after the meeting, and went home with a feeling of heaviness and unease in my heart. What was wrong? Didn't I have the faith? Didn't I believe that God was willing to heal me, too?

I got ready for bed, being careful to brush my teeth the proper way. I was depressed to see that my clean toothbrush soon became bright pink. I padded into the bedroom and opened my Bible, but I couldn't concentrate on what I read. Impatiently, I began to pace up and down.

It was true that my condition could hardly be considered a serious illness. But, I reasoned, isn't God the Lord of every aspect of our lives? And doesn't it then follow that He is as concerned about the relatively minor problems as well as the major crises? After all, the small, everyday occurrences and problems, when added together, make up the very warp and woof of our lives. Then, as if in confirmation, the words of Jesus flashed through my mind—words spoken when He was trying to convince His followers of God's love for them: "The very hairs of your head are all numbered." (Matthew 10:30)

Suddenly I knew what I had to do. I stopped pacing and placed my hands on either side of my face. "Oh, Lord," I prayed earnestly, "touch me and heal me now. I know, Lord, there are others who are much sicker than I am, but, please, dear Father, I need a healing. . . . I believe You can do this if You will. I believe . . . I believe. Lord, help my unbelief! Thank You, Lord. Thank You. Be it done unto me, according to Your will."

I opened my eyes, letting my hands drop to my sides. I felt a sense of peace stealing over me. I felt so tranquil, that I was suddenly very sleepy. I crawled under the covers, and, mumbling a prayer of thanks and praise, drifted off to sleep.

Curiously, for the next several days, I didn't think too much about the operation. Somehow it no longer seemed so important or frightening.

Monday arrived. By 1:15, I was reclining in the "hot seat," as I had come to call the dentist's chair.

"Open up, let's have a look," said Doctor Shapiro. He began to probe. "Hmmmmm," he said, after a moment. He stepped back, adjusted the mirror and looked again. After a few minutes he stepped away once more, and, not even waiting to lay down the pick, he said, "Just a minute, I'll be right back."

A faint thrill of hope began to stir within me. In a few minutes Doctor Shapiro had returned with his colleague, Doctor Klineman, who took the probe, and stepping close, peered into my mouth. "I don't believe it. I just don't believe it," Doctor Shapiro was saying softly, somewhere in the background.

"You can sit up for a minute, if you'd like," said the dour-faced Doctor Klineman, adjusting the chair.

"What's the matter?" I asked, half-anticipating what was to come. I had the feeling that we were performing in a rehearsed scene, and I knew all the lines.

"I'm not going to operate," said Doctor Shapiro. "There isn't any infection. We've looked and it's all gone. Your gums are healthy. I just can't understand it."

A wave of relief, mingled with joy, flooded over me.

"A remission, it was just a remission," Doctor Klineman insisted. "It sometimes happens."

"Look," I said, cautiously at first, my face beginning to flush with excitement. "I don't want to minimize any of the preparatory work that Doctor Shapiro did, but we believe in faith-healing in my church." I took a deep breath and plunged on. "I asked God to heal me and I believe He did." I felt a shock of embarrassment at what I had just said; yet I was glad that I had been able to say it.

"I still don't understand it," Doctor Shapiro said, shaking his head in disbelief as he packed his equipment away.

A few minutes later, as I rode down in the crowded elevator, I had the urge to shout to everybody that I was cured, *I was cured!* It was a miracle! Had I actually shouted I'm sure they would have carted me off to Bellevue Hospital, which was just across the street.

I stepped out into the cold of First Avenue, my heart light within me. "Thank You, Lord! Thank You!" I kept saying to myself as I waited for my bus. I was literally overflowing with joy and praise.

And, as I waited there in the cold street, I knew in a deep intuitive way that whatever the future held, God had given me a sign of His very real concern for me. *"The very hairs of your head are all numbered."* It was as if I weren't walking by faith anymore, but by sight.

I didn't get a job right away. There were many anxious days and nights. But often, when I was at the point of darkest despair, I would suddenly remember the wonderful sign He had given me—the touch of His hand upon my life—and in that moment I would take heart to go on.

I thought Mama was asking for too much. But Mama didn't think so. And neither did God.

THE IMPOSSIBLE PRAYER

Patricia Houck Sprinkle

The summer I was eight, our family lived in the country five miles out of Wilmington, North Carolina. Daddy was the preacher for two rural Presbyterian churches composed largely of Dutch immigrants who had established a thriving bulb and flower industry there.

Our home was one of an irregular string of houses along the highway, separated from one another by bulb fields, farm fields, and, on one side of us, a nursery. The owners let my little sister and me gather violets to bunch and sell for our own flower business, so I felt somewhat proprietary about that nursery.

But to Mama the nursery was mainly a nuisance. About once a day, someone would come to our house wanting to buy bushes, and Mama had to stop whatever she was doing and tell them to go next door. At times, the interruptions made Mama angry. But one day the nursery provided Mama with an adventure in prayer.

That spring, Daddy had become ill. I couldn't see anything wrong with him, except that he needed a lot of naps and didn't want to play with us children as often. Then he went to the hospital for a few days. When I was allowed to visit him, I was shocked to see that he had begun to turn a strange shade of yellow—even his eyes were yellow. I couldn't figure it out and got a little afraid.

In early summer, Daddy's doctor diagnosed nephritis, a serious kidney ailment, and he called in a specialist. Although they tried many treatments, usually painful, he was getting progressively worse.

One hot Saturday in August, Daddy awoke at 5 a.m. in severe pain. Our doctor insisted on driving all the way out to our house rather than having Mama take Daddy to the hospital emergency room. After he had given Daddy something to ease the pain, he asked Mama to walk him to his car, and I followed along.

The doctor told Mama, "If this continues, there is no real hope. You need to begin to consider what you and the girls are going to do."

When the doctor left, Mama went into the kitchen and sank into a chair. Dropping her head on her arms, she began to pray frantically between sobs. "Oh, God, don't let Sam die," she pleaded. "What can I do? What can I do?"

I put an arm around her shoulders. "Isn't there somebody else who can do something?"

She looked at me searchingly. "There must be, but I don't know who." Then she lowered her head again and prayed. "Who can help, God? Who?"

"Don't you know any other doctors?"

"No," she said. She looked away, remembering. "The only person I know in medicine is Laura Brennon.* We were friends in high school. She became a nurse. Last I heard, years ago, she was a supervisor in some big hospital somewhere, but I don't know where."

"Can you find out?" I asked.

"I doubt it," she said. "I'm sure she's married, and I don't know her name now."

As our minds sometimes do in trouble, Mama's seemed to fix on Laura, until she had an overwhelming desire to talk to her old friend. Mama closed her eyes and said, "God, I want to find Laura. Can she help Sam?"

We heard tires on the gravel drive and two car doors slam. Mama quickly slapped some water on her face, and we went to see who it was and what they wanted.

Two complete strangers stood there, a middle-aged couple looking toward the nursery. The man said, "Hello. We are interested in some of your azaleas."

"That's the next house," Mama said automatically. Then, as the strangers turned to leave, she blurted out, "Who are you?"

**name has been changed*

"Mr. and Mrs. Adams," the man said, starting to get into his side of the car, "from Winston-Salem. We're just passing through on vacation, and we saw the nursery."

Mama ran down the steps toward the woman. "Are you Laura Brennon?" she demanded.

The woman gasped. "Why yes, I am—or was. Who are you?"

"Eddis Byers, from Grover."

As Laura hurried to give Mama the conventional Southern hug of greeting, she exclaimed, "Why Eddis, I wouldn't have believed this could happen in a million years. What a coincidence!"

"No coincidence," Mama breathed. "Providence." Then she told Laura that Daddy was ill, and how she had been feeling a strong desire to find her just before the car arrived. "Would you just look at Sam and give me your opinion?"

Immediately Laura followed Mama into Daddy's room, and, while chatting casually as a friend of Mama's, she scanned his face. When they returned to the living room, she said, "He looks like a mighty sick man, Eddis, but I've seen sicker get well." Then she gave Mama the name of a kidney specialist to call first thing Monday morning. "We live near the hospital," she said as they were leaving, "and you can stay with us as long as you need to."

That weekend Mama alternated between thanking God for the miraculous way Laura had appeared and wrestling with when to go to Winston-Salem—and how. We talked about it. School would soon start, and Mama taught fourth grade. Could she leave Daddy in Winston without her? Could we afford for her to miss some school, perhaps a whole semester? Would they hold her job if she did? Sunday evening as she still struggled with these questions and poured out her thanksgiving that Daddy might, after all, have a chance to live, a new thought came to her.

She closed her eyes and prayed, "God, You answered my prayer in a way I could not possibly have imagined. Now I know that You could heal Sam here in Wilmington, if You want to. Show us what You want us to do."

I said, "Mama, aren't you asking God for too much?"

"That's impossible," she said. "After the way God used that nursery to bring Laura back into my life before the prayer was out of my mouth, I'm never going to hesitate to ask Him for anything."

Early on Monday before Mama could call Winston-Salem, our local kidney specialist came to the house. "Mrs. Houck," he said, "this weekend I have thought of one more treatment we might try with Sam. It's painful, and I can't guarantee it, of course, but I think it might just be the cure we've been looking for."

"I'm sure it is," Mama said firmly.

That was more than 20 years ago. Recently Daddy celebrated his sixtieth birthday by painting the eaves and all the trim on his home. I telephoned him to give him the greetings of the day.

"Sixty years," he said. "Isn't that something? I'm asking God to let me have at least another twenty more."

I laughed. "Don't push your luck, Daddy."

"Why not?" he said. "Didn't your mother teach us all that you can't ask God for too much if you've got the faith for it?"

A PRAYER FOR ONE WHO IS ILL

Lord, Thou hast suffered, Thou dost know
The thrust of pain, the piercing dart,
How wearily the wind can blow
Upon the tired heart.

He whom Thou lovest, Lord, is ill.
O come, Thou mighty Vanquisher
Of wind and wave, say, Peace, be still,
Eternal Comforter.

Amy Carmichael

"You'd better think about hanging it up," a team of doctors advised me. But I was determined to play football.

NOT ON MY OWN

Rocky Bleier
Running Back, Pittsburgh Steelers

"What did you do in civilian life, son?" the Army doctor in Tokyo asked me, after he'd finished examining the bandages on both my legs.

"I was drafted by the Pittsburgh Steelers as a running back, before the Army drafted me," I said bitterly.

The doctor's eyes searched mine.

"Well," he said gently, "your football days are over. Thank God you're not permanently crippled."

I wasn't thankful. I was mad. And I was scared. Not of the pain—I was used to punishing my body. I was afraid of being a "gimp." And I wouldn't accept the doctor's diagnosis. I was determined to make my legs run again.

Back in Vietnam, my platoon had been attacked by a large force of North Vietnamese. We were cut off. Close-quarters fighting. I was hit in the left thigh by small-arms fire. I went down. Collapsed even before I felt the pain. "God, no," I pleaded. "Not my legs." Then a grenade exploded right at my feet. Shrapnel tore into both legs, shattering bones in my right foot.

I started crawling toward cover, dragging my legs. *I can make it,* I thought. Then I started to pass out. At that moment a black soldier I'd never seen before came and picked me up. Under fire, he wrapped my arms around his neck and lifted. Then, carrying me on his back, he started to the rear. Two miles away there was a landing spot for evacuation helicopters.

He carried me a mile and then collapsed. But stretcher bearers found me and got me to the choppers. I never knew his name, but I'll never forget him. When I could do nothing for myself, God sent him. He saved my life.

The war was over for me. They patched me up and sent me back to the States. Eventually, I found myself in Fort Riley, Kansas, waiting to be discharged. It was July, 1970. I was an out-of-work rookie football player with a 40 percent disability rating from the Army. But I was too stubborn to accept the doctor's verdict. I intended to try out for the Steelers that summer. My foot felt pretty good. I figured I only had to get my wind back to get into shape again.

I hadn't had any real exercise since being wounded, four months earlier. I thought I'd start with a light workout, so I set my alarm clock for an hour and a half before reveille.

It was a clear spring morning. I remember how the dew on the prairie grass glistened in the pale dawn light. As my footsteps crunched onto the cinder track, a needle of pain jabbed my right foot. The toes didn't bend much anymore. They didn't *look* bad. They just didn't work. I loosened up with some stretching exercises, then started jogging at an easy pace.

Within half a mile I was gasping for breath, struggling and stumbling.

"No!" I murmured in shock, remembering how easy a two-mile run had once seemed. "This can't be. *It can't be!*"

But I wouldn't give up.

Tough, agonizing weeks followed before I could run any distance. I didn't even worry about my lack of speed.

The Steelers, unfortunately, had to. I reported to preseason camp and took a beating. I was tired, sore, limping. When the coaches timed us in the 40-yard dash, their stopwatch put me dead last, slower than the biggest lineman in camp. And I was supposed to be a running back!

Head Coach Chuck Noll told me his decision. "It doesn't look like you've got a future with us, Rock," he said tersely. "Maybe you can build yourself up enough to try again next year."

Next year! How often does a comeback like that happen? How can a guy manage to become a better athlete while he's getting older, and sitting idle? I was five-feet-nine, too small for the pros anyway, everyone said. Maybe I should give up.

But I wouldn't. I underwent another operation, to repair damaged muscles and restore movement to my injured foot. And, though I took a job with a Chicago insurance firm, I still forced myself into a rigorous after-hours exercise program.

The worst days of football training camp are the first weeks—a period of tough physical workouts, twice a day. Even conditioned athletes sometimes collapse in the summer heat.

Well, I decided I would punish *myself* that way for the whole year. I exercised before work, at lunch breaks and in the evenings. At the end of a day, I had to force my legs up the steps of a railroad overpass on my running route. *Can't do this anymore!* my body cried; my will forced it on.

I punished my body every day for a year. I wanted to be a running back.

When the 1971 summer training camp opened, I reported early with the rookies to take advantage of the extra workout time. And there were some hopeful signs. Muscles that had been tight or useless the year before now surged with new strength; joints stiff before my operation felt loose and flexible again. My speed—never outstanding—was suddenly respectable. There was hope . . . I knew it . . . believed it . . . willed it.

Then the first day of regular camp, I pulled a hamstring muscle. There was this sharp, knifing pain in the back of my leg. Every athlete knows what that means—out of action, maybe for the season.

"You'd better think about hanging it up, fella," a team of doctors advised me. "You'll only keep getting this sort of injury. That kind of scar tissue builds up in your leg. You want to ruin yourself for life?"

Even Coach Noll gently advised me: "Maybe you should think seriously about staying with the insurance business."

The message was there, plain as day: *Quit!*

I felt betrayed—by my own body. How could *it* do this to *me?*

Even though I knew the end of my athletic career might come any day, I accompanied the team up to Green Bay, where we were to play the Packers in a exhibition game. It was a chance to visit my family in Appleton, Wisconsin.

And I could have a serious talk with an old friend, Father Al Lison.

His six-foot-two frame was still lean, though his salt-and-pepper hair showed a bit more white, perhaps. But he was still the man who had guided me through high school. Father Al had the knack of asking the right questions and listening in the right places. In a few moments, after he'd seated himself in our kitchen, I was telling him everything that was on my mind. I told him about my years of sweat and uncertainty. I told him about my latest injury, and Coach Noll's suggestion.

"I guess it's time to decide whether you've tried long enough, Rocky," he said gently. "How do you feel about it?"

I didn't answer for a long time. Finally I said, "I made a promise back in Vietnam. When I was lying there wounded, I prayed that if I survived I'd do the best I could with my life. I didn't say I'd become a priest, Father."

We laughed.

"I wouldn't make a good priest. But I thought I would make a good football player. I promised I'd keep on trying."

Father Al smiled. "I guess you're learning something about life now, Rocky. A lot of things require two wills—yours *and* God's. We used to talk about how the Lord must have had His hand on your shoulder, because of how well you did in high school and at Notre Dame, remember? Well, the hand's still there, Rocky. But do you feel it? Or are you just trying to make it on your own?"

It was a surprising idea. Maybe pure, hard grit and punishing training weren't enough.

I went back to the Steelers' camp with renewed determination—and something more. I was waiting to feel His hand on my shoulder.

No one was looking for me to be a star ball carrier, but there are many other jobs for a professional football player. When coaches asked me to block, I'd put my head down and do the job. When I was told to cover kickoffs, I tried to be the first man downfield. And each day that went by without reinjuring my hamstring, I breathed a silent "Thanks" to the Lord.

When the team roster was posted after final cuts, my name was on it. I'd made the Steelers!

Success didn't come in one big wave. Talking with Father

Al had prepared me for the gradual, uneven way God's will can unfold in a person's life. So I lived with the restraints and setbacks. For several seasons, all the game action I saw was special team play—such as the kickoff team and punt coverage. When I *was* sent into the regular lineup, I was generally used as a blocker for another player. I didn't mind. I hadn't set any conditions on the direction of God's guiding hand.

But the season climaxed by the 1975 Super Bowl still remains special to me. That was the first year I managed to break into the starting lineup. Besides blocking for our great 1000-yard rusher, Franco Harris, I became a useful part of our offense in my own right, running and catching passes.

I'll never forget the day of the Steelers' first Super Bowl game. It wasn't our victory over the Vikings in New Orleans I remember as much as a single moment before the game.

It was early. Most of the spectators had not yet crowded into the huge, open bowl of Tulane Stadium. I had put on my uniform and all alone silently walked through a passage out toward the field. At the mouth of the tunnel, I stopped and my heart jumped a beat.

"Lord," I said, "I can hardly believe You've put me here. The Super Bowl! I couldn't do it on my own. A lot of the players are out here today because they're fast or strong or naturally great athletes. I'm not any of those things. And now I realize—that's the gift you gave me. In Your will, my will worked."

Early in the fourth quarter, when the game was still close, Terry Bradshaw handed off to me. I was tired, late getting to the hole opened by our line—two Vikings closed it up. The lines slammed together. Dust, heat, sweat, tired bodies crashing together, punishing one another in an effort to triumph over the opponent. That's sport. I summoned up enough energy to step sideways, and found a bit of running room on my own—enough to make a first down.

As I walked back to the huddle, one of our linemen slapped his big hand on the top of my helmet and said, "Attaboy, Rock. Never give up. If we can't do it for you, do it on your own."

Behind my face mask, I just grinned. I knew I could never do it on my own.

Ada Leas wasn't just another old lady. She was my friend. And she needed my prayers.

A PRAYER FOR ADA

Stan Coleman
Guideposts 1979 Youth Contest Winner

"Old Ada's pretty bad," my father said.

I looked up quickly, questioning him with my eyes.

"Oh, Stan," he said, "I've doctored lots of patients, and when they get to be that old you have to prepare yourself, because there really isn't anything medicine can do."

That was fine logic for adults, but to me, a child of 11, it made no sense at all. Ada Leas wasn't just another old lady, she was my friend, so it hurt to hear my dad talking so frankly. I knew he was right. Ada had looked sick the last few weeks when I had delivered her paper, but I, a child, hadn't noticed how very sick she was.

As I delivered papers the next day, I could hardly wait to see how Ada was feeling, to see if my father was right. Finally coming to her door, I looked carefully for any sign of the kind smile that usually greeted me. It wasn't there. The old chair where I placed the paper so that Ada wouldn't need to bend was there. It was the chair I sat in during the summer when she showed me the black and white post-cards she and her late husband had bought in California. The chair was still there, along with that familiar smell of age, but the smile was nowhere.

"How's Mrs. Leas?" I asked my father that evening. I knew he had been to see her.

"She was pretty sick last night," he answered over the paper. "Had to give her a shot."

"You give her a lot of them, don't you?"

After setting the paper down and seeing my worried look, he added, "Son, we do everything we can, but God didn't mean for these bodies to live forever. You need to understand that."

I knew that we all grow old, but I couldn't understand why my father accepted Ada's sickness so calmly when he had prayed for my healing when I had the flu.

The following week, when collecting time came, I was afraid to go to Ada's house. "What if she is so sick that she won't recognize you? What if she isn't even there? What if? What if?" my mind screamed again and again. My fears hushed after I knocked, went inside and found my friend rocking slowly in her chair.

"Hello, Stanley," she said.

"Hi," I answered nervously. "I'm collecting."

"Oh, yes. How much is it?"

"A dollar-ten."

"Oh, dear. Would you hand me my purse? It's over by my bed. Did you find it?"

"Yes," I said, and handed it to her.

"I think I have the money right here," she said as she fumbled through her purse. "A dollar-ten did you say?"

"Uh huh."

"Here's the dollar, and here's the ten."

"Thank you," I said, avoiding her eyes.

Then, without saying a word, I gave her the receipt. I wanted to speak, but my tongue was a prisoner of the room's awkward silence.

"How are you feeling?" I finally managed.

"Oh, not so good. My arthritis has been hurting me, but your father was here last night, and he gave me a shot. I felt better today, so I decided to get out of bed and sit here. One mustn't lie around too much. I'm feeling a little worse now though."

"Would you mind if I prayed for you?" I blurted without taking time to think. (Now that I'm older, I realize I should have said, "Oh, that's too bad," or "Well, I hope you get to feeling better," but I was just a child who didn't quite understand the ways of an adult.)

"Yes, please do pray," she replied.

I suppose she thought I'd meant later, at home before I went to bed, because she looked rather surprised as I dropped to my knees and took hold of her hand.

"Father," I prayed, "heal Ada Leas, and let her know You're the One responsible."

I stopped, afraid to continue, scared of what I'd just prayed. What if it wasn't God's will that she get well? I knew God wanted the best for everyone, but what was the best? I didn't know, but again the words came without my mind's help.

"I believe You hear my prayer, God. In Jesus' name—Amen."

I rose feeling strangely warm. Ada, still holding tightly to my hand, was smiling that same lovely smile I had seen so often before.

"Thank you, Stanley," she whispered.

"Sure, ah, good-bye," I said, close to tears.

A moment later I was outside among the fallen leaves, feeling warm despite the cool fall temperature, wondering if I had prayed against God's will. Wondering if. Wondering if.

God didn't answer my questions right away, but gradually Ada's midnight calls came less and less frequently. She began to smile more, and when spring came, she even started walking uptown to the grocery store—something she hadn't done in years.

"Trying to put me out of a job, son?" my father asked one night.

"Huh?"

"Ada has hardly been sick since the day you prayed!"

"Oh, well . . ." I stammered. I hadn't told anyone and was surprised that he knew.

"I think it was a wonderful thing you did," my father said. "It meant a lot to Ada, too. In fact, she hasn't stopped talking about it. It's a miracle, son. At the rate she's going she'll live to be a hundred."

That was six years ago. I no longer deliver papers and Ada (now 89) doesn't live in the house down the street. She sold it last year and moved to a nursing home. I'm busy with my job, school, wrestling and my future plans, so I don't visit her very often. I did see her a few weeks ago, though. When I walked into her room, I found her in a rocking chair, but the moment she saw me she jumped up hospitably.

"Stanley!" She kissed me. "You've grown so much. Here,

sit in my chair."

"That's okay. I'll sit on the bed."

"No, I sit in my chair all day, and it's good for me to get up and move around."

I didn't argue further and sat down.

"Well, I bet you've been keeping busy lately," she began.

"Yes, I just came from wrestling practice."

"Oh, yes, you like wrestling."

"Yeah, and what have you been doing?"

"Well, I went into town today . . . saw my brother . . . he's been sick you know . . ."

We talked for a few minutes about small things. I listened some and responded when I should have, but my mind was wandering while I studied my friend. She seemed surprisingly full of life and love, not at all like the sick woman I had delivered papers to. She had changed, but then, so had I. *Maybe*, I thought, *I'm too much of an adult*. If I prayed the same prayer again, would it be something less, something more adult, like, "Be with Ada, God," or "Comfort Mrs. Leas," instead of "Heal her."

Most of all I wondered, as I talked with my smiling friend, how much God would do if I always prayed with the faith of a child.

YOUR SPIRITUAL WORKSHOP

WHEN YOUR WELL RUNS DRY

Pain and suffering leave deep scars on our minds and bodies. Here are methods to renew our strength.

- You have nursed someone through a serious illness: husband, son, close friend. They recover; the strain is over. But you find yourself in a terrible slump.
- You have done your best to help someone who means a great deal to you. Your efforts, however, are misunderstood and disharmony results. You are exhausted.
- You have worked hard meeting a series of business crises. With the worst over and things going all right again, you suddenly feel terribly depressed.

Or perhaps the reason for your slump is not so obvious. It can be hidden in the secret mysteries of the body's chemistry or in the delicate adjustment of the nervous system. It can come from wrong-doing. But when it happens—as it does to all of us—the fact is that our well has gone dry. The power has drained from our life. In such a state we are vulnerable to illness, temptation, discouragement—in fact, all the evils that befall us.

Tiredness may be traced to a physical ailment so a doctor's examination is the first logical step. But in 90 per cent of such cases your physician will not find anything organically wrong. He may not describe it this way, but what you have is *malnutrition of the spirit*.

How do you replenish the water of life? How is the spirit fed? Follow the plan suggested on the following pages:

ep 1. Admit Your Helplessness

Accept the fact that your fatigue, depression, slump is a normal occurrence. We all go through it at various intervals. So sit down in a comfortable chair and admit your inability at this point to run your own life efficiently. At this low ebb you can't do things well, so don't put large demands on yourself. If you can't pray, don't try to. If you can't believe, don't try to. If you can't perform as well as you would like to, don't expect top performance of yourself.

John Keats, a poet and wise man, used to call this process "diligent indolence—the power of passive existence." For the very yielding process begins to change the chemical imbalance inside you. At this point the well will begin to fill very slowly from the bottom, the way a wound heals from the bottom.

ep 2. Resume Your Normal Routine

Meanwhile, of course, the routines of life go on. The next meal must be prepared, an assignment done, an errand performed, a deadline met. So you get up and do what you have to do even though you still feel physically and emotionally spent.

Keats had his own method of resuming work. "Whenever I feel *vaporish* (the word our grandfathers used for this condition), I rouse myself, wash, put on a clean shirt, brush my hair and clothes, tie my shoestrings neatly—all as though I were going out—then all clean and comfortable I sit down to write."

It is a proven fact of life that the way you feel does not necessarily determine what you can do. At the time of very bad health and a great emotional upset in his life, Beethoven, who was deaf, wrote some of his greatest music. Robert Louis Stevenson had severe hemorrhaging spells and chronic lung trouble while he was writing his greatest works.

You will find that you can do what you have to do; and sometimes when you feel least like doing it, you will do it better than you realize.

Step 3. Seek Out Another

After years of experience, one minister became aware that numerous people were coming to him simply because they were at low ebb. They would open the conversation something like this, "Normally I can handle things like this myself, but I have come to the point where I need to talk to somebody." The minister learned to listen with receptive warmth and not try to play God. A prayer together, the recommendation of a Scripture passage to read, possibly a book suggestion—nothing too detailed. Yet he learned that while a person may go away with only a cup of water, it often was all that was needed to prime the pump.

A visit with a courageous shut-in or a trip through a hospital ward often will work a quick therapy. Bringing comfort to someone in worse straits than you can bring on a surge of gratitude and begin the inner filling-up process.

Sometimes you can get help from a person you meet between the covers of a book. Try reading Deitrich Bonhoeffer's *Letters From Prison* or Joni Eareckson's *A Step Further*. You may find yourself saying, "If they can have this kind of strength under the conditions of their lives, surely I can find strength to do what I have." You may find your well beginning to fill up, fed by the wells of others who have much to give.

Step 4. Find Water for the Soul

There are times, of course, when you need more than just a person. Perhaps people depress you. So you go away for some rest, but the deadness is still there. This kind of weariness lies not in the mind or body, but in the soul. When the soul is sick, the body and mind soon register the defect.

To restore the soul, you must have new heart for life. And the secret of a fresh interest in life does not lie on the surface. It lies in the recovery of God's purpose for you. *He restoreth my soul.** This is the Spring that never fails.

To restore malnutrition of the spirit, seek out the Person of Jesus Christ. Read everything you can find about Him. Pour over the Gospels. Seek Him through the communion table. In every possible way, get as close to Him as you can until you feel His Spirit flowing through you.

The sacraments of the church will replenish the spirit.

*Psalm 23:3

The act of confession, taking communion bread, prayer, the singing of hymns—all can help you make connection with the extraordinary vitality of Christ. And if you continue to reach out for spiritual nourishment you will some day come to know what Jesus meant when He said, *Whoever drinks of the water that I shall give him will never thirst; the water that I shall give him will become in him a spring of water welling up to eternal life.* **

ıggested Prayer

When our energies recede and our vitality is inadequate to meet the needs of the day, help us, O Lord, to learn to sit still, to do nothing; and then to give us the will to rise up to do the things we have to do, and go to those who can fill our empty wells, even unto Christ whose well is never empty. Amen.

**John 4:14, RSV

The Unlimited Power of Prayer

LORD, GUIDE ME

Chapter 4

Every day there are decisions to be made which can alter the course of your entire life. Do you know that God will guide you? He has promised to lead you safely through life. But to receive His guidance you must first ask for it. Hear the words of Jesus: Ask, and it shall be given you; seek, and ye shall find; knock, and it shall be opened unto you. (Matthew 7:7)

The people who speak in the following stories asked God to guide them. When they did, He led them safely down paths they might never have discovered alone. Here are the stories of an 84-year-old jazz singer, a directionless army veteran, a young couple contemplating marriage. . .nine remarkable true tales of people who prayed for guidance and received it. Let their stories inspire you to bring God into your daily decision-making. He will show you the safest course for your life's journey.

This popular singer on the Lawrence Welk Show *struggled for many years to find his niche.*

IN THE MORNING OF MY LIFE

Tom Netherton

I grew up believing that nothing in life was permanent. My father was a career Army officer, constantly being transferred, and we rarely lived on the same post for more than a year.

Each move meant a new start for me—a new community, a new school, a search for new friends. In one of the high schools I attended I saw a notice on the bulletin board about auditions for a musical the drama club was putting on. I went just to have something to do. I found myself sitting with some boys who were heckling the kids on stage. Finally one of the kids challenged us: "If you guys think you can do any better, come up here and prove it."

In a rash moment I said, "Okay."

I went up on stage. I was nervous, I was embarrassed and I was scared to death. I sang *Almost Like Being In Love* and by the time I was finished I was far from in love with myself or with my performance. Head down, I hurried out of the auditorium.

Next day, on the bulletin board, I was astonished to see my name. I'd been given the lead in the show!

More important to me was that I had found an entree into the new life forced on me whenever one of my father's military transfers would come up. I could always join the singing groups at school or at the local church. But I never thought of singing as a career. I never thought I was good enough to make a living at it.

After graduating from high school, I enrolled in the University of Minnesota. I started the semester with enthusiasm, but in just a matter of weeks I had completely lost interest in my classes, the people and student life in general. Maybe it was the newness of it and the fact that I was anonymous, but I felt so alone.

When the Vietnam war intensified, I decided to join the Army. It was a decision that would change my life.

Through Basic Training and later in Officer Candidate School I considered becoming a Green Beret or a paratrooper in Vietnam. But when my orders came, I was assigned to Panama, not Vietnam.

I had begun to smoke a little and to drink. After all, that's what soldiers are expected to do. In Panama I sang at night on off-duty hours at the piano bar of the Officers' Club. I went snorkeling and skin diving off Tobago Island. During the day I led my men on training maneuvers in the steaming Panamanian jungles. At night I partied with Panamanian friends. But there was a longing, a deep longing inside me, going far beyond the tropical days and nights. Nothing seemed to satisfy it.

One day a friend asked if I'd like to hear a Major Ian Thomas speak at church. Up to this point in my life, church for me was more social than spiritual. It was something nice people did on Sunday. But I didn't have anything else to do, so I went along with him.

During the service I sensed that something strange was beginning to happen to me. The message was rich with love and power. I sat among all those strangers and felt a sudden surge of expectation. There was no voice from Heaven. No bolt of lightning. No thunder. But as I sat there, I met my Savior.

"Take my life," I whispered, "and use it any way You want to. Jesus, I give myself to You."

In that moment I knew that by giving my life to Him, I would be empowered by the Holy Spirit to be the kind of man God had always intended me to be. Everything became clear to me. I had spent my life trying to "be good" and "do good" just to get other people's approval. But now I felt free. Free from fears and, best of all, free from the haunting worry that my life wouldn't count for anything. My life belonged to Jesus, and I trusted Him completely in everything.

I got out of the Army in 1969. I got a job with a company that made artificial plants. I dipped dried twigs and leaves in wax for Christmas decorations, making $2.50 an hour, hoping for better things to come. Then I changed jobs and went to work in a shoe store. Selling shoes was tiring and annoying. But I had promised the Lord that everything I did was for Him . . . so I sold shoes for the glory of God.

"I asked for red, not brown."

"Yes, ma'am, I'll get them for you."

"I changed my mind. I'll see the brown."

"Yes, ma'am, I'll get them for you."

As I worked I prayed. After a year, with a little money in the bank, I put my last box of shoes on the shelf, brought out the last pair of shoes to a customer and said good-bye. I decided to go to Bible School and train for missionary service.

At first I was sure that was what the Lord wanted me to do. But as I got involved with the school programs and began to sing for the students and faculty I felt a twinge of longing in my heart to sing again.

My counselor called me into his office. "There's been some criticism, Tom. Your singing is a little too worldly for the church."

"But I sing from my heart."

"Well, Tom, you *croon*. If you could change your style . . ."

Rebellion, bitterness, hurt—all welled up inside me. I prayed, "Lord, do You really want me to become a missionary? Is there something else You want me to do? All I can think of is singing. Tell me what You want, Lord."

The answer came in my next thought: "I want you to sing for Me." Right then and there I called a local theatrical agency. They had an opening for me to sing with a popular singing group in a supper club in St. Paul. I believed it was God's sign to me. I left the Bible School with the love and prayers of my instructors and counselors.

It was great to be performing again! I prayed for the people in the audiences and I was careful about the kinds of songs I sang. More engagements followed and I went to

Chicago to perform with a new variety show. But when I objected to some of the material and refused to sing it, I was out of a job . . .

I decided to become a one-man gospel show. With borrowed money I got a van and sound equipment, thinking that churches all over the country would pay to have me come and sing for them. But I got in over my head. I couldn't earn enough even to pay for the gas to get to a church to perform; and many churches just didn't have the money to pay me at all. Depressed and defeated, I gave up and went home. Would I ever really amount to anything?

My spiritual life went into a swift decline. I'd never been in such dismal circumstances since becoming a Christian. Other guys my age had careers and college degrees. "I'll never amount to anything," I grumbled. There were no singing jobs open, no job openings at all, and I didn't want to go back to selling shoes. I was full of self-pity and anger. I couldn't figure out why God had allowed me to fail so miserably. After all, I had earnestly wanted to serve Him, hadn't I?

The days turned to weeks . . . and to months. Finally one night, after nearly a year of doing nothing but feel sorry for myself, I began to think I was wrong to be angry with God. I went into my bedroom and got down on my knees. "Forgive me," I prayed. "I know I've been selfish and weak." I felt sick to my stomach, as if the ugly thoughts I had allowed to fester within me were finally stirring.

"Please forgive me, Lord. Please do with me what You want. I'll try not to complain." Tears slid down my cheeks. I determined to trust God in *all* things and to thank Him in *all* circumstances.

Nothing changed right away. I still struggled with depression until the next summer when I got a job as a singer in an outdoor musical pageant in Medora, North Dakota. The owners, Harold and Sheila Schafer, gave me a small part. I thanked the Lord for helping me. I had no idea that He had only just begun.

The show had been running a few weeks when Sheila asked me if I would like to meet her friend, Lawrence Welk, and try to get an audition with him. All I'd wanted to do that summer was earn enough money to pay my bills and get close to the Lord again. I felt that the last year had been such a disaster that I needed time to read the Bible and get to know Him better.

"Lord," I prayed, "if this takes my attention away from You I don't want it." And I put the idea of auditioning for Lawrence Welk out of my mind.

Then three weeks later Sheila announced, "Lawrence Welk is in Bismarck playing golf and we're taking you to meet him." Now I grew excited, but I was afraid to get my hopes up. In a borrowed outfit (white shoes, white pants, blue sweater) and with a pianist just in case he asked me to sing, we went to the Apple Tree Country Club. Sheila left me in the lobby to go find Mr. Welk. Soon she came running across the lobby to me. "Come on! He's on the second tee!" She grabbed my hand and ran with me through the club and across the green to where he was about to putt the ball into the cup. "Now don't be nervous," she said, "it's just Lawrence Welk." They embraced and chatted like old friends and I stood there in my white pants and shoes feeling very nervous indeed.

"Ah! This is the young man you were telling me about?" he said.

I put one white foot forward. "How do you do, sir."

"He's a nice-looking young man," Lawrence Welk said to Sheila, surveying me. "Do you play golf?"

"No, not well, sir."

"That's all right. Come with me and be my caddy." So I walked alongside him as he played golf. We talked about the Lord and being a Christian in show business. He said, "Tom, Christians have to make themselves known and stand up for what's right and wrong. That's what I want on my show." We walked up to the club for lunch. Then he asked, "Is there any way you could manage to sing for me?"

"Well," I said, "I just happen to have brought an accompanist . . . "

I sang the first number, then a second one. During this second number he whispered to Sheila, "If I ask him to sing a third song that means I like him."

I finished the song, and he said, "But you had one more song to sing for me, didn't you?"

Sheila beamed, and I sang *I Asked the Lord*.

Mr. Welk applauded and gave his famous smile. "Tom, we don't have any openings on the show just now. But in six weeks we're performing in St. Paul. How about singing on that show and I'll see how the audience likes you?"

I don't remember what I ate. To me the lunch was manna from Heaven!

On the 125-mile drive back to Medora I asked my accompanist, Dwight Elrich, "What do you think are my chances of actually getting on the Lawrence Welk Show?"

He shook his head in a way that said, "Hopeless."

"Tom," he said, "I don't want to sound discouraging, but just look at the odds. It's a national television show. Think of all the singers in the country he has to choose from. I wouldn't get my hopes up."

"I guess you're right," I said, and put out of my mind the hope of ever appearing on the Lawrence Welk Show.

The summer season at Medora came to a close. I packed my suitcase and headed back to Bloomington, Minnesota. I had no idea where I'd work next. I knew I didn't want to go back to selling shoes.

A few weeks after I got home a couple of my friends and I were down in the basement listening to records. The telephone rang. Then my mom appeared at the top of the stairs.

"Tom, you'd better come to the telephone. It's— it's Lawrence Welk!"

"Hellooooo," said one of the most familiar voices in America, "guess who this is!"

It really was Lawrence Welk. "Tom, I just want to make sure you'll be in St. Paul when we do our show."

"Yes, sir, I'll be there!"

"Just sing the songs you sang for me in North Dakota; that'll be fine." He was so gracious you'd have thought I was doing him a favor just agreeing to show up.

The St. Paul Civic Center, where Lawrence Welk was performing, is a huge complex covering several blocks.

"Stage door?" The man in the lobby by the ticket window didn't even look up. "There ain't no stage door. Maybe you mean the loading dock. There's a loading dock. Round thataway." He gestured with his shoulder. "Keep following around the building."

The doors along the building were closed and unmarked. I could hear the cars whistling past on nearby I-94 and the wind was doing terrible things with my carefully combed hair.

Finally I came to a door marked EMPLOYEES ENTRANCE. Inside, I found that the backstage area was just a cavernous end of the auditorium. Squinting through the darkness, I saw no people.

"You're two hours early," a man in coveralls told me. "The Welk bus hasn't even showed up yet. You can wait around if you want to."

"Thanks." At least I had time to comb "Mr. Kenneth Hair Styles for Men" back into place.

Finally the cast members began to arrive. I watched them coming through the employees entrance, and I thought of the many times their voices had filled our living room and mingled with the sounds of my brother and me wrestling and the smells of dinner on the stove.

Jim Roberts, one of the vocalists, asked me who I was waiting for. I told him that I would be singing in the show today. He was so friendly, I felt I had known him for a long time. He called pianist Bob Ralston over and introduced us. "Oh, yes. Lawrence told me about you. Let's go over your numbers. I'll be accompanying you."

As we quickly rehearsed my numbers, I saw the performers, one by one, come out of their dressing rooms in their makeup and costumes. I felt self-conscious, as though I had hayseed on my lapel or chicken feathers in my ears.

As the musicians took their places in the orchestra, I saw Lawrence Welk coming toward me. He was dressed in a powder blue suit, shirt and shoes, and looked smaller than when I saw him in North Dakota. He was smiling warmly. "Are you ready to sing for the people today, Tom?"

"Yes, sir."

"That's good. I'll be putting you on in the middle of the show, so you just stand by and be ready. You're not nervous, are you?"

"I think I am, Mr. Welk . . . a little bit."

"I'm glad you admitted that. Shows you're honest. Well, a little nervousness never hurts a performance. It actually makes it better."

Then, taking lively little steps, he hurried on stage to the thundering ovation of his fans.

Bobby and Cissy were doing their dance number when I stepped into the shadow offstage to pray. "Lord, I commit this night to You. I'm going to have peace now that you are in control of this performance as well as my entire life. If I do well, fine. If I do badly, then I'll know it's not Your will that I get a job with Lawrence Welk."

The minutes ticked away. I watched Arthur Duncan tap dance, Gail Farrell play the piano, Anacani sing, and then I heard Mr. Welk's voice near me. "Are you ready now?" He pulled some notes out of his jacket pocket and read them over. "At the end of this number by the orchestra I am going to introduce you."

I swallowed. *Dear Jesus, help me.* I felt as if I were back in high school ready to go on stage for the first time in the class play.

Then I heard Lawrence. "Ladies and gentlemen, I have a very special surprise for you today. I want to introduce you to a young man I met in North Dakota—come on out here, Tom, and say hello to the folks." My feet moved and I was smiling and striding across the stage to the microphone. The spotlight shone on me and followed me across the gigantic stage.

"His name is Tom Netherton and he's from Bloomington, Minnesota." (Thunderous applause.) "I've asked him to come and sing for us today."

I heard Bob play my intro and I began the song, *I Asked the Lord*. When the song was over, I heard an eruption of applause that stunned me.

"Just listen to that applause!" Lawrence shouted. "Just listen to that audience! That was Tom Netherton, ladies and gentlemen! Tom, come over here! You'd better sing another song."

My intro began and I started, *I talk to the trees* . . . .

When I finished the song the audience was clapping and shouting and waving their arms in the air. I had never heard anything like it in my life. I bowed and started off the stage.

"You can't just leave the stage when the audience is giving you such an ovation!" Mr. Welk shouted into the microphone. His baton was stuck under his arm and he was applauding, too.

"The audience is always right, Tom," he said. Then, holding onto my sleeve, he turned to the audience and said, "Well, what do you think of him? Do you like this Minnesota boy?" The crowd shouted its approval.

Then Lawrence was talking to his audience as though he

were talking one-to-one to old friends. "There's only one thing I can do, folks. Tom, how would you like to come out to Hollywood and be on my television show?"

My knees weakened. Hire me right *here?* On stage? In front of 19,000 people?

What did I say? Did I stutter? Did I say "yes" or did I say "sure"?

The crowd went absolutely wild. Right before their eyes an American dream had come true. Hometown boy makes good.

There, amidst the clamor, I whispered a silent prayer, "Dear Jesus, thank You." Well-wishing people were shaking my hand, patting my back, talking all at once, asking for my autograph. I felt overwhelmed, but I also felt very sure that this was what the Lord wanted me to do.

The dawn was breaking—bright and beautiful. It was the morning of my life.

Lead me Lord
Lead me in Thy righteousness
Make Thy way plain before my face
For it is Thou Lord
Thou O Lord only
Who makest me dwell in safety

The Concord Anthem Book

Falling in love was easy. But did God really mean for us to be together forever?

WILL YOU TAKE THIS MAN?

Peter Jenkins

In 1973, Peter Jenkins began an extraordinary walk across America. He had become so disillusioned about his country that he thought of leaving the United States for good. Instead, he decided to give it one more chance before abandoning it.

Two long years of walking and working with his countrymen, from Alfred, New York, down the Appalachian Trail, through the Deep South to the Gulf of Mexico, brought him to the realization that what he was searching for was God. He found Him in an emotion-packed confrontation at a revival meeting in Mobile, Alabama. What follows is his amazing story of falling in love in New Orleans and how God guided him, even in love.

Almost 1900 miles had passed under my feet. Ahead and down the coast was New Orleans where I hoped to live for a while and get a job. I had started out on my walk with a feeling of dullness and desperation. Now, as I moved on, I was fueled with a thrill and expectation of new discovery.

I approached New Orleans, the enchanting city, the city that never sleeps, from the eastern edge and camped one last night in the open fields, trying to decide what to do. I wanted to write an article for the *National Geographic* about what had happened to me on my walk and I needed to earn some money to continue. After all, I still had more than half of the country to cross!

The next day I remembered Bill Hanks, a seminary student I had met at the revival in Mobile. Recalling his invitation to stay with him if I was ever in New Orleans, I stopped at a gas station and found his number in the shredded telephone book. His friendly voice told me to come to the New Orleans Baptist Theological Seminary just four miles farther. I walked on past beer-can-littered parking lots, concrete shopping centers and bus stops full of loitering people to the seminary. When I stood at the elegant brick-and-wrought-iron gates under thick palm trees that sheltered the school from the roaring city street, I felt uneasy. This was so different for me. I had given up any idea of partying and living in the French Quarter. But a seminary? My old friends would pass out if they knew I was here.

Bill and his wife welcomed me and showed me around the campus. To my alarm he had gotten permission for me to rent a room in the men's dorm. But there was no question that it would be as quiet as a soundproof closet. There would be no loud music, no attractive Southern belles. I'd be like a monk, able to think, to relive my walk and start writing my article about it. So I moved into the dorm.

My first weekend on campus I went to a party for the seminarians. Scanning the room full of proper preachers and students, I saw her. Her hair was black and freer than a waterfall. I had never liked black hair, but at that moment I loved it. Every gesture she made was precisely right—not too much movement, not too little. A student was making a speech, but all I could do was look at her. At the end of the unheard speech, it was time to get in line for food. She turned to get in line and caught me staring. Her dark eyes seemed to respond. I wanted to get near her. I wanted her to notice me. I heaped my plate with barbecue beef and baked beans, and dropped half of my cake across the floor as I walked slowly to my chair. I couldn't even get near her! When the party ended we were still lifetimes apart.

Weeks passed and I didn't see her again. I thought and thought about the girl with the shining black hair. I looked for her at every turn, but she had disappeared.

One night as I was on my way to eat at a local diner I heard happy screams coming from the girls' dorm. Then a guy came crashing out the door followed by a full pitcher of water aimed at his head. He got soaked and I heard riotous laughter, wonderful laughter, permeating the fog-thick solemnness of the campus. I felt drawn to it. I heard more laughter as I got into the hallway. A full-scale water fight was in progress!

Then I saw her again. She wore a soaked football sweatshirt and jeans. I froze. She broke her deerlike stride and cut right toward me and dumped water all over me. It was like a test of some kind. I seemed to pass it when I smiled and then laughed. She ran off and stopped at the kitchen door where everyone was filling water jugs, and then glanced back at me. I ran after her as she laughed and pounced into the kitchen where all the seminarians were in friendly battle. Neither she nor I said anything, but we both knew a powerful spark had been ignited.

Soon the crazy water war was over and we all laughed and mopped up water for half an hour. Some of the girls drifted back to their rooms and five of them and I rested around the kitchen table. The air was filled with expectation.

Then I spoke. I told them why I was on campus, where I was from and where I was going. They didn't understand—except for the gentle black-haired girl.

I blurted out, "Could any of you girls show me around New Orleans? It's almost Friday and I'm ready to see the sights."

The girl I hoped would answer said, "Sure, I'll show you around."

"Great," I responded, playing it cool. "By the way, what's your name? Mine is Peter Jenkins."

She acted surprised that I didn't know her name. "I'm Barbara Pennell. Come tomorrow night at seven-thirty." She stood straight up and walked to the door. Turning one last time, she glanced my way. "Bye, Peter."

I knew I had met my match.

Barbara was studying for her master's degree and had almost finished her first year. I was working on my article for the *National Geographic* so I continued seeing her that summer from June into the fall. We saw each other daily, if only for lunch between her classes and my writing. Or we'd stroll around the campus at night, sharing and discussing every issue known to man until midnight. There was never a minute we didn't have something profound to talk about. Never had I found anyone with whom I could talk over everything. We would say good night and hours later I would throw rocks at her window to wake her so we could say one more word to each other. By fall we were so deeply in love we talked about getting married.

It was mid-October when things went wrong. Our volcanic love began to cool along with the weather and winter breezes from the Gulf that made the pecan trees drop their golden fruit all over the campus. The reality of what lay ahead sobered Barbara. A former yearbook queen at college, she had never been camping or hiking in her life. She belonged in a southern mansion, escorted down the winding steps with a camellia in her beautiful black hair. She realized that if she married me she would have to walk from New Orleans to the Pacific Ocean. She would have to walk the rest of the way across America with me.

The harsh fact of actually walking over 3000 miles frightened her. She became confused and began to ask advice from friends. Her roommate thought she could handle the walk and that our marriage was a great idea. Others thought the idea of our marriage was crazy and senseless. Everyone wanted to help. Our love became less and less sure of itself.

Finally Barbara said we should stop seeing each other to find out if our love was true. Maybe we weren't being honest with each other and needed to be apart to find out. She couldn't take the indecision any longer. All the blood drained from my face when she told me we would have to break up. I wasn't a person who gave up easily, but I had the feeling that this was the end.

Other men who had been attracted to Barbara moved into her life. The days of separation stretched into weeks. Our love seemed to be dying as the sad days crept by. I knew we would never get back together. I wanted to forget her and go back on the walk, but I couldn't.

It was November 15, 1975. I passed by her dorm and gazed up to her second-floor window. I heard footsteps behind me and turned.

"Barbara!" I shouted.

Before she had time to say a word I kissed her on her tear-streaked cheek. She smiled through eyes that looked as if they had cried enough to overflow the Mississippi. Her face was tight and tired. I wanted to pick her up in my arms and comfort her, now that I knew she had been hurting, too. I didn't care if we were in the middle of the campus; just being near her was healing my churning emotions.

"Peter," she said softly, "these past weeks have been terrible for me." Her face looked as if it were going to crack and shatter.

"I know; it's been horrible for me, too," I answered.

I hoped she would say she couldn't live another minute without me.

Then she said, "I can't take this torture of not knowing what I should do. I've decided to go to church with you one last time. If we don't get a sign, or if something doesn't happen, everything is over with us for good."

This ultimatum seemed impossible!

"Barbara, let's go out to dinner and we can talk about it some more. All right?"

"I'm sorry, Peter," she sighed. "I plan to spend the rest of the day and evening in my room, resting and thinking. If something definite doesn't happen in church tomorrow, I really mean that it's over. I can't take another day of this."

Her eyes looked hollow and I knew she was telling me the truth.

"I'll be praying for a sign, Peter," she muttered while walking away.

My heart sank. Since when did anything happen in church to give anyone a specific sign? I resigned myself to going to church with her in hopes that I could talk sense into her, but I knew nothing could happen.

Sunday morning dawned cool for a Louisiana November day. The sky was blue as a robin's egg and the mockingbirds seemed to sing happier. But I felt so helpless when I called for Barbara. Our drive to church was quiet and strained. She said she stayed up all night in the little chapel of the women's dorm, praying. I guess she believed anything was possible, even a word from God. I doubted it.

The church foyer was full of people waiting to be ushered to their seats. As we walked across the blue carpet down the long aisles my hopes for a seat in the rear were snuffed out. They were filled. We self-consciously moved toward the front and were seated in the first row. We sat together, listening to the choir. I was in such a state of helplessness that if a flock of angels had appeared to sing for me, I doubt it would have lifted my breaking heart. I knew this situation was impossible and nothing would happen. God never did anything like that.

When the ministers entered I was shocked to see the pastor pushing an old lady in a wheelchair. He introduced her as Mom Beall who had come all the way from Detroit to preach a special message. She was at least 80 years old. She looked sickly and pale and her hair was fluffed, light red. Here I had just reached the point where I believed in God, and now an old woman in a wheelchair was going to preach! It was impossible for anything to happen to save Barbara and me now. I wanted to slip out the side door and not waste any more time.

A microphone was bent down to Mom Beall and she began to speak. Her voice was as quiet as a leaf dropping to the ground. First she told us about all the snow in Detroit, but said that the Lord God in Heaven had told her to come to New Orleans regardless of the weather. She didn't know why she was to come, but she had learned to obey.

"Everyone please turn in your Bibles to the book of Genesis, chapter twenty-four," she said.

The pages in hundreds and hundreds of Bibles turned with a sound like walking through a pile of leaves. *Whoosh, whoosh, whoosh.*

The old and wise lady began to tell us a story from the Old Testament. It was like sitting at your grandmother's feet and listening to her kind and gentle voice as she began to tell a story.

The story was about Abraham and his son, Isaac. Abraham was old and about to die, but he wanted to find a wife for Isaac. He sent his best servant to Mesopotamia with many camels and gifts. Mesopotamia was Abraham's homeland and he wanted Isaac to have a wife from there. The servant stopped in a city called Nahor to water his camels and get a drink. It was hot and dry when the servant reached the well. He prayed, "O Lord God, let the maiden who says she will water my camels be the one whom Thou hast appointed for Thy servant Isaac."

Mom Beall continued the story sweetly. I sat fascinated and had forgotten about the aching situation with Barbara and me. I had to know how this story would end.

She told how a beautiful maiden named Rebekah came to

the well with a water jar balanced on her slender shoulders. When she saw Abraham's servant at the well she drew water for him to drink. Then she began to draw water for his thirsty camels. The servant knew this was the girl for Isaac. When she left, he followed her home with the jewelry of silver and gold. He planned to ask her if she would come back with him and marry Isaac.

"The next day," Mom Beall told us, "Rebekah's family called her to them because they knew the servant was ready to ask her to marry Isaac and they wanted to know her answer." Mom paused. Her pause was long and over a thousand people were totally silent.

Suddenly she pounded the arm of her wheelchair with her right fist and half yelled and half quavered, "Will you go with this man?"

The simple phrase burst through me with a surging power; it echoed and shot through my body like holy electricity. This was Barbara's sign!

Again, with fantastic power, Mom shouted those words from Genesis: "Will you go with this man?"

The impact of that message pushed Barbara back into her cushioned chair. She was sort of slumped down, her eyes staring nowhere. She had prayed all night, yet this direct message from God seemed to shock her.

"Will you go with this man?" Mom's lily-white hand banged the wheelchair, emphasizing each and every word. Barbara gasped as though each hit her heart with the force of a sledgehammer pounding on iron. She sat up straighter, blood flushed her pretty face and her hair seemed to stand out fuller than before.

One last time, Mom cried, "Will you go with this man?" I couldn't believe this was happening. I looked over at Barbara again. She knew I knew. Her eyes were wide and clear except for the crystal tears that gathered in the corners. She leaned close to me and whispered, "Peter, I'll go with you."

Very slowly we stood as the service ended. I wished I could slap myself in the face just to be sure all this had really happened. Even though I believed in God, I had thought this kind of thing was impossible. Yet, in that church on that November 16 in 1975, among a thousand people, God had pointed His finger at the two of us.

The lights of the tall sanctuary dimmed and everyone

began to leave. Coming toward us against the flow of people was a smiling man with dark hair. When he got to us he stopped abruptly. He handed me a plastic container which I recognized as a cassette tape and said, "We record all our services here at Word of Faith. Perhaps you'd like to have this." God had not only given us the sign Barbara had prayed for, now He was offering us proof!

"Thanks," I said, stunned. Barbara was staring ahead, deep into what had happened to us. She hadn't noticed the tape.

As we stepped through the doors into the glaring Louisiana afternoon, Barbara leaned toward me and said, with wonder in her voice, "Peter . . . Peter, did that really happen?"

I felt the cassette in my pocket. Someday we would listen to it, and hear those words again that joined us together.

"It sure did," I said. "It sure did."

I reached down to take her hand. From now on that's the way we'd be, hand in hand.

Our morning experiments in prayer turned into a lifetime of shared adventures with God.

THE COFFEEPOT EXPERIMENT

Catherine Marshall

The scene is forever etched in my memory. It was a winter evening, 1959, soon after my marriage (after ten years of widowhood) to Leonard LeSourd. The setting was our new home in Chappaqua, New York, a sprawling white house with red shutters. We were gathered around the dinner table for our first meal as a new family with Len's three children: Linda, age ten; Chester, six; Jeffrey, three. My son Peter, 19, was away at Yale University.

I had lovingly prepared food I thought the children would enjoy—meat loaf, scalloped potatoes, broccoli, a green salad. Len's face was alive with happiness as he blessed the food.

But then as Chester's big brown eyes regarded the food on his plate, he grimaced, suddenly bolted from the table, fled upstairs and refused to return.

"Let him go, Catherine," Len said. Then seeing the stricken look on my face, he explained ruefully, "I'm afraid my children are not used to much variety in food. Mostly I've just fed them hamburgers, hot dogs, or fried chicken from a take-out place."

Had Len and I but known, that disastrous scene was but a foretaste of what lay ahead. The following morning Linda's hostility erupted when she refused to wear the clothes I had laid out for school. The two boys wanted to room together, yet were forever fighting like bear cubs. That next night when they started scrapping again, Len summarily removed Jeff to another room. The little guy sobbed himself to sleep.

Later on that same night after Len and I, exhausted, had just fallen asleep, the shrill ringing of the telephone awoke us. It was Peter. "Mom, I got picked up for speeding on the Merritt Parkway. I'm at the police station." We agreed to post bond for Peter's release.

Yet all these troubles were but surface symptoms, the tip of the iceberg of difficulties. Flooding in on us day after day were the problems of parents and relatives, together with the children's emotional trauma from six housekeepers in ten months. Even Peter was still suffering from the loss and shock he received as a nine-year-old when his father, Peter Marshall, died.

How do you put families broken by death or divorce back together again? How can a group of individuals of diverse backgrounds, life experiences and ages ever become a family at all? I knew I didn't have all the answers, but I also knew Someone Who did.

So I began slipping out of the bedroom early while the children were still asleep for a quiet time of talking-things-over prayers, Bible reading and writing down thoughts in my *Journal*.

During those early morning times slowly there dawned the realization of something I had not wanted to face: Len was one of those men who felt that his wife was more "spiritual" than he, somehow had more Christian know-how. Len liked to point out that I was more articulate in prayer. Therefore, he was assuming that I would take charge of spiritual matters in our home while he would handle disciplining the children, finances, etc.

I already knew how many, many women there are who find it difficult to talk with their husbands about religion, much less pray with them. How could I make Len see that "spirituality" was as much his responsibility as mine? "Lord, what do I do about this one?" I hurled heavenward.

Somehow the answer was given me that nagging a male about this would not work. My directive was to go on morning by morning with the quiet time, but otherwise, refuse to accept that spiritual responsibility for the home. The assurance was given me that God would work it out.

After a few more days, Len became curious about why I was getting up early. Persistently he questioned, "What are you *doing* each morning, Catherine?"

"Seeking God's answers for my day. I know He has them, but I have to ask Him, then give Him the chance to feed back to me His guidance. You see, if I don't take time for this as the kickoff of the day, it gets crowded out."

"That would be good for me, too," was Len's reaction. "After all, we're in this together. Why not set the alarm for fifteen minutes earlier each morning and pray together before we start the day?"

Thus an experiment began that was to change both our lives. The next day at a local hardware store I found an electric timer to plug into our small four-cup coffeepot. That night I prepared the coffee tray at bedtime and carried it to the bedroom. The following morning we were wakened by the pleasant aroma of coffee rather than an alarm clock going off.

We drank our coffee, and I started to read at a spot in Philippians. But Len wanted to get on with the prayer. "You start, Catherine," he said sleepily.

"But how are we going to pray about this problem of Linda's lack of motivation to study?" I asked. A discussion began. It got so intense that time ran out before we got to actual prayer.

Len agreed that we needed more time. Our wake-up hour went from 6:45 to 6:30 to 6:00. Discipline in the morning meant going to bed earlier. It became a matter of priorities. The morning time together soon changed from an experiment to a prayer-shared adventure.

By this time, Len, always methodical, had purchased himself a small five-by-seven brown, looseleaf notebook. He began jotting down the prayer requests, listing them by date. When the answers came, those too were recorded, also by date, together with *how* God had chosen to fill that particular need. Rapidly, the notebook was becoming a real prayer log.

Not only that, as husband and wife, we had found a great way of communication. Bedtime, we already knew, was a dangerous time to present controversial matters to one another. When we were fatigued from the wear and pressures of the day, disagreements could erupt easily.

Yet when we tackled these same topics the next morning in an atmosphere of prayer, simply asking God for His wisdom about it, controversy dissolved and communication flowed easily.

Perhaps an actual page out of the brown notebook best tells the story . . .

Prayer Requests—
December 15, 1959

1. That we find household help so that Catherine can continue writing *Christy*.
2. That Peter will do more work and less playing around at Yale.
3. That Linda will be less emotional about the clothes we ask her to wear and more motivated in her studies.
4. That Chester will stop fighting with his brother and accept his new home situation.
5. That we can find the way to get Jeff toilet-trained.

Morning by morning the requests piled up and up . . . Linda's rebelliousness, a personnel problem at Len's office in New York, a friend with cancer; guidance as to which church to attend; a relative with a drinking problem; very close friends with difficulties with their children—and on and on.

We were learning more about prayer: that specific requests yield precise answers. So we did not simply ask for household help, we recorded a request for live-in help, a good cook, someone who loved children, who would be warm and comfortable to live with.

The day came when Len set down the answer to this in the brown notebook—middle-aged Lucy Arsenault. She was sent through Len's mother who had known her in Boston years before. Finding her enabled me to resume writing *Christy*.

The answer to Jeff's little problem came through the homely advice of the country General Practitioner near the farm in Virginia: Irrepressible Jeff was simply too lazy to get up and go to the bathroom, too well-padded with too many diapers. Waterproof the bed, take all diapers off, let him wallow in wet misery. It worked—miraculously.

Now unless we had been recording both the request and the answer, with dates, we might have assumed these "coincidence" or just something that would have happened anyway. But with those written notations marking the answers to prayer, we found our gratitude to God mounting. The prayer log was a marvelous stimulus to faith.

Not that everything always worked out the way we wanted. We found that prayer is not handing God a want-list and then having beautiful answers float down on rosy clouds. God seemed especially interested in our learning patience and to trust *Him*, rather than man's manipulative devices for answers. Also, His timing is certainly not ours: Most answers came more slowly than we wished, and piecemeal. There continued to be some health problems. Two Marshall grandchildren died soon after birth. I worked for two years on a book I finally had to abandon. It took 12 years of anguish and many different kinds of prayer before Linda's life was turned around. But when the turning point came, it was with beautiful timing.

One of the best answers of those early days was Len's dawning realization that unless he became the spiritual head of our home, Chester and Jeffrey were going to grow up considering religion as something for the womenfolk. He had always considered his prayers too "bread and potatoes." But the two boys liked that. So, as Len continued to say grace and lead the family prayer time, the boys began praying too—as if it were the natural thing to do.

Thus our husband-wife morning prayer time has set the tone and direction of 20 years of marriage. That original coffee-timer (still operating although with many new parts) is one of our most cherished possessions. We know that neither one of us, or both of us, without God, have the wisdom to handle the problems which life hands us day by day. But as early morning prayer partners we have added assurance that "where two or three are gathered together" in His name, God is indeed with us. We know that communication between us, and between us and our children, has opened up. We can be sure that our morning prayers to God have mutual support and we know, from our prayer log, that those prayers are answered.

Why don't you go out and buy yourself a coffeepot and a timer? Try awakening to the pleasant aroma of coffee. Try approaching the problems of the day, partnered in prayer and with a fresh mind, and you may find—as Len and I have—a lifeline to cling to all day long.

I would need every bit of skill I had as a doctor to save this boy's arm. And every bit of faith.

THE HEALING OF LITTLE ROBERT

Dr. John Graham

It had been an exhausting day at Schumpert Hospital that Thursday, April 7, 1977, and I had just kicked off my shoes and stretched out on the lounge in our den when the telephone rang.

The voice was tense: "Dr. Graham, this is the emergency room. A four-year-old boy whose arm was ripped off above the elbow in a farm accident is being rushed in. We wanted to give you plenty of warning."

He said that the sheriff was rushing little Robert Hyatt from Many, a town about 100 miles from Shreveport, and should be at the hospital in an hour. The arm, which Robert's father found in the tractor mechanism, was being sent in the same ambulance.

I put down the phone and stood for a moment, my mind racing. Though I had replanted fingers and thumbs, this would be my first attempt at replacing a severed limb. Could I do it?

Almost numbly, I drove to the hospital where I delivered my microsurgery instruments to be sterilized and let the nurses know we would use the electric zoom microscope. After notifying X-ray and the lab of the boy's arrival, I walked across the street to be alone in my office.

I spent a few minutes refreshing my memory on the anatomy of the upper arm, then sat quietly at my desk going over each step of the replantation.

My mind clear on it, I leaned forward on the desk and

prayed: "Dear Father, oversee every decision that will be made concerning this little boy. Help each person in that operating room do his best work."

I asked for confidence, faith and wisdom and prayed for Robert's family to be given strength. Lifting my head, I gazed at the wall before me. On it was a long string of certificates, plaques and diplomas telling the story of where the Lord had brought me over the years.

It had been a rocky road. Four years ago as a successful ear, nose and throat surgeon here in Shreveport, I had an experience with Jesus Christ. My new faith had brought me ridicule, joy and surprises. The most surprising was His guidance that I study plastic surgery. To the consternation of friends and family, I sold my well-established practice and moved my wife and five children to Miami where I studied under the eminent plastic surgeon, Ralph Millard. After that came more grueling work and study in Norfolk, Virginia. Pat and the children endured privation, uncertainty and the confusion of relocating without complaint. But my heart suffered for them. Then, at age 38, when most doctors are comfortably settled in their practice, He brought me back to Shreveport.

Now, I looked to Him again. "Lord, if this is what You have prepared me for, I feel humble. For, like Paul, I know that 'I am what I am by Your grace.' May You and You only be glorified in all that I do."

The distant whine of a siren interrupted my thoughts and I hurried across the street to the hospital as the sheriff's car swung up to the emergency-room ramp. Television and radio crews flooded the entrance.

The anxious-faced sheriff raced into the emergency room with the little boy in his arms. Another man followed carrying a bucket filled with ice; it contained the severed arm.

The boy's parents, Gerald and Linda Hyatt, anxiously watched from a corner of the room. The child lay quiet on the examining table. I pulled back the blanket from his left shoulder only to flinch as any father would. Splintered white bone, gray, threadlike nerves and bloody flesh and veins dangled from the stump of his arm. I reached into the crushed ice and found the little arm. It was cold, white and stiff. The fingers were clenched as if his fist had tightened during the accident.

I took the limb into X-ray where the technician almost fainted when he saw it. Within minutes, the anesthesiologist's infusion was going and blood was drawn for necessary crossmatching. Robert's vital signs appeared to be stable and we brought him into X-ray to take views of his chest and shoulder. The operation would begin soon.

Then we faced a complication. While I was studying the X-rays, Bill Fox, a local orthopedic surgeon, walked in. He had been contacted by physicians in the boy's hometown for the bone work.

"John," he said, "we will need to send him to Louisville, don't you think?" Louisville has a center where several successful replantations had been made. Bill, who had not known that I had been called in on the case, said that his partner, Clint McAlister, was at this moment phoning Louisville to have Robert transferred there.

I looked at him in concern. It would take hours to get a plane, fly to Kentucky, unload and transfer Robert. By then much vital time would be lost.

"No, Bill," I said, "we're ready to go here right now; I don't think we should waste any more time."

He studied the floor for a moment, then looked at me. "Why don't we put it before the family since we haven't done anything like this in Shreveport and Louisville is experienced and successful?"

I nodded, and he led the way into the family group and presented the situation. Robert's father said: "If Louisville is the best, then let's go there."

All I could think was: *Lord, Your will be done.* I picked up the phone to arrange for air transport when Bill Fox stopped me. "Hold it, John. Louisville just told us to do it here rather than to make the transfer. We have a microsurgeon here and the delay would cause more muscle death."

Robert was wheeled into surgery as his parents stood in the hall weeping and praying. As I scrubbed for the operation, I prayed silently for a clear mind.

Robert was soon asleep under anesthesia. Dr. McAlister and I divided into two teams. With Ben Dowden, my scrub assistant, we scrubbed and draped the arm stump. Then, using the zoom microscope, I began searching the stump for the brachial artery, median, ulna and radial nerves and as many veins as I could find.

At another table, Dr. McAlister worked with his assistant, Rick Chapell, on the arm, meticulously identifying the opposing vessels and nerves I had found. This complete, McAlister skillfully repaired the fractured bone. He first shortened it about an inch to take any strain off the microsurgical repairs we would make. Then, small steel rods fastened the ends of the bones together.

Now my work began. With the severed nerves, arteries and muscles in conjunction, Ben and I first had to find a piece of vein from another part of Robert's body to graft the important severed arm artery. It had to be the same three-millimeter size. We found it in the groin area of Robert's leg.

Using the zoom microscope, I began to suture in the graft, using a nylon filament so light that it would float in air were it not secured by the tiny needle. The needle itself was small enough to slip through a human hair.

I settled down to the meticulous step-by-step process. Each stitch had to be perfectly placed, each knot perfect, otherwise it would have to be removed and the process repeated. About ten sutures fastened each vessel, and whenever a graft was used there had to be twice as many sutures.

Working under 25- to 40-power magnification is mentally and physically exhausting. After an hour of this I wanted to stretch and walk around the room. But I couldn't even take time to pray; I had to fasten my complete attention on the exacting task, knowing deep down that I had already asked for help.

I continued linking the severed blood vessels, suturing the saphenous vein graft—the vein from Robert's leg—to a large vein adjacent to the brachial artery. Then I did a primary repair on one other vein in the area. I glanced at the clock. Almost two hours had gone by. I went back to the brachial artery; finally it was repaired.

Now, I stepped back for a moment. Every vessel I could find was connected. When the clamps holding the blood back in Robert's upper arm were removed, this would be the moment of truth.

With a silent prayer, I released them.

Exclamations of joy filled the operating room as blood pulsed through the repaired arteries and veins. Robert's hand and arm began to become warm and pink.

As I watched, I felt that I knew in some small way the joy our Father must have experienced with each act of creation.

I looked at the clock on the wall. It was midnight. "It's Good Friday, everyone!" I announced. "What an Easter blessing!"

But there was still much work to do. Exhausted, I went out to talk with the family as Dr. McAlister now began dissecting the nerves in the forearm to prepare them for repair. After a short rest, I returned and prepared to stitch the opposing ends of each nerve together under the microscope.

Each nerve is composed of ten to 20 tiny bundles of fibers like a cable or twisted strands of spaghetti. I endeavored to line fiber up end to end and then patiently stitched the tiny microscopic sutures that held these clusters together. It would take months for the nerve growth to reach the muscle, but the quality of repair this very night would determine the use Robert ultimately would have of his hand.

Finally, I was able to look up and signal completion. At 4:30 a.m. on Good Friday, April 8th, we brought Robert out of surgery and he was taken to the intensive care unit for recovery.

I stood leaning against the wall as he was wheeled out of the room. I took off my scrub suit, changed and then I went into intensive care to check on him.

His mother and father were there with Robert. He was still sleeping, but he was whole, his arm propped up on a pillow, glowing a healthy pink with normal pulse beating strongly at the wrist. And suddenly it came to me. In answer to all my striving, heartache and agony of the last five years, God had given another Easter gift: a symbol of resurrection.

Amazing what can be done at 84—if you have a little faith and a lot of spirit.

I'LL BE LISTENING, LORD

Alberta Hunter

When Mama died in 1954, it was as though my life stopped, too. Show business had meant everything to me—the bright lights, the music and the applause—my, how I loved the applause! But now, it all meant nothing. I never wanted to sing again.

Sitting alone in our New York apartment, I tried to sort my whirling thoughts. Mama and I had been very close—much closer than most mothers and daughters. Best friends, we had lived together for the past 25 years. In fact, it was for Mama that I ran away from home in 1903—from Memphis, Tennessee, to Chicago. I was eight years old.

Mama was a maid in a white brothel and my stepfather was a Pullman porter. Often they didn't get along. More than anything I wanted a better life for my mother. I also wanted to sing. When I heard that girls were earning up to ten dollars a week singing in Chicago clubs, I knew I had to go there. So one day, when Mama sent me to the store to buy a 15-cent loaf of bread, I hopped a train instead. I was never scared—not for one minute. I knew all along that God was taking care of me.

My first week in Chicago, I worked in a boarding house peeling potatoes, and made five dollars. I mailed two dollars home. When I was 12, I got my first real singing job at a club called "Dago Frank's." That job paid six dollars a week. Dago Frank's was a dark, smoky place that attracted a tough crowd—not exactly a good place for a youngster. But even then, I knew God was looking out for me. Several white call girls who worked there took care of me like mother hens. "Be a lady, Alberta," they'd say. "Don't take money or gifts from anyone. Stay away from cigarettes and whiskey." They even helped me with my school work. And while I was there I just naturally learned the music and discovered I could sing.

By the time I was in my 20s, I was singing at the best clubs, writing hit songs like *Downhearted Blues* for Bessie Smith, and rubbing shoulders with the likes of Al Jolson and Louis Armstrong. My childhood dream had come true. Mama came to Chicago. Later, we moved to New York City.

Our years in New York were exciting; I played on Broadway, made dozens of recordings, helped organize the first black USO unit, toured around the world and starred in my own national radio show. The best times of all were those rare evenings when I was home, and Mama and I would sit at the kitchen table and talk.

But Mama was gone now. A deep sense of loss washed over me. There would be no more talks. Never had I felt so alone. There was so much I wanted to tell her—so much I wanted to do for her. The memory of one particular conversation echoed hauntingly.

"Honey," Mama would say, "when you're doing all your singing, do you think you could ever mention the Lord? He has been so good to us, you know."

"Yes, Mama," I'd answer, avoiding her glance. "You're right." Then, I would quickly change the subject. Often I wanted to mention the Lord, but I couldn't. To do so might jeopardize my career. People might not understand. They would think I was "odd." So, I had kept silent. Not once in all my 62 years had I ever mentioned His name in my act.

Now my heart ached with remorse for those years. With Mama's death, my career lost all its meaning—like some fancy-painted glass bubble, broken to bits. With penetrating sharpness came the painful realization that all my life I'd been singing for the applause and fame. I'd been giving to get. Now, I just wanted to drop out of sight and give, somehow . . . for Mama and for God. I would find a way.

But how? Singing was all I knew.

That night, alone in the apartment, alone with distant city noises, I prayed.

"Lord," I said, "I've forgotten You. Help me now to

forget myself, to somehow reach out and help others. Help me to give without expecting something in return."

The room was quiet. Dark and silent. Even the traffic seemed to stop.

"I'll be listening for Your answer, Lord," I whispered. "I'll be listening real good."

The day after Mama's funeral, I was walking home from the market when I passed the Harlem branch of the YWCA. A sign in the window announced classes for practical nursing. Casually I read it, kept on walking, then—not really knowing why—turned around, went back and read it again. *Nursing* ... I shuddered. Just walking into a hospital made me sick. Still, I couldn't seem to take my eyes off the sign. Something very important was happening; I knew I couldn't stop it. From deep down inside me, I heard a voice say, "Do it." It was the Lord. I had no doubt. Strong and reassuring, His peace took hold of me as I walked through the door and into the interviewer's office.

The nursing program, I learned, would take three years to complete. Most of my classmates would be high-school graduates; some had attended college. I would be required to take a test to earn the grammar-school diploma I'd never had. I watched as the interviewer filled in information about me on the application form. When the point of her pen approached a certain blank box, I flinched.

"Age?" she asked, raising a curious eyebrow.

"Fifty," I said hesitantly, hating to lie, but afraid not to. The question was never raised again.

Three years later, I passed the New York State Board of Education tests and was capped as a licensed practical nurse. I will never forget that day. That little white cap with its smooth black velvet ribbon was, for me, like a priceless crown from Heaven. "Lord," I said out loud, reaching up to make sure the cap was pinned securely on my head, *"thank You."*

I began full-time work at the Goldwater Memorial Hospital on Roosevelt Island, where most of the patients suffer chronic and terminal illnesses. My tour of duty was 3:30 p.m. to midnight. It was a new life for me and I loved it. The rewards were simple: a heartfelt look of appreciation from a young man whose eyes remained his only means of expressing himself—his spirit trapped in a body racked with multiple sclerosis; or the joy that lit the face of another young man, also helpless, at the sight of his parents when they unfailingly came to visit him every day.

My days had a comforting sameness. I rarely went out socially. Some people must have considered my life monotonous—but I thrived on it. My heart was continually touched, my faith renewed, by the small doings of each day. I often thought of Mama. And I prayed to God constantly for protection and guidance.

Days slipped into weeks, months, years . . . when suddenly, as abruptly as Mama's death, I was faced with the shocking news of my mandatory retirement. There could be no exception to the rule. Already, the hospital staff had generously allowed me to work five years beyond the usual retirement age of 65. "But Alberta," they explained, "at seventy, you must stop."

Seventy! I winced. *If they only knew the truth.* I was 82. Still, it just about killed me. For the second time in my life, I felt stranded, alone, with no direction—no sense of purpose. This time, however, I knew what to do.

"Lord," I prayed on the eve on my retirement, "I've got a few good years left in me—please help me live them out right. Show me what You want me to do."

The room was quiet. Dark and silent, like that night so long ago. I felt my eyes burn with the memory.

"I'll be listening for Your answer, Lord," I whispered. "I'll be listening real good."

I'd kept up many of my friendships from the old days: jazz musicians, singers, club owners and the like. Often they called to ask me out. Usually, I would refuse. But when my jazz pianist friend, Bobby Short, telephoned to invite me to a small party for Mabel Mercer, I hesitated. For some strange reason, I couldn't say no. I couldn't say anything. With the same force that had gripped me that day outside the Harlem YWCA, the Lord had hold of me again. "Go," that inner voice seemed to say. "Go."

"*Alberta*?" Bobby's voice had an anxious edge.

"Yes, Bobby," I answered, "I'm here. And yes—I'll go to the party."

As I hung up the phone, I began to hum. Something important was in the air; I could feel it. And whatever it was, there would be no stopping it. All I could do was let it happen. There was a real peace in knowing that God was in control.

The party was at Bobby's charming old high-ceilinged apartment opposite Carnegie Hall. I arrived in good spirits and—before I knew it—was having a ball. Encouraged by friends gathered around the piano, I agreed to sing. The moment I opened my mouth, it was as though a cork popped inside me; a flood of long-forgotten melodies, lyrics, rhythms came flowing out. It was glorious.

The next morning, I was awakened by a phone call from Barney Josephson, a long-time jazz patron and manager of "The Cookery," a Greenwich Village supper club. Barney had been talking to some people from the party, and asked me if I might consider returning to work. At first I hesitated, but he had such a nice manner—so honest and sincere—that I agreed to come and visit him. Well, we talked no more than five minutes and I was convinced. It was time to sing again.

That was in October, 1977. I've been at The Cookery ever since, six nights a week. Sundays, I rest. It's a lot like the old days—the bright lights, music and applause. But there is one important difference: Not one show goes by when I don't somehow squeeze in a good word for our Lord. I know some people in the audience think my ways are kind of old-fashioned; they find the old gal's faith rather quaint—charming. But I'm not doing it for effect. I'm doing it because it's the truth.

There is a God, and He's just waiting for us to reach out to Him. God is personally interested in each one of us, and wants to answer our prayers. He's easy to find: You just call on Him, and ask Him into your life. But here's the secret: *You've got to take time to listen for His guiding voice.* If you just *listen* for the Lord, He will whisper in your ear, take you by the hand and lead you where He wants you to go—for your own good.

This, I think, is the most important lesson I've learned in all my 84 years.

Mama knew it all along.

"If God is willing"—that's the cornerstone of this doctor's faith and work.

THE REMARKABLE DR. ROSEN

Ruth Stafford Peale

The first time I realized I had a hearing problem was when I tried to listen to my watch tick and found I couldn't. With my left ear I could still hear it, but not with my right. When I consulted a doctor, he confirmed that I had a serious hearing loss. At that point, he wasn't sure why.

Months of tests and examinations followed. Fortunately, the hearing in my "good" ear remained normal. But if a person sat on my "deaf" side, I had to twist my head awkwardly to hear. It was troublesome and a bit frightening at times.

It was during this time that I learned to have a feeling of compassion for people with hearing problems, which has never left me. A blind person or any disabled person arouses sympathy immediately. But many people are insensitive about deafness or partial deafness in others. They can't "see" the affliction, and so they tend to be impatient with it. This causes a lot of unhappiness, because there are 14.5 million people in the United States alone who are hard-of-hearing or deaf.

My doctors finally came to the conclusion that my problem was otosclerosis, an overgrowth on a tiny bone called the stapes inside my right ear. This bone is the smallest in the human body; ten of them would just about cover the small fingernail. It's shaped like a stirrup, and is the closest bone to the auditory nerve. Sound makes the stapes vibrate. This stimulates the nerve, which in turn sends the sound-message to the brain where its meaning is deciphered. But in my case the stapes had become rigid, unable to vibrate or react to sound.

Time went by. More treatments and one operation didn't seem to help. Then one day by chance (or was it chance?) I happened to mention to Dr. Louis Bishop, our personal physician, that I had this problem. Louis' wife Kitty, who had a similar problem with both ears, had just been greatly helped by an operation performed by a Dr. Samuel Rosen. A new technique, they told me. A real breakthrough. They urged me to go and see Doctor Rosen in New York. I did, and met a most remarkable physician.

Doctor Rosen was in his 70s, gentle, reassuring—fatherly was the word that described him best. I told him about my problem and asked if he could help me. He smiled. "If God is willing," he said.

He used the same phrase from time to time during subsequent visits when I came in for testing. One day I ventured to ask him why. "When my parents prayed," he said, "whether it was a prayer of supplication or of thanks, they always ended it with, 'If God is willing.' That's a cornerstone of my faith and work."

Doctor Rosen told me that his parents were immigrants. His father had peddled crockery, and his mother had suffered from severe asthma. He recalled that one morning, when he was six years old and preparing to go off to school, his mother had such a severe attack that she could not catch her breath.

"To a child that meant that she would suffocate," Doctor Rosen said. "A doctor came and gave her some medicine, which relieved her, but I would not go to school. I sat by her bedside all day. When I told her that one day I would be a doctor and cure her, she took my hand in hers and said only, 'If God is willing.' "

Doctor Rosen's mother died when she was quite young. His older brothers pooled their labor, their savings and love to send him through medical school. For over 40 years Doctor Rosen has been an ear surgeon at Mt. Sinai Hospital in New York City and has taught ear surgery in its medical school. In his early days he was baffled by otosclerosis, as were all ear specialists. They knew what it is, but not what causes it. The standard surgery, called fenestration, took over four hours, and required the removal of the second of three bones in the middle ear. Sometimes it helped; mostly, it didn't. It usually left the patient dizzy for weeks, even months, and often totally deaf.

Like many dramatic discoveries in medicine, Doctor Rosen's was an accident. Or was it?

One day, in 1952, while operating on a woman who had had a hearing loss for over 20 years, he was startled to find that her stapes was not entirely rigid, even though otosclerosis had been diagnosed.

"I wondered how many times fenestration was performed on patients like her," Doctor Rosen told me. "I decided that from then on I would first try to test the stapes with a long, thin needle to see if it was rigid before I operated."

In the next five operations the stapes were rigid. So was the sixth, in the case of a 42-year-old engineer, who had been almost deaf for 15 years. But when Doctor Rosen inserted the long needle to make the test, the engineer suddenly shouted, "Doctor, I can hear you!"

"I knew something remarkable had happened," he recalled. "But what?"

He did not remove the bone from the ear; the engineer recovered his hearing. Afterward, Doctor Rosen tried desperately to recall every detail of what he had done. His nights became sleepless, as he tried to find the answer to the question: "How can I do deliberately what I did accidentally?"

For the next 18 months, after his day's work was done, he performed autopsies, studying the tiny stapes. What was its structure? How much pressure could it take? How could he get through the complex labyrinth of the ear to try to move the stapes without damaging it or the other fragile bones?

He designed and made at least three-dozen special instruments. None worked. When he finally made one that promised to work, it broke the arms of the stapes. The search seemed endless, the frustration was deep. I asked him what had kept him going.

"Only the Lord knows how the human mind works," Doctor Rosen said. "But there was something that filled me with hope. How do you reinforce hope? You pray. I did, every day."

One night, he twisted the delicate sides of one instrument in the hope that it would grasp the neck of the stapes, its strongest part, without damaging it. He wiggled the instrument, and gasped when it moved the base of the stapes—without breaking it. He tried it again and again, and finally murmured, "God *is* willing!" He labeled the instrument "The Mobilizer," and used it 400 times before he ventured to try it on a living patient.

"Until then I don't think I really understood what my parents meant when they ended their prayers with 'If God is willing,' " he said. "I do now. It could not have happened without His help."

After a series of successful operations, (each takes 30 minutes and requires only a local anesthetic), Doctor Rosen published his findings in medical journals. He was invited to demonstrate and teach the procedure all over the United States and the world. He had done so in 45 countries including Arab and Iron Curtain nations. He always leaves the special set of surgical instruments behind when he departs. He has trained over 1000 doctors to perform the operation, and they in turn have trained others. Doctor Rosen charges no fees for such teaching. Over 750,000 people have been spared possible deafness in this chain of unquestioning love.

On the morning that I arrived for my operation in 1969, I prayed that God would guide Doctor Rosen's gentle hands, and prayed for the strength to accept the outcome, no matter what it was. Doctor Rosen began his work. There was complete silence. About 25 minutes later I thought I heard someone speaking. Was it a fantasy? No. The voice was whispering, "I love you." I looked up in amazement. Doctor Rosen was bending over me, smiling, his lips close to the ear that had been deaf. Now the sound was coming through in the form of the three most beautiful words in any language. "Oh, Doctor Rosen," I said, "I love you, too!"

Doctor Rosen continues to be an active and sought-after consultant. At 80, he feels spiritually and physically ready for any challenge.

Doctor Rosen's latest challenge is to find a cure for nerve deafness, a problem that has baffled medical science for generations. When I asked him if he thought one day he might find the answer, he smiled. "If God is willing," he said.

None of us believed she would find her husband, but she had an unshakable faith that proved us wrong.

THE SEARCH

John Gleason

It happened years ago, but the incident sticks in mind and memory. Perhaps I can make you see why.

It was October, 1938. I had just graduated from Northwestern University and wanted to see something of the world before settling into a career. With $350 saved from a summer job—quite a lot in those days—I was heading for Puerto Rico and the Virgin Islands, places that seemed romantic to me.

In New York I boarded a rusty old coal-burning freighter. At first there seemed to be just three passengers besides myself: a bright young civil engineer from Michigan, a worried-looking old man in a white linen suit and a stately, charming woman who turned out to be Mrs. Charles Colmore, wife of the Episcopal Bishop of Puerto Rico, who was returning there after a visit to relatives in the United States.

We made friends quickly, the way you do on a sea voyage. Then, two days out of New York, a young woman with dull blonde hair appeared on deck for the first time.She was in her early 20s, much too thin. She looked so pale and wan that we instantly pitied her. She seemed a bit wary of us male passengers, but she accepted Mrs. Colmore's invitation for tea in her cabin.

"It's a strange story," the bishop's wife told us later. "She comes from a little town in Pennsylvania and she's on her way to the West Indies to look for her husband. He evidently left home several months ago after a violent quarrel with the girl's mother over his drinking and his inability to find a job and support his wife properly. The girl finally heard a rumor that her husband had gone to the West Indies. She still loves him, so she left her old dragon of a mother, and now she's on her way to find Billy—that's her husband's name: Billy Simpson."

"You mean," I said incredulously, "she's going to leave the ship when we get to San Juan and start looking? Why, that's crazy! There are hundreds of islands in the Caribbean; maybe thousands."

"I told her that," the bishop's wife said, "but it didn't seem to make any impression. She just says she'll find him. How, I don't know. But she seems absolutely sure of it."

"It would take a miracle," the old man said, thin and intense in his white tropic suit and brown wool cap.

"It would take a whole hatful of miracles," I muttered.

"Does she have any friends where she's going?" asked the young engineer. "Does she have any money?"

"No friends," said the bishop's wife. "And almost no money. Ten dollars, I think she said. Not even enough to get her back to New York."

When we heard this, the rest of us dug into our pockets and raised $25 to give to this strange waif of a girl.

"This will help you find a place to stay when we get to San Juan," the bishop's wife said when she presented the money in front of all of us. "And I'm sure our church there will help find enough for your return passage home."

The girl murmured her thanks. Then she said, "But I'm not going home. I'm going to find my husband."

"Where? How?" asked the old man. He had been fired from his bookkeeping job after 30 years with the same company. Now he was moving to Puerto Rico, where he hoped his experience would outweigh his age when it came to finding a job. I couldn't help thinking that he was seeking an answer to his own where and how as much as to the girl's.

The girl shrugged and smiled a little. She had the oddest smile—sad, fateful, dreamlike. "Prayers," she said. "My prayers. A few years ago, I asked God to send me someone to love, and He did, and I married him. Now I'm asking God to help me find my husband again. That's all. Just asking. And I'm sure He will."

The engineer turned away. "Not rational," he murmured, and I nodded. He was a tall, friendly fellow on his way to become a plantation overseer on Santo Domingo. He was a couple of years older than I, and it made me feel like a man of the world to agree with him. The old man said nothing. The bishop's wife looked thoughtful. We didn't discuss the matter again.

Time passed, trancelike, the way it does on shipboard, the girl leaning against the rail watching the flying fish skitter across the cobalt sea, the engineer and I on the fantail listening interminably to his record of *Once in Awhile*, the old man asking the bishop's wife for ideas about getting a job in Puerto Rico.

We docked in San Juan early one morning. I was scheduled to catch another boat that afternoon for St. Thomas in the Virgin Islands, and so had a few hours to kill. The others were going to look for an inexpensive hotel where the girl could stay while she figured out her next move, whatever that might be. The engineer and the old man needed a place to stay, too. The bishop's wife had delayed her own trip to Ponce, where the bishop was, in order to give some reassurance to the girl. "I've got to see her settled somewhere," she said to me privately. "And then I'll ask some people at the church to keep an eye on her. She has this unshakable faith, and I've done some praying myself, but . . ."

"But she needs that hatful of miracles, doesn't she?" I said.

Mrs. Colmore smiled. "A great big hat," she said. "A God-sized one, perhaps."

In the smothering heat of midday we walked all over the old city of San Juan, finding the cheap hotels—all rundown establishments infested with fleas and bedbugs. Finally the bishop's wife suggested that we get on a bus for the little neighboring town of San Terce. She thought accommodations might be more attractive and more available there.

So we clambered onto a bus for San Terce, but all the hotels we found in this pleasanter suburb were too expensive. Finally, exhausted under the hot sun, the bishop's wife, the old man and the girl sat down on a sidewalk bench. The young engineer and I continued the search and, amazingly, we found a pleasant, clean and inexpensive hotel within a block.

We tried to register for the group, but the clerk insisted in broken English that each person register individually. So I went and brought the others into the lobby, where they lined up before the registration book. When it was the girl's turn to sign, she picked up the pen, glanced at the page, dropped the pen—and fainted.

The clerk dashed for some water. The engineer and I put the girl on a couch, and the bishop's wife bathed her forehead while the old man patted her hand. After some water, she came to slowly.

"Heat too much for you?" I asked sympathetically.

She shook her head. "No ... Billy."

"Billy?"

"He's in the book," the girl whispered.

We jumped up to take a look. There, scrawled after a date two days before, we read: "Billy Simpson."

"Billy Simpson! What room is he in?" I asked the clerk. I couldn't believe it.

"Simpson?" the clerk said. "Oh, he got a job. He come back after work. Not here now."

"This can't be," the old man said almost angrily when the clerk's description of Billy Simpson seemed to fit the girl's. "She must have had some idea that he was here!"

Still lying on the couch, the girl didn't hear, but the bishop's wife looked at us. "No, I'm sure she didn't," she said. "Otherwise she would have come directly to this hotel on her own, wouldn't she?"

Nobody could answer that. It was obvious that there could be no final answer until Billy Simpson came back from work—by which time I was supposed to be on the boat that sailed overnight to the Virgin Islands.

Now, I know that in a good story the narrator does not remove himself from the scene just when the climactic episode is coming up. But this is the way it all happened. I guess real life doesn't always write the script the way a good playwright would.

Anyway, I had to go. The engineer shook my hand and wished me well. The bishop's wife gave me a letter of introduction to the Episcopal minister on St. Thomas, a Reverend Edwards. The old man said he would come and see me off.

The boat for St. Thomas was belching smoke, more of a ferry than a ship. As we neared the gangway, the old man spoke. "The real reason I wanted to come along was to ask you something. Do you think that prayer really led that girl to her husband?"

"I don't know," I replied uneasily. "There's always coincidence. But this is certainly a big coincidence."

He took my arm. "I wonder if prayer could help me?" he said. "I just wanted to ask you. I don't know much about it."

"Neither do I," I said. "Why don't you ask the bishop's wife? She prayed for the girl, you know."

"Do you think I should? I've been a bit afraid to."

"Sure," I said. "Ask her. And if I hear of any jobs in the Virgin Islands, I'll write you at the hotel."

"Thanks," he said. "Have a good trip." He waved to me from the dock after I was aboard.

When I arrived, Reverend Edwards invited me to stay with him, charging only $10 a week for room and board. Settled in, I spent my time sight-seeing, chatting with natives at the docks, writing, relaxing, learning all I could about the islands. Evenings I often visited with Reverend Edwards after dinner. One night I told him about the girl on the boat and the missing husband and the prayers, and probably my tone clearly indicated my doubts about it all.

The old clergyman said: "Don't ever be afraid to believe, John. You're too young to have a closed mind."

With time, the girl and Billy Simpson almost slipped from memory. But one day I mentioned the incident to two new friends of mine, deaconesses who lived next door to the church.

"Why," said one of them, "that Mr. Simpson sounds like a Mr. Simpson we had here at the church clinic. He came from Antigua with a very bad case of the D.T's. We practically had to chain him to a bed."

"And then," said the other, "one day he suddenly became alert and insisted on getting up. Our Danish doctor said he'd better stay with us for a time, but Mr. Simpson was adamant. He said he had to get to San Juan to see someone. When we asked who, he said he didn't know. He just had to get to San Juan. That night he caught a small power boat going to Puerto Rico. We gave him $20 to get him there and maybe enough for a room. That's the last we heard of him. Now this!"

We compared dates, and this "Mr. Simpson" would have landed in Puerto Rico three days before my group arrived in San Juan from New York. He could have reached that hotel two days before we had, as the register showed.

I had to find out. I wrote the bishop's wife, gave her my news and asked for hers. In two weeks, her answer came: "Yes, it was the right Billy Simpson. His reunion with his wife was one of the most touching things I've ever seen. Now, there have to be several events to consider, miracles possibly. One, Mr. Simpson's sudden cure from alcoholism in St. Thomas, which he confirms; two, his strange compulsion to get to San Juan, which he couldn't understand himself at the time; three, the guidance that led him to that particular hotel; four, his finding a good job within 24 hours, after not being able to get a job for months; five, the guidance that took our group to that hotel, a hotel which you yourself found. For me, these events add up to a hatful of miracles that can be explained in only one word: *Prayer*. The Simpsons are living happily in San Juan now. Not long ago they gave me $50 to use for charity, and so I am enclosing $20 for your friends who helped Mr. Simpson while he was ill."

I sat with Mrs. Colmore's letter in my lap for a long time.

A week later, I received a letter from the old man. He had gone to Ponce with the bishop's wife, found a good job, joined the church and become very happy in it. He wrote: "When we were all at the hotel that day, Mrs. Colmore said that maybe there was a lesson in the experience we had just shared. I believe there was. For me, the lesson was that some people instinctively know the power of prayer, but others have to learn it."

I couldn't argue with that.

These days, 40 years later, my mind is no longer so young, it is no longer closed, and I am no longer afraid to believe.

YOUR SPIRITUAL WORKSHOP

IT PAYS TO ENRICH YOUR PRAYER POWER

Peter Funk

How to have an increasing sense of God's presence in your life.

There was a time when my monthly feature in Reader's Digest, was titled "It Pays to Increase Your Word Power." One day DeWitt Wallace, founder of the Digest, suggested that the word "enrich" be substituted for "increase." At first I balked, but after mulling over the two words and comparing them, I perceived what he saw and I had missed.

Increase means to become greater in size, amount, degree, etc.—a straightforward word, plain and simple.

Enrich is another kind of word, altogether. It suggests depth, wealth, abundance and profusion. There is grandeur and promise to the word.

Enrich has all those meanings for your prayer life. As a secular Franciscan in the Episcopal Church, I work as a spiritual counselor, and I've seen lives transformed through prayer. As your prayer power is enriched, so will be every other aspect of your life.

Here are some suggestions that I've seen work for people and which can enrich your prayer life. Try them during the four stages of prayer I've outlined here for at least 15 minutes a day for the next three months. I guarantee you will have an increasing sense of God's presence in your life and be in a better relationship with yourself and others.

tage One: Be Still . . .

The goal of the first stage of prayer is to become aware of God's presence. Before you begin to pray try to calm your mind.

Most people will be helped to achieve a state of stillness if they try to follow these points when they pray:

- When possible pick a quiet spot and let its peace make you receptive.
- Allow your body to relax; it will help to clear your mind.
- Realize that God is there with you. A friend I treasure, an Anglican Franciscan friar named Brother David, taught me that when I pray, whether alone or in church, I should say the following: "Oh my God, *You* are here. . .Oh my God, *I* am here . . . Oh my God, *we* are here." This strengthens your awareness that you are with God and He is with you.
- Don't pray immediately but sit in silence for a minute or two.
- Begin your prayers by thanking God for loving you.

tage Two: Get Rid of Stumbling Blocks

As you pray, ask God to help you get rid of all the excess baggage of fears, resentments, jealousies, hidden guilt or unworthy desires that may be encumbering your mind and heart. Remember that Jesus said to forgive anyone whom you resent before you begin to plead your own case before God.

Try these simple block-removing steps:

- If there is someone you dislike, picture the person and yourself together; then pray for this individual and imagine God lifting the resentment off your heart until your relationship is transformed.
- Review the activities of the day—is there anything you should or should not have done? If there is any shadow of omission or commission, tell God.
- Ask for forgiveness. No matter what you have done, you will be forgiven.
- Accept it . . . and then forgive yourself.

tage Three: Ask with Confidence

Once you have accepted God's forgiveness, be confident. Claim His aid, comfort and mercy for others and for yourself. This is the stage of prayer in which we make our petitions and needs known to God. Don't be afraid to bring small concerns or material and monetary problems before God. He is interested in all your needs. The following suggestions will be helpful:

- Prepare your list of concerns beforehand. Write it out if necessary.
- Pray for others first—not in false humility, but because there are so many that need your aid and God's blessing. Pray for specific problems in the world, our country, your church, your friends.
- Visualize some specific person with a problem or need and visualize him helped or healed. Rely on the promises of the Bible for such help.
- As you start to pray for yourself, pray for your spiritual health first, then for your physical well-being, and finally for material things.

Stage Four: Listen

Once you've asked God for help, begin tuning your mind and heart for His answer. Remember that "Hear, O Israel" is one of the Bible's most ancient prayers. It means to listen.

"Hear" also means "take heed." That means to obey the commandments, to act on God's word and in His will. Don't let your prayer life cease when you open your eyes or unclasp your hands.

Love is the binding thread of all life and all God's works. It's the work you can do—a touch of the hand, a friendly glance, a comforting remark, a selfless action, a constructive suggestion, a sharing of grief, a going out of your way. An act of love is a prayer in itself.

Try these follow-up exercises:

- Recommit yourself to the Lord at the end of each prayer.
- Make a contract in each prayer to do something that very day.
- Keep a follow-up diary. What did you do to help a certain prayer to work?
- Keep your eyes and ears open. Watch for the hand of God in daily events.
- Read your Bible daily. The Word found in Scripture gives you concrete foundation on which to build your life. The

Bible is perhaps the greatest tool in preparing for prayer and enriching your prayer life—the goal of which is gaining closer union with God.

If I had but one gift to give to my children, it would be for them to know with certainty that at any moment each of us can reach out and be with God in prayer. When this happens, you are in Him and He is in you. And your life is enriched beyond all measure.

The Unlimited Power of Prayer

LORD, GIVE ME HOPE

Chapter 5

Jesus said, "Lo, I am with you always, even unto the end of the world." (Matthew 28:20) What a marvelous promise! You can count on Him. He is with you. He is your reason for hope.

When you feel discouraged or depressed or defeated, believe God is with you. The people in the following stories did just that. Some faced difficult tasks with a quiet confidence that God was with them; others met Him in the midst of their struggles; all discovered that a seemingly impossible situation could be overcome when hope rests in God.

Hope is more than wishful thinking, it is a quiet certainty grounded in the trust that God is with you. You can trust in His goodness and expect Him to help you.

Pray for hope. Then let this chapter inspire you to reach for the highest—confident that God is with you and will remain with you . . . even unto the end of the world.

All we had were six hoes . . . and a lot of problems.

HATTIE'S GARDEN AND HOW IT GREW

Hattie Fields

I knew how these old people felt. They had worked in gardens almost all their lives, raising fresh vegetables and greens, but now they were too old or too sick to grow anything for themselves. Most of them didn't have a place to make a garden anyway, and they were too poor to buy what they needed at the store. A lot of them were just going hungry.

Working with a community-help program, I would go to their homes, carrying food to them, and they would say, "Hattie, have you got any vegetables that you can spare?" Or, "Oh, if you could just bring me a bunch of turnips."

I had been a farm worker myself for 20 years and I knew something about raising crops. But I couldn't see any way to help these poor people. Farm land is expensive around the Florida Everglades, and nobody I knew of was going to just up and hand over a piece of his farm for nothing.

When I would pray I would often mention the problem to the Lord. "Lord," I said one time, "I don't think I could find somebody to give even Your angel some land to raise something for free."

Right then a little voice whispered back: "Didn't I say that if you walk upright, I will give you your heart's desire?"

I wasn't sure that I was hearing anything but my own heart talking. But it got me thinking.

One day I was driving by the Glades Correctional Institution, a prison farm near Belle Glade, and I noticed a piece of black, mucky ground alongside a ditch. It didn't look like it was being used. So I decided I'd go see the prison farm's superintendent about it.

When I got up to the main building, I just went in and told the man at the desk that I wanted to see the superintendent.

"You have to see him by appointment," he told me.

"Well, just give me an appointment," I said. And believe it or not, he did.

So the day came for the appointment, and I went back out there. I was taken right into the superintendent's office. He seemed like a nice man, and when I told him I'd like to use that patch of land, he said, "What do you want with those thirteen acres?"

I didn't know it was that much land. "One acre will be enough," I told him. "Even the ditch bank will do. All I want to do is try to raise some fresh food for these old people on fixed incomes, and the ones that can't hoe and make a garden for themselves."

"You mean to tell me you want to make a garden?" he said, looking at me like he didn't think an old lady like me could ever do such a thing.

"I want to try," I told him.

"I've got to write the State to get approval," he said. "But if they say it's okay for you to have an acre to work on, it's okay with me, too." I thanked him real sincerely and went out of there rejoicing, but still wondering if it could be so.

Well, I wasn't going to leave it entirely up to the State officials, so I called my praying band together, a little group who get together and tell God what we need. And the band started telling the Lord about that land.

A few weeks later the superintendent called me and said, "I want you to meet with me." So I went out to the prison farm again, and when I went in to see him, the superintendent said, "Mrs. Fields, I got you the whole thirteen acres. The State said okay."

I thought I'd faint. But I gave the superintendent a big smile and said, "Okay, thank you, sir."

Then I began to think of how I was going to work that land. I didn't have a tractor, a hoe or anything else. "I'm going to need a tractor to disk the land with," I told the superintendent.

"Well, that's one thing I can't help you with," he told me. "The regulations just don't allow for that."

I had the land, but what could I do with it now that I had it? "Oh God," I prayed, "help me think."

There is a government-assistance program called Manpower that helps poor people find jobs. So I went over there and talked to the director. "I'm going to need somebody to help me grow the old people's garden," I said. "It would be a chance to help some men help themselves."

I gave the Manpower people the information they wanted, and the director told me, "We'll see what we can do."

On the morning that we were to get started preparing the ground, I went out to the prison farm and waited for whomever the Manpower people would send me. Nine men showed up; I thanked the Lord.

When I told the nine workers what we were going to do, one of them said to me, "Okay, lady, where's the tractor?"

"Oh Lord, honey," I said, trying to make them understand how hard they were going to have to work, "we don't have a tractor. We only got six hoes." That was all I'd been able to borrow.

"You think we can make a farm with six hoes?" he said. I told him, "We're going to try it." I knew the Lord had provided for us so far; I just had to have the faith to believe He would keep it up.

It was the summertime then, and that old Everglades sun was beating down on us out there. I wasn't sure anything would grow in that heat; it just seemed like it would burn up anything we planted. But we went to work, planting the seeds that the county had given us.

We beat that ground with our hoes; we dug; we planted. We beat; we dug; we planted. After a while, something green started coming up. As it grew more and more, we could see that it was something we hadn't planted. It was a long, silky-looking grass that I'd never seen before.

I knew that strange grass would just choke out our little vegetable plants, if they ever came up. So we started attacking that grass with our hoes, trying to chop it out. But the more we fought it, the more it grew. It just kept coming up.

"Lord," I said, "now I'm going to waste all those seeds that the county gave me. The Manpower people are going to come out here to see what we're doing with their money, and they're not going to see a thing but this good-for-nothing grass. I don't know what else to do, Lord."

Then I went over to the men, standing there with the muddy hoes in their hands, sweat pouring off their faces in that hot sun. "We're just going to have to give it up and let the grass grow," I told them. "Let's just hoe around the ditch bank and let the people know we're still out here trying to do the garden."

The men were shaking their heads, starting to move over to the ditch bank. Then I said, "Wait. We ain't done all we can do. We're going to join hands and we're going to pray."

They looked at me like I was crazy, but they linked their big, rough hands and we prayed. "Lord," I said, "bless this crop. We're Your people, Lord. Let the crop come up. Bring it up, Lord. Bring it on up now."

Well, that grass kept growing. It grew so high, it started to bend over, and it would blow around in the air, like strands of silk, the prettiest and strangest grass I had ever seen. And we kept working around that ditch bank, cleaning out around there, so we could plant some more, and letting the prison farm superintendent know we were still out there working.

After about a month, while I was there at the ditch bank with the men, a voice whispered to me and said, "Why don't you walk over there and see if that strange grass has died?" I thought maybe the sun was getting to me, to be hearing voices like that. But the urge was so strong that I just had to go do it.

When I started heading that way, the men asked me, "Where you going?"

"I'm going across the field to look at that strange grass," I told them.

"For God's sake," one of them said, "don't put us back in that stuff."

"Just stay where you are," I told them, and I walked on across the field.

When I got over there, I could see the grass was taller than ever. But it had bent down like an umbrella over the rows, so thick you could hardly see down through it. As I walked through it, I looked down. And there in the rows, shaded by the grass, were the biggest, prettiest turnip greens you ever saw!

The sun was high in the sky, and I wiped the sweat from my face and said to myself, "I knew it was too hot in this sun. I'm seeing what I can't believe I'm seeing." I wiped my eyes again and looked again. Yes, that's what they were—the prettiest greens I ever saw.

I called out to the men. "Put your hoes down and come running!"

"What do you see?" they yelled back. "A snake?"

"No, I don't see a snake!" I shouted. "Just come running!"

They came jumping and running over. When they got close, I said, "Just look under there," pointing down to the strange grass. They pulled the grass back and saw those big, pretty greens for themselves.

"This ain't ever been in history before that the crop grew under the grass!" one of them said.

"But it's in history now," I said. "You can see it. The Lord has suffered it to be so. He caused it to grow so it could protect our crop for the old people."

Then the men began to rejoice and thank God, and I was praying, "Thank You, Lord! Thank You!"

We began to pull the greens and carry them out to the truck. We started distributing them among the poor, every day. And the more we distributed, the more grew under that grass.

One of the farmers from around Belle Glade saw the turnips and the mustard greens we were carrying to the poor families. "Where are you all getting such pretty greens shipped from, this time of year?" he asked me.

"Just come and see," I told him.

When he came out to our garden, he couldn't believe what he saw. "Where did you get this grass to hide your crop?" he wanted to know.

"It came directly from God," I said.

After the Lord gave us such a crop of greens—more than the 300 poor families we were giving them to could eat—we started planting other vegetables. We planted okra, squash, corn, hot peppers, bell peppers, collard greens, lima beans. And God made it all grow for us. It was just beautiful. Some families began working special little plots in the 13 acres. And the nine men kept on gardening the rest, giving the vegetables to the sick and the blind and the other handicapped and old people who can't do field work for themselves.

That all happened five years ago, and we have made many a crop since then. But that grass never did come back again.

When I tell people how the Lord did that miracle for the people who would share in our garden, they don't know what to make of my story of how the Lord took care of us. One woman said to me, "Well, that's sure a beautiful philosophy."

"It's not a philosophy," I said. "It's a real thing. God is real. He did it. And you can believe it."

GOD ANSWERS PRAYER

I know not when He sends
the word
That tells me fervent prayer
is heard;
I know it cometh soon or late,
My part is but to pray and wait.
I know not if the blessing sought
Will come in just the guise I
thought.
I leave all care with Him above,
Whose will is always one of love.

Source unknown

Out of tragedy the Lord was indeed showing His love for us.

A BLESSING OUT OF SORROW

Andre Thornton
First Baseman, Cleveland Indians

It was a typical Sunday in the Thornton household in suburban Cleveland, Ohio. The baseball season had just ended, and despite the gloominess of that October day in 1977, my wife, Gertrude, and I had attended church that morning with Andre Jr. and his little sister, Theresa. Then, after a leisurely supper, we had gone back to church for the evening service.

When we returned home that night, we finished our packing for our trip home to West Chester, Pennsylvania, to attend the wedding of Gert's kid sister. We often travelled at night—there was less traffic and the children slept.

A light drizzle was falling as we bundled into the van for the eight-hour drive. We waited a moment in the driveway, in the chill darkness of the van, as Gert prayed, asking God to give us a safe journey.

We hadn't gone very far before the drizzle turned to driving sleet. Amid the shadows and the flitting lights from the highway, I could see the children peacefully asleep under a warm blanket.

By the time we had crossed the border from Ohio to Pennsylvania and were climbing into the mountains, the sleet had begun to freeze on the road. We still had a good four hours of driving ahead of us. Switching on the CB radio, we listened to the other drivers complaining about the unexpected storm. The friendly chatter made us feel less apprehensive.

When we got to the Pennsylvania Turnpike near Pittsburgh, I took the wheel. As we switched places, little Theresa sleepily opened her eyes and asked if we were at her grandma's house.

"No, darling, not yet," Gert replied. "You want to come up here, with Mommy?" Andre stirred in his sleep when Gert picked up his sister, but he didn't waken. We continued on our way, with little Theresa curled up on her mother's lap. She soon dropped off again.

As we headed higher into the mountains, I slowed to 40—vans aren't the most stable vehicles—and the road was like glass. Then the wind, funneling down through the mountains, began buffeting us again and again.

"Wow . . . that wind has got to be at least fifty, maybe sixty miles an hour!" I exclaimed. Just then another blast hit us, almost lifting the van off the road. I could feel the back wheels slipping.

Desperately I fought to straighten the van, but it didn't respond; we were skidding sideways across the highway. Gert began to scream. Suddenly, a guardrail appeared starkly white out of the driving sleet . . .

It was dark and wet and cold. I was on my feet, stumbling forward through icy grass. As in a dream, I could see cars parked up on the road, with flashing blue lights. There were voices, but they sounded far away.

The van had flipped onto its roof. "Andy . . . ! Andy . . . !" I cried, clawing at the wreckage. Hands were pulling me back. "Dear Jesus, I've got to get my wife and kids out!" I screamed, trying to shrug off the hands holding me back.

"Take it easy buddy," a voice said close by, "we'll get them out." I turned to see strange faces peering at me through the pouring rain.

"Gert! Where are Gert and Theresa . . . ?"

"Don't worry about them, we'll take care of everything," one of the strange faces said . . .

I was in a brightly lighted room, trying to get up off a table.

"Relax, Mr. Thornton," a nurse said, placing a firm hand on my arm. "You're going to be all right."

I looked and saw little Andy lying on the next table. His eyes were open. "Daddy . . ." he said weakly.

"Where are my wife and Theresa?" I asked, staring at the pitiless white tiles of the ceiling. Leaning over and looking into my eyes, the nurse said gently, "Mr. Thornton, I'm sorry . . . but your wife and daughter didn't survive."

"Oh . . . no! Oh, dearest God, no!" I moaned, turning my face away. I lay there and cried as if I'd never stop.

After a while, I tried to pull myself together; there was little Andy to think about. They let me go to him. I held him in my arms and told him that his mother and sister had gone home to be with Jesus.

He was only five and didn't quite understand. He didn't cry, but there was a great sadness in his dark eyes. *Why couldn't he see his momma and little sister again?* There was really nothing I could do to answer the needs of this little boy. Only God in His infinite love could give him the comfort and peace he needed.

A minister came and sat with me. We bowed our heads and, through our tears, thanked God for all the good years Gert and I had shared. We asked Him to welcome Gert and Theresa into His kingdom, and for the strength to go on serving Him.

A short time later, they released us. Andy had not even been shaken up and I had escaped with only a nasty bump on the head. The minister drove us the rest of the way to Gert's parents; the family had been informed of the tragic news by phone.

The wedding was cancelled. In a house where there was to have been the joy and laughter of a marriage celebration, there was instead the tears and heartbreak of a funeral.

Before the service, my wife's cousin, Betty, approached me. Gert and I had both tried to share our faith with her, but she resisted. Now, tearfully she asked how the Lord could do this to us? Was this the way He repaid commitment and trust? It just didn't make sense to her.

Taking her hand, I said, "Betty, right now I don't understand it either. All I know is that the Lord never makes a mistake. I've got to trust Him; He's all I've got to hang on to."

Andy and I stayed about four days and then returned home to Ohio to pick up the threads of our lives. There was pain and a cruel void where my beloved wife and child had been. But God was there, too, helping me again, through the hardest time of all.

During those dark days, I think the sweetest times were those spent in silent, contemplative prayer, when I simply sat in God's holy presence without uttering or even thinking a word, just letting His comforting strength touch me and fill the void of my loss.

When baseball season resumed in the spring, some of the players on the Indians were surprised that I was back and functioning, that I wasn't broken up, bitter or angry.

My game actually improved, as the record was to show—five more home runs and 35 more runs batted in than in the '77 season.

One day, just into the season, I drove in two runs to win a game. Later, in the locker room, after the crowd had cleared out, one of my teammates approached me as I was finishing dressing.

"That was a terrific game, Andre," he said.

"Thanks," I replied, sensing he wanted to talk about something else.

"Uh . . . Andre, I don't know exactly how to put it," he said, shifting his weight self-consciously from one stockinged foot to the other, "but how do you do it? I mean . . . after what happened to your family. If it had been me, I'd have gone nuts, but you seem so . . . well, together."

I turned to him and, choosing my words carefully, said, "If I were alone in this, I might have gone crazy, too. But I'm not alone: God comes to you in a strong way at times like this if you seek His help. He lets you know He's there with you. He's all I've got to hang on to."

"You know, Andre," my teammate said, "I used to be religious, but I kind of got away from it."

"Look, why don't you come out to Baseball Chapel meeting on Sunday morning; it's a real comfort before a game to spend some time in prayer."

"I think I will," he said, his face brightening. "Thanks a lot, Andre."

Several months later, I received a call one night from my cousin, Betty. "Andre," she said in a quiet voice, "I've accepted Christ as my personal Savior. I wanted you to be one of the first to know . . ."

"That's wonderful, Betty!" I replied. Just before we said good-bye, I added, "You know, Betty, I hope you don't mind my saying this, but you were always so self-assured and independent."

"Andre," she said, "Gert once told me that some day I'd feel a need for the Lord, only I didn't believe it, until she died . . ." Her voice broke at the other end of the line.

"I understand, Betty," I said, tears suddenly in my eyes.

"At the funeral," she continued, "when everybody else was so broken up, you were so calm, so peaceful. And I knew how much you loved Gert. I didn't understand it, but I said to myself that if you could have such peace on the worst day of your life, then I wanted it too."

Out of tragedy, I thought, the Lord was indeed showing His love for us. His comforting power, and His ability to change lives.

A CONFEDERATE SOLDIER'S PRAYER

I asked God for strength, that I
might achieve,
I was made weak, that I might
learn humbly to obey.
I asked for health, that I might
do greater things,
I was given infirmity that I
might do better things.
I asked for riches, that I might
be happy,
I was given poverty, that I
might be wise.
I asked for power, that I might
have the praise of men,
I was given weakness, that I
might feel the need of God.
I asked for all things, that I
might enjoy life,
I was given life, that I might
enjoy all things.
I got nothing that I asked for—
but everything I had hoped for.
Almost despite myself, my
unspoken prayers were
answered.
I am, among all men, most
richly blessed.

Which was stronger—Mama's faith or my doubt? By Thanksgiving we'd know.

MAMA'S WONDERFUL WASHING MACHINE

Florence Carnes

Mama's wash machine defied description, so let me try to describe it. It was made entirely of wood except for two metal gears centered on a hinged lid, with an arm running to the side of the tub. On this arm was a socket with an upright wooden handle. Extending down from the gears into the tub was a round dolly from which hung four appendages, worn smooth by years of agitating. (As a child they reminded me of the part of the anatomy of a cow from which we got our milk.) On the back of this machine was clamped a hand wringer, which was one degree better than wringing clothes by hand.

In summer Mama's wash machine stood under a crooked box elder tree, close to a black wash pot in which Mama heated the water. Come fall it moved inside because Minnesota winters did not take kindly to washing clothes outdoors.

In addition to being very inefficient, this wooden mechanism had another more grievous fault. It needed one human being, preferably young and strong, to push and pull its handle back and forth, which set the wooden dolly in motion. When the right arm tired you tried it with the left. If you were right-handed your left arm gave out even quicker. Excuses like going to the privy or needing a drink or just being tired usually didn't work with Mama.

We washed clothes by the bushel, and with only our wooden friend to help us it was almost an all-day job. Every week or so we had to boil the white clothes in the ebony pot, with homemade lye soap to help our inefficient friend. Usually by three o'clock the last pair of overalls would be draped over the fence, since we had long ago run out of clothesline.

It was 1934. Not only were we in the midst of the Depression, but the crackling hand of the second year of drought held our prairie farms in a firm grip. There was no money for such frivolous things as new wash machines. So on this particular Monday in May, through the patient, persistent and ofttimes despairing urgings of Mama, we finally finished the last bushel of clothes. I was 12, and by far the laziest of the lot, so I might have been the main reason why Mama made an announcement the next day of a very definitely made-up mind.

"I am going to raise some turkeys this summer and sell them in the fall and buy a new wash machine." When Mama spoke with that kind of firmness, it was as good as done. No more human slaves because the new washer would have its own power plant, a gasoline engine.

Now raising turkeys was not as easy as raising ordinary fowl, so the day after Mama's announcement a small brooder house was moved down the pasture. As we helped Mama get ready for our small charges, my brother Victor, who was just a little older than I, stopped white-washing the walls and frowned. "Are we going to have to carry feed and water this far every day?" he asked.

I frowned, too. "Mama, this must be a quarter of a mile from the house!"

Mama stopped what she was doing. "Yes, I know it is far from the house, but as I told you, turkeys can't be raised near chickens. It is going to be a lot of hard work and there won't be much time for playing and reading. Are you still willing?" When she said "reading," she looked at me. Mama knew my weakness. I was in the middle of a book I'd scrounged out of the attic. We looked at each other, then at Mama. We all nodded solemnly.

"Then let's get busy," Mama said briskly.

The day came when the small turkeys were brought home. Mama lifted them gently from their box onto the clean litter. The lamp under the hover had been lighted and it was comfortably warm in the small house.

"Mama, they sure are small," my younger sister, Joyce, said, looking as doubtful as I felt. I wasn't sure what I had expected, but it was not these small things running aimlessly about on their little stick legs. The new wash machine did indeed seem far away. Then Mama sat back on her heels and looked up at her ring of doubting Thomases.

"I want you all to trust that we will raise these turkeys, sell them and get enough money to buy a new wash machine. I want you never to doubt that for one minute." In Mama's voice and look there was no doubt. Well, if Mama believed it, I believed it, too.

Through that hot, dry summer, we children helped Mama carry gallons of water and, it seemed, tons of feed for our precious charges. One miserably hot day in July we found a dead turkey. As we raced back to the house to show Mama the dead bird, in my young, faithless mind all the turkeys were already dead and the new wash machine had vanished. Not so Mama; we spent the better part of that hot day catching turkeys, while she fed each one medicine with a medicine-dropper. The next few days were anxious ones for me. Mama told me I was the worst worrier she had. We lost only six from the disease.

But one hot, sultry night my young faith hit the skids again. Joyce and I were wakened by the beginnings of a storm. Overshadowing the immense relief I should have felt that the drought was broken at last was my fear for the "wash machine" turkeys.

"That wind sounds awful strong," Joyce said anxiously. Downstairs we could hear Mama quietly stirring about, "praying on hoof" again. Then we heard the kitchen door open and close. Jumping out of bed and peering out the now streaming window, we could barely see Papa hurrying to the pasture with a flickering lantern.

"Papa is going to check on the turkeys," I said somewhat relieved. The wind was getting stronger and we could see sheets of rain when the lightning flashed. We waited. Then he was back, but the lantern was moving too quickly across the yard.

"Joyce, something is wrong. Papa is running." We grabbed our clothes and ran downstairs.

"Mama, what is wrong?" Fear twisted my stomach into a hard little knot.

"The turkey house has blown away," Mama said too quietly.

"Blown away!" I wailed. "Are they all dead? What are we going to do?"

"Now, Florence, there is no sense in that," Mama said sternly. "We are going to have to go out and gather them up and see how many we can save."

By this time the whole family was roused. After instructions from Papa, we headed for the pasture with baskets to rescue our investment. I went with fear and trembling. Lightning was high on my coward's list. Papa shouted over the storm that the lightning flashes would help us find the turkeys. I considered that a doubtful blessing. Those stupid birds just sat in the mud and water waiting to die. They were easier to catch that way, but I sure had less respect for them. Mama had built a low fire in the cook stove while we rounded up unhappy, sodden turkeys. She warmed and dried them in the oven until they recovered from their baptism.

As the sun crept over our eastern hills, I returned from my last trip. I'd survived the lightning and most of the turkeys were safe. The smell of a rain-washed world and the sight of a perfect rainbow were too much for me. I tossed my empty basket high in the air and shouted, "We made it, we made it, and I'm starved to death." Papa, coming across the yard, smiled and shook his head.

After their baptism of fire and water the turkeys thrived and grew fat. But now I had a new worry. We had lost ten from the storm and four more in September.

"Mama, do you think we are going to have enough money for the wash machine?" I worried.

"Florence, you are the limit. Why do you worry so? Of course we will have enough," Mama scolded.

Finally Thanksgiving week arrived. The hour glass had run its course and the turkeys were fully grown. The prospect of the new wash machine glowed bright and shining until I saw Papa and Richard kill the first turkey, then I disappeared. I'd worried so much over those birds that I'd developed a certain amount of affection for them.

They were left to cool on Monday night, then on Tuesday morning they were packed into a barrel. As we drove to the produce market, my hands were cold inside my warm mittens and there was that knot in my stomach again. The turkeys were weighed and Mama tucked the check in her pocketbook.

"Did we get enough money?" my mind screamed, but my lips couldn't make a sound.

Joyce and I followed close on Mama's heels when she walked into the Coast To Coast store. "Yes, Ma'am, may I help you?" a clerk asked.

"You may," Mama replied. "I'd like that 'Challenger' washer over there in the window." Mama had evidently picked out her wash machine much earlier. The clerk slowly removed the tag from the machine and brought it back.

"That will be seventy-nine dollars, Ma'am."

Mama opened her pocketbook, removed the check and laid it on the counter. My heart was beating so fast I couldn't breathe too well and my cold hands were sweating inside my mittens. I stretched my neck to see the amount on the check. My jaw dropped and I stopped breathing. The check was for seventy-nine dollars. I looked at Mama. She looked at me and smiled.

A precious lesson learned by a hard-headed kid. Mama had said, "Thank You, Lord, for helping us raise these turkeys." But she hadn't said it on a cold day in November. She said it on a day in May—the day she brought the turkeys home.

Everyone knows it takes awhile for seeds to grow. What about prayers?

WHEN THE POPPIES BLOOMED

Lorena Pepper Edlen

Spring can be beautiful in the high desert country, but I saw no beauty that Monday morning when I started for work. Driving from my small New Mexico farm into El Paso, Texas, my mood was as black as a winter midnight. I had learned over the weekend that my daughter-in-law Susan had obtained a divorce from my son David. Such was her bitterness and estrangement, she had threatened to change her name and disappear with my two small grandsons if David or any of his family attempted to see little David, 7, and Michael, 5.

My thoughts kept churning and racing and colliding with one another. The harsh treeless desert and barren mountains formed a fitting backdrop for my despair. Part of my mind tried to fight down the resentment I felt toward Susan. Other parts experienced a sick numbness from grief over the loss of my only grandchildren and fear for their safety.

I arrived at work and was glad to see that Carlotta Towle had come back to work after a six months' layoff. A devout Christian, she had listened many times while I poured out my worries about my son's unhappy marriage. Carlotta always had such an air of serenity and a loving smile. Her black eyes, which could sparkle with laughter, registered sympathy that Monday when, after our initial greeting, I told her of my sorrow over the divorce and Susan's ultimatum that we could not see the children.

"My prayer group has been praying for Susan," Carlotta said thoughtfully.

All the bitterness suddenly welled up inside me. "You've been praying for Susan? Well, it hasn't done any good!"

Somewhat aghast at my outburst and too frustrated to add an apology, I turned to my desk.

I threw myself into my work in an effort to keep my worries at bay, but they hovered just beyond my consciousness. On my way home, they all came rushing back. I now had the added burden of knowing I had been rude to Carlotta, who deserved much better from me.

I was so upset that I drove past my regular turnoff and instead took the route that ran along the base of the Franklin Mountains. These foothills of the Rocky Mountains, rising from a desert floor, usually had a soothing effect upon me. Often they made me think of Psalm 121: "I will lift up mine eyes unto the hills, from whence cometh my help."

I certainly needed help now, but I knew the source of it was not these hills. Then, as I topped a small rise, the sight of a wide vista of brilliant golden color suddenly assaulted my vision and flooded me with joy. The poppies were blooming!

The normally monotonous stretch of olive drab plants and rocks between the road and the mountains was blazing with the gold of California poppies. They swayed in the slight breeze on the slopes away from the mountains and even part way up the mountainside. There were acres of them. I was lost in their beauty. It was impossible to be surrounded by them and not feel joy and know the glory of God.

And then I remembered the story of the poppies.

A native wildflower, it grew only sparsely along the Franklins until, in the 1930s, a local newspaper spearheaded a drive for funds for poppy seeds. Eventually pounds had been sown from an airplane along the base of the mountains. Then came spring and all the excitement died because the poppies did not come up. Years passed and, if anyone remembered the poppies at all, it was with wry regret that the big experiment had failed.

Then, one fall and winter there was an unusual amount of rain. That spring the seeds—dormant for years—

seemingly overnight burst into bloom.

Now when I needed evidence of God's love, I saw it in the loveliness of the poppies. The ache in my heart was gone. Peace replaced it. "God, bless the boys and both their parents," I murmured.

God's time is not man's time. If seeds can produce blooms almost 40 years after they are planted, prayers will certainly bear fruit even if you can't see the results right away. The seeds that had turned into those golden blossoms under the right conditions were the proper kind of seeds to grow poppies. It would take the proper kind of prayer and the right conditions if my prayers were to be answered. I would ask God to show me how to pray, and I would keep on praying for my son and his family for as many years as were required.

"Dear God, rain down your love upon them. And thank You, God, for letting the poppies bloom."

A PRAYER FOR FULFILLMENT

Make my mortal dreams come true
With the work I fain would do;
Clothe with life the weak intent,
Let me be the thing I meant;
Let me find in Thy employ
Peace that dearer is than joy;
Out of self to love be led
And to heaven acclimated,
Until all things sweet and good
Seem my natural habitude.

John Greenleaf Whittier
from Andrew Rykman's Prayer

My mind was filled with images of fear, but the painting changed everything.

THE FINGER-PAINTED PRAYER

Sue Kidd

It certainly didn't seem like the kind of morning for a crisis. I sat in the kitchen where the May sun reclined against the windows, geraniums bloomed red on the sill and finger paintings trimmed the refrigerator door. With husband off to work and children off to play, I lingered over a late breakfast, savoring a moment of quiet and a mug of coffee.

I propped my feet on my son's soccer ball that rolled around under the table, and smiled at his paintings plastered across the refrigerator. Such an artist, my four-year-old! I loved his bright, bold pictures—a tall house on a green hill, a smiling stick figure in a rocket ship, a line of giant-sized daisies, an orange butterfly. They brought out the picnic in me.

Picnic! The idea brought a wiggle to my toes. An hour with nothing but a grassy knoll, a spring breeze and a peanut butter and jelly sandwich. That was just what my husband, Sandy, needed. He had been so tired and pale lately. A month ago the doctor had noticed a small patch of pneumonia in his lungs. Sandy had never really got over it. In fact, I'd been badgering him to have another checkup. If he wouldn't have a checkup, he'd at least have a picnic.

I was trying to remember where I had stashed the picnic basket, when the phone rang. I reached up to the phone on the wall. It was Sandy.

"Hey! Let's have a picnic for lunch," I blurted out before he could say why he had called. "I'll bring the kids and meet you in the park. Deal?"

There was an interminably long silence on the other end—so long, I became uneasy.

His voice was subdued, almost a whisper. "The picnic sounds nice . . . but not possible."

Somehow I knew that what came next would be painful. It was all there in the strange quietness of his voice.

"I dropped by the doctor's on the way to work," he said. "You'll never believe this. He just admitted me to the hospital. My chest X-ray looks suspicious."

"Suspicious?" I said weakly.

"That little spot he thought was pneumonia has advanced rapidly. He thinks it could be a malignancy."

I sucked in my breath, stunned.

"Don't worry, just concentrate on getting pajamas over here. I don't look so charming in this little white gown." He laughed. It was strained, somebody else's laugh.

We hung up. I sagged in the chair, gripping the sides till my knuckles hurt. A mental picture flashed in my mind with such terrible clarity that I could hardly get my breath. My husband, 30 years old, taken away by some dreadful disease.

"Oh, God!" I cried. "Please not this!" But even as I said the words, waves of fear from that grim picture washed over me. I stumbled on through a prayer for my husband's life, his health. But deep inside something had already knotted in my stomach. It was doubt.

I called a baby-sitter and began to straighten the kitchen at a near frenzied pace. All the while I prayed, prayed while the knots tightened in my stomach and that terrible picture left spots before my eyes.

I picked up the grape jelly from the table, bent down and scooped up the soccer ball from the floor. Then I did something so absurd, so preposterous, I still can't fathom it. In all that rushing about and frantic praying, I mixed up the simple matter of putting away the jelly and putting up the ball. Before I knew it, I was standing in my son's room, blinking at the grape jelly sitting on his closet shelf. It sat between a yellow dump truck and a space patrol helmet, in a spot usually reserved for the soccer ball. Naturally I wondered if the ball was in the refrigerator.

I plopped back on Bob's tiny tot table, leveled by this silly blunder, finally forced to sit down and take stock. Tears spattered down my face. I was in a deplorable state of distraction—putting jelly in the closet, a ball in the refrigerator, knots in my stomach and that picture, that dreadful picture in my mind. I had always hoped when problems came, I would meet them with steady, reassuring faith.

"But look at me!" I said out loud. "Just look at me. All this praying, and I'm going in feverish little circles of doubt and fear. Where is my faith?"

I looked toward the shuttered windows splintered with sunlight, as if some answer might materialize. But I saw only that same silent image of losing my husband. It swamped me with fear.

I couldn't face Sandy like this. I wiped my eyes and prayed a desperate prayer. "God, show me how to find faith."

I retrieved the jelly from the closet and plodded back to the kitchen. Bob ran ahead of me, a streak of flushed cheeks and blond, wind-blown hair. He went straight for the refrigerator and swung open the door.

"What's my soccer ball doing in here?" he asked.

"Never mind."

"But what's it DOING in here?"

"Don't ask silly questions," I said, peering in at it. The thing was bigger than a ten-pound ham. I picked it up—ice cold. I dropped it in his hands and led him to a chair.

"Daddy's in the hospital," I said.

Bob turned the ball over and over in his hands, silent. His daddy had given him that ball. They had often played on the lawn, kicking and catching. I wondered if Bob was thinking of those times.

Bob and I had prayed together when his dog got sick and it seemed only right to do so when his daddy was ill. But I wasn't sure I had any prayers left. They had all run aground in doubt. But I looked at Bob hugging the ball and heard myself ask, "Shall we pray for Daddy?"

He nodded and bowed his head. "Let Daddy get well and play soccer ball with me. Amen."

I ruffled his hair and bit my lip. He skipped happily to his room, leaving me more fearful than ever.

When the baby-sitter arrived, I stopped by Bob's room to say good-bye. He sat at his table under the shuttered windows, up to his elbows in finger paint.

"I made a picture of me and Daddy," he said, proudly.

I peered over his shoulder. "Very nice." Suddenly I stopped cold and bent closer.

An over-sized ball of yellow sun hovered in the upper corner of his paper. It was wedged in a wobbly strip of blue sky. On a green hill stood a tall stick man and a short stick boy. The stick man held an unmistakable soccer ball. The stick boy held up his hands for a catch. On their faces were gigantic red smiles.

I knelt beside the table, my heart beating strangely. This was his prayer! His prayer in a picture.

It was as if God was saying to me, "You wanted a way to find faith? Here it is. Put your prayer into a picture, a mental picture so bright and bold, there can be no room for doubt and fear." It seemed logical. To rid myself of the unyielding, frightening picture, I must replace it with one more vivid.

Bob shoved the picture in my hands and zoomed off to play. Holding that tangible bit of childlike faith, I prayed. It was a small prayer, but with a vivid new image to go with it. I simply looked at Bob's painting and whispered, "Yes, God. Make it happen . . . just like this." I closed my eyes. I concentrated. I pictured my husband on a green hill, under an enormous yellow sun and brilliant blue sky, playing ball with Bob. Nothing more. Nothing less.

The knots in my stomach seemed better. Definitely better.

For the next two weeks my husband lay in the hospital undergoing surgery and tests in an exhausting search for a diagnosis. Each day I clung to my picture.

One afternoon in the hospital room, the doctor brought us the diagnosis. A progressive fungal disease had invaded Sandy's lungs. It could spread to other organs, destroying vital tissue as it had in his chest. There was one possible cure. Only one. It was a precarious drug to be dripped into my husband's veins for six weeks. But would it work for him? Was it in time?

I looked at my husband, so thin, pale and weak. A surge of fear threatened. I closed my eyes. It was there, rooted in my mind. Green hill, blue sky, golden sun, and Sandy, smiling and healthy, romping on the lawn with his son. The fear subsided. A steady, reassuring faith filled me. I believed it!

That evening I taped my son's finger painting front and center on the refrigerator as sort of an exclamation point to the faith God had brought blooming into my life.

Then one shiny July morning, soon after my husband came home from the hospital, I looked out the patio door. I caught my breath. It was happening.

Bob and his daddy stood on the green hill in our back yard, smiling gigantic smiles and holding, what else, a soccer ball. I craned my eyes to the sky. A tremendous yellow sun sat snugly in a corner of the bluest sky I'd ever seen. Bob lifted his hands for the catch. His daddy kicked the ball. It sailed through the air.

I stood at the door, awed by this tender little moment in time, when God seemed to pause in our backyard and put the finishing touches on a four-year-old's finger-painted prayer. In that moment, I knew that with God and a bright, bold prayer in my mind, anything was possible. Anything.

A prayer to remember when you're ready to give up.

HOLD ME UP A LITTLE LONGER, LORD

Marjorie Holmes

Whenever I am asked, as I frequently am, what single quality a parent needs most, I immediately answer, "Endurance." Not faith or patience or even love, vital though they are, but sheer physical and emotional endurance. The ability to make it through another night, another day.

Through those times when conflicts, complications, problems, swoop down upon a family like a flock of clamoring birds, demanding help, comfort, instant solutions. When there doesn't seem to be enough of you to go around (but there is). When it seems you'll surely collapse (but you don't). Days when the sheer number and nature of the difficulties become funny. Or weeks, sometimes months when sickness and troubles strike in sequence like a soap opera, another dire episode beginning just as the last crisis is being resolved.

My journal records the highlights of a typical day so hectic that a woman (or yes, a man) can only pray, "Hold me up a little longer, Lord." *Teachers' meeting, no school. Planned to sleep late then set out flowers. Phone rang at dawn, kid who wanted to buy Mark's car said to meet him right away at bowling alley. Told Mark I'd follow and bring him back. Lost Mark at stoplight, couldn't find the bowling alley. Finally got there; Mark had phoned, his car for sale had broken down! Called his dad to come get him. Mark distraught . . . Home to discover big mess in kitchen and the cake Melanie was baking to surprise a sick friend burning while she giggled on the phone. Cake ruined. Melanie distraught . . . Upstairs, Mickie in throes of making new dress for big date. Sewing machine snarling. Dad, who can fix it, still off trying to fix Mark's car. Mickie distraught. I find oilcan and by some miracle fix it, but get oil on dress. Mickie tries on dress and howls, "It looks awful!" Oil won't come out, dress doesn't fit. Both of us distraught . . . Mallory bursts in to remind me Scout uniform has to be done up and all patches on for parade at three o'clock. He rushed off with pals for ballgame in yard and breaks window. Dog throws up . . . I wash, iron, sew, bake and try to patch up cake, dress, window, dog and people until dark . . . Flowers didn't get planted, but they will. Everybody happy tonight, everybody survived. We do somehow.*

God does see us through such days. He not only holds us up, He gives us an extra burst of strength, sometimes at the very moment we think we'll go to pieces, like that window glass. I vividly remember that was my own moment of near-explosion—when that ball came crashing into the house. I opened my mouth to scream, but instead began to laugh. Suddenly the whole day seemed like a comedy, exasperating, but challenging my performance and ingenuity as a woman. I felt suddenly renewed in energy and spirit, ready to cope with whatever came next. God even fortifies us with a sense of humor that gives us a second wind.

There are other times more serious. Years ago, when I was expecting a third child and the older two were small, I nursed them alone through a series of illnesses, even as I struggled to finish a novel. It was during World War II; we had moved to a strange city, my husband was away. First measles, then mumps, then only two days after Mickie was back in school, and I was back at the typewriter, her little brother climbed fretfully on my lap. I was so tired and frustrated I tried to put him down—then realized, with a start of fear, that once more his little body was hot. I opened his shirt, examined his chest; again he seemed to be broken out. Wearily I trudged to the phone to tell the pediatrician, "The measles must have come back."

"Are you sure? I'll be right over." She was a fine woman, who actually made house calls in emergencies. "I'm afraid it's worse than that," she said, putting away her stethoscope. "It looks like scarlet fever. You'll have to be quarantined."

Mickie raced in, elated at all that was happening at school. She struggled not to cry when I told her. "I won't get it, Mommy," she promised bravely. "I'll help you." But she did get it, and was a very sick little girl. Night after night I changed sweat-soaked sheets, bathed burning foreheads, held spoons of medicine or cups of water to parched lips. Day after day I rocked and sang and cut paper dolls and read stories. And when they napped and I should have been napping, I went to bed with a portable on my knees and pecked out a few more paragraphs.

Did the quarantine last three weeks or three years? It seemed an eternity. Scarlet fever was considered so contagious then nobody could come near us. Not even help, if we could have found it, not even my husband if he'd been in the city. We kept in touch by phone and it was arranged that he fly home the minute the quarantine was lifted.

At last the day came when the yellow warning was peeled from the doorway. We were out of prison! And their father would be home that night. "We won't fumigate," Dr. Bates said, "but you'll have to go over every inch of the upstairs with disinfectant, burn everything burnable, and of course wash and air the bedding. The children must be bathed and shampooed and put out in the sun while you're doing it. And by all means work in a nap for yourself if you can. You'll need it."

My head whirled, but I felt fired with joyous new confidence and strength. I wanted everything sparkling anyway for my husband's homecoming. But it was a day to remember, a day that was to demand almost super-human speed, strength and endurance . . . Running up and downstairs with disinfectant and shampoo and towels. Into the basement to start the washing (in a small lingerie machine never meant for sheets; they had to be wrung out by hand). Into the yard to struggle with a clothesline that didn't want to stay up, then start hanging things out—away from the smoke of the fire where the children were forlornly saying good-bye to the books and toys and teddy bears that had comforted them in their misery. Their wet heads made them look like just-hatched birds, especially in the skimpy faded garments I'd dug out for them to wear until the contents of their bureaus could be sunned on a balcony. I thanked God for that balcony, for it was close to the bedrooms. I had to drag the mattresses only down a hallway to reach it for their airing and sunning.

The children had to be watched; they were so excited to be out they were racing about and I was afraid of a relapse. When the little boy climbed the fence and ran down the street I spanked him when I caught him. Then we both cried, hugging each other on the steps. The breakfast litter still faced us when we all came in for lunch at three o'clock—with the scrubbing of woodwork and floors and windows not even begun. And it was about that time that a refrain began to sing itself in my heart: "Hold me up a little longer, Lord. I'll do it, I'll get it all done, I've got to! Just hold me up a little longer."

And He did. Like the miracle of the loaves and the fishes, time and strength were provided. By five the last of the washing (the curtains) was on the line. By six the stripped house smelled like a hospital, but was shining. By 6:30 the fresh, fragrant sheets were back on the beds (Mickie helping). By 7:30 the children were fed and dressed and watching out the window. And tired, bone-tired, but filled with a marvelous sense of triumph at all that had been accomplished, I was shakily putting on lipstick and listening for the sound of a taxi in the driveway.

But when my husband came in, exclaiming at how great we all looked, I collapsed in his arms. The Lord had held me up as long as He really needed to, I guess.

God gives us the endurance to survive these trials with children, and to survive the deeper, more complex emotional trials which almost no family is spared later on. Perhaps the physical ones are just rehearsals for the impending larger crises we will be called upon to face, and surmount: Quarrels. Temptations. Stormy romances. Problems concerning jobs or college or sometimes even the law. Disappointments far more significant than a ruined cake or car or dress. Healings that can't be achieved just by carrying medicine to a feverish child. Protection that can't be provided by simply scrubbing down a house.

But this I know: whatever life asks us to face, we need not be afraid. God will see us through it, hold us up as long as we need Him. I knew it then; I know it now.

After all, he always has.

"Lord," I prayed, "help me do a good job. Take away my fear ..."

MY TURNING POINT

Ed Asner

My heart was pounding as I stood in the shadowy wings of the University of Chicago's theater. It was summer term, August, 1951, and the intermission for our student production of T.S. Eliot's *Murder in the Cathedral* was nearly over. I could hear the sound of the audience returning to their seats. Nervously, I tugged at my belted costume. The musty purple garment was unlined and scratchy.

I was playing the lead role—Thomas à Becket, Archbishop of Canterbury in the year 1170. Becket was a Christian martyr, a man who lived and died in 12th-century England, in loyalty to his faith. So far, the play had gone well—but I was more than a little nervous about the upcoming final act.

Back in high school in Kansas City, Kansas, I had performed in many radio dramas, but this was my first try at stage acting. Since I'd been in college, I had dabbled in a lot of subjects, but acting was the only thing that held my interest. For this reason, more than any other time in my life, I wanted to do a good job.

Restlessly, I tapped my foot.

Don't worry, I told myself. *You know your lines. You'll do fine.*

But the anxiety I was feeling ran deeper than the usual case of opening night jitters. From the first rehearsal, I had felt unsure about the Becket role. There was a part of his character—the essence of the man—that I couldn't grasp. His relationship with God seemed so intense, so personal. I couldn't understand it.

Hey, I told myself again. *Take it easy*. But I couldn't stop worrying. Amid the confusion of backstage activity, I mentally reviewed the script, considering the events leading to the big final scene—Becket's martyrdom in Canterbury Cathedral. Under my breath, I murmured his final words of faith, hoping that this time I might somehow experience first-hand what Becket felt. It was my last chance.

"For my Lord"—I paused dramatically, waiting for inspiration—"I am now ready to die."

But nothing happened. As usual, the words came out flat and empty. In the silence that followed, I flinched with the bitter realization that I would probably never be able to put myself in Becket's shoes, no matter how hard I tried.

But, I asked myself, *how could I be expected to? I was a 20th-century American Jew. What could I possibly have in common with a 12th-century Christian martyr*?

The more I brooded about it, the more discouraged I became. This wasn't the first time my faith had seemed a stumbling block to my hopes, dreams, desires. Memories of growing up in Kansas City as one of less than 100 Orthodox Jewish families in a city of 120,000 came flooding back. . . .

It was four p.m., on a gray and muggy afternoon. I was a chubby little kid, waiting after school for the city bus (which was late) that would take me to the streetcar, that would take me to another city bus, that would finally drop me off at Hebrew school.

All the other kids were having fun playing football or basketball, and visiting each other's houses and eating peanut butter and jelly sandwiches. The sound of laughter caused me to look up as a group of classmates approached, grinning and joking and taking playful punches at one another. When they saw me, they waved hello, and stopped for a minute to talk. Then they moved on. I liked them a lot—and I think they liked me, too. But they knew I was different.

As I watched them walk away, I tried to ignore the hollow pit in my stomach. My fingers reached deep into my jacket pocket and curled around the soft, flat *yarmulke* that had been tucked there since morning. I would put it on this afternoon before entering the synagogue for lessons with the rabbi.

Sometimes I wondered what it would be like not to be

Jewish; to be able to play with the other kids after school; not to have to wear a skull cap; to worship on Sunday instead of Saturday.

But then I chased away such thoughts with warm recollections of home and family behind the red brick walls of our two-story house on Oakland Avenue . . . the sweet aroma of fresh-baked *challah* wafting from Mama's always bustling kitchen; the candlelight magic of sundown seders; the mystery and wonder of shared prayers and songs around the dinner table on High Holy Days.

Still, I had to face the fact that when I was away from home, I was lonely. Sometimes a deep fear gripped me—a cold, hopeless feeling that I would never have friends, never be accepted, never be "normal."

At moments like this, my best friend was my imagination. While waiting for the bus to Hebrew school, I entertained myself by lapsing into fantasy about my favorite Biblical characters. Like a mighty army of superheroes on parade, they thundered past the reviewing stand of my mind. First came Abraham, wise and faithful patriarch. Then came his son, Isaac, with grandson, Jacob—who later became known as Israel—and great-grandson, Joseph. Fearless Samson followed, his spectacular mane blowing in the wind. Daniel was there, too, flanked on either side by a pride of protective lions, like so many loyal dogs. All passed by in glorious procession. Then, finally, came Moses. His face shone brilliant with the light of the Lord. His eyes were ablaze with his vision of the Promised Land—the land he would safely lead his people to, but would never reach himself. *Truly*, I wondered, *these were all great men of God; men who lived and died in loyalty to their faith* . . .

"Ed!"

I jumped, startled. It was the stage manager.

"Five minutes to curtain," he said.

"Thanks," I acknowledged.

At the thought of going onstage, my old anxiety returned with staggering force. I felt like a little kid again—afraid of failing, afraid of being rejected. Suddenly—and quite unexpectedly—I heard myself saying, "Lord, help me do a good job. Take away my fear. Let me *live* this role; let me *be* this man, Becket, who died so bravely so long ago. Don't . . ." I hesitated. "Don't let our differences stand in the way."

As I took a deep breath and walked on stage for Becket's final scene, my heart was racing.

Why, I thought frantically, *should this time be any different from the rehearsals*?

But this time, something was different.

God must have heard me, because suddenly I understood that the God Becket prayed to and died for was none other than the same God of my childhood—the same God Who spoke to Abraham, the same God Moses saw face-to-face. The differences between Christianity and Judaism were great, certainly. Yet there was this tremendous heritage that we shared; faith in one Father, Creator of us all. Where once it seemed that Becket and I were strangers, now I knew what we had in common. Finally, I understood the man.

"For my Lord," I heard my voice ring out with newfound conviction, "I am now ready to die!"

The words shot out like blazing arrows into the darkened theater. They must have hit their mark; the performance earned good reviews. From that night on, I knew I was destined to be an actor.

Most importantly, I knew that never again would my faith be a stumbling block to my hopes, dreams, desires. Rather it would serve as a mighty bridge to meet them.

MIRACLE POWER

Prayer is reaching
beyond human scope,
Past reason, past logic,
past yearning, past hope.
Available always
through faith every minute;
Prayer is a power
with miracles in it.

Viola Jacobson Berg

This 1977 Heisman Trophy winner learned that in life, as in football, the going can be tough.

LONG YARDAGE

Earl Campbell
Running Back, Houston Oilers

Early last December I stood before a crowd of 1500 people in the elegant Grand Ballroom of the New York Hilton Hotel, feeling more nervous than a freshman at registration. I'd been named the winner of the 1977 Heisman Trophy, the award that said I was the best college football player in the country, and I was there to accept it.

From up on that speaker's platform, with the microphones in front of me and the TV lights on me, I could see how far I'd come to be there. My father, B.C. Campbell, had died of a heart attack when I was nine years old, leaving Mama to raise 11 children in a tiny, tin-roofed house on the outskirts of Tyler, Texas, about a million country miles from the Grand Ballroom of the New York Hilton.

I could remember the time, shortly after Daddy died, when Mama called all us kids together and told us, "I'll do everything I possibly can to feed you and put clothes on your backs and get you through school. But I can't afford to pay fines or bail anybody out of jail. So we're gonna have a rule here: Everybody behaves himself and stays out of trouble."

Mama lived up to her part of the deal. She took every kind of job you can imagine to keep us together and fed and clothed. She worked in the rose fields, she scrubbed other people's floors, cooked, babysat, anything she could find. And more often than not she would wait until all of us had eaten before she would sit down to the table. She always wanted to make sure we were taken care of first. Later, I was going to remember how Mama never quit working and trying.

But at the time, I didn't pay too much heed to what she had said. By the time I was in high school, I was drinking and smoking, habits financed by my hustling with a pool cue and shooting craps. I was doing the whole big-shot number. I wasn't spending one minute thinking about my future. One day I'd get out of school, I figured, and get enough money together to buy a car and just bum around.

I'd acquired the nickname of "Bad Earl," and Mama kept trying to keep me from living up to it.

She'd point out that because I was one of the outstanding players on our high-school team, there were a lot of little kids who were looking up to me. "They're gonna be awful disappointed in what they see if you don't straighten up," she said.

Mama wasn't talking only to me. She was talking to the Lord about me, praying that I'd see how foolishly I was acting. Mama had taken us to Sunday school and church when we were kids and had tried to teach us to look to the Lord to help us handle our problems. One day, after I'd come close to getting into some serious trouble, I remembered Mama's words.

Our little house sat near the road, and behind it were woods, where the sweet-smelling pines were so thick you could almost get lost there. I decided I'd just get off by myself in those woods and think awhile. After I'd walked a ways, I stopped and sat down under a big pine tree. I could see a cloudless, clear blue Texas sky up through the pine branches, deep into the heavens. I felt real close to God then, closer than I'd felt in a long time, and I spilled out my heart to Him.

"Lord," I said, "I know I'm doing things all wrong. But I can't seem to help myself. Would You take over?"

As I sat there, I began to feel more at peace, and the Lord just seemed to speak to me through Mama's words. "The Lord gives each of us a gift," she had said, "and He expects us to use it. I think yours, Earl, is the ability to play football."

By the time I graduated from Tyler High School, we had won the state championship for our divison, I had been named to the All-State team, and a number of colleges had offered me scholarships. I chose to go to the University of Texas. When football practice started that summer, I went off to Austin confident that I had direction in my life.

At the end of my freshman season at Texas I was named an All-Southwest Conference back. In my sophomore year, I gained 1118 yards rushing, was picked for several All-American teams and was pretty sure I had a shot at the Heisman Trophy and at playing on a national championship team.

But just when everything was going so well, I got hurt. I injured a leg muscle during spring practice and no matter what I did about it, I couldn't get it well. When the season began in my junior year, I was still limping and was overweight. I sat out three games and didn't do very well in most of the ones I did play in.

The harder I tried, the more frustrated I became. People were expecting me to perform, and I just wasn't able to. I ended the season with only 653 yards, and we didn't even win the Southwest Conference championship.

I thought about quitting football entirely. In the locker room one day, full of pain and defeat, I sat looking at my leg, thinking I was up against a situation that I simply wasn't able to handle on my own. I'd tried and failed.

Then, as before, almost in desperation, I prayed. "I can't do it by myself, Lord," I said. "I don't know what else to do but ask for help."

Of course, I knew God wasn't going to zap me and make me suddenly well and able to play again. So I went to work again to do my part. I did everything I could to prepare myself to play in my senior year. I worked with weights, spent hours and hours exercising on the stationary bicycle, did 200 to 300 situps a day. I became the most familiar face in the training room.

I also got me a little sign and hung it up in my dorm room, as a reminder. It said: "Lord, Keep Me Going."

By the time the season was to start, my leg felt a whole lot better. I had got my weight down from 242 to 220, and I felt strong and ready. We opened the 1977 season with new enthusiasm and a new coach, Fred Akers, and we quickly won our first three games without too much difficulty. I scored seven touchdowns in those three games, making me the nation's top scorer at that point in the season.

After that came the really crucial tests. We beat Oklahoma, Texas A&M and Texas Tech, *all* strong rivals. We clobbered most of the other conference teams and knocked off the one remaining contender, the University of Arkansas. By then our Longhorn team was rated No. 1 in the country in both the AP and UPI polls. Man, we were riding high!

There was just one more thing needed to make it a perfect season—the national championship. All we had to do was beat Notre Dame in the Cotton Bowl and we'd have it locked up. We were going into the game with an 11-0 record. We had the College Coach of the Year in Fred Akers. We had Brad Shearer, who had just won the Outland Trophy as the best college lineman in the country. We had the game site practically in our back yard, Cotton Bowl Stadium in Dallas.

We weren't long into the game, though, when we started running into trouble. We couldn't seem to hold onto the ball, and we fumbled away scoring opportunities. Their defense was like a mine field that kept blowing up under us.

We lost big—38-10. And on national television, too, where everybody could see. When the final polls came out the following week, it was Notre Dame that was the national champion, not Texas.

We still had our undefeated regular season, and just getting to play in the Cotton Bowl was something. But we were almost sick with disappointment.

In the dressing room after the game, among all our glum, tired and frustrated players, sportswriters from all over the country poured in, asking questions, trying to get us to talk about the game, about what had gone wrong and how it felt to end the season on such a negative note.

What could I say? I wondered. Then, suddenly, I remembered something my mother used to say to me. I could almost hear her telling me, "Earl, when you fall, get up as quick as you can. The Lord understands and forgives. He says, 'Hey, it's okay; start over and try to do a little better next time.' " I grinned as the words came back to me.

". . . Get up as quick as you can . . . The Lord understands . . . Do a little better next time."

All right! I thought. Now I knew what I could say, and do, about it.

America's popular inspirational author shares some secrets for an all-too-familiar problem in some marriages.

SO YOU MARRIED A SKEPTIC

Catherine Marshall

The letter I was about to answer posed an all-too-familiar problem:

> I married a skeptic, a man who had no Christian background. At first this meant little to me since I thought I could change him. That hasn't worked. We've been married eleven years and have three boys. The boys and I go to church, but I cannot get my husband to go. Inevitably our sons are going to count Christianity "a woman's thing" of lesser importance since it doesn't matter to their father. How clearly I see what blessing and happiness could be ours as a family if we could live together in Christ.
>
> Tell me—how can I pray? What can I do?

Having never been married to a skeptic, I could scarcely answer my correspondent's question from personal experience. But I could share with her the experience of friends whom I know and trust. Their advice is surprisingly consistent.

Treena Kerr, wife of the "Galloping Gourmet," Graham Kerr of television fame, is an especially articulate representative of this group. Four years ago Christ delivered Treena from the pit of drugs, alcoholism, and a disintegrating marriage. Soon after that she was given clear-cut instructions about how to relate to her husband, Graham.

"Put a golden zipper on your mouth," she was told. "Say

not a word to Graham about what has happened. No Bibles or religious books or tapes lying about the house. Pray secretly. Don't go rushing to religious meetings—not yet."

One night as Treena was reading her Bible in the bathroom, one verse seemed written in fire: ". . . you wives, be submissive to your husbands, so that some, though they do not obey the word, *may be won without a word* by the behavior of their wives." (I Peter 3:1, RSV)

Treena was excited to see in print the verification of the "golden zipper" instruction that she had been given directly. But, she thought, that "behavior of their wives" suggested another dimension.

"Tell me, Lord," she asked in prayer, "what behavior of mine will get that result?"

"I chose you as a woman," the reply came. "Being a woman is a glorious thing. But it doesn't mean to be in competition with your husband. Put him first. Putting someone else first is love in action. Love him with My love. Set yourself to do what pleases him and leave the rest to Me."

What pleases him . . . That can vary so much from man to man. If he prefers freshly-brewed coffee rather than instant, then take the time for it. Make his favorite dessert. Dress up just for him. Give him some undivided attention. Find special ways to help him carry his responsibilities.

In Treena's case it took just three months for her prayers for Graham to be answered. "During most of that time," she told me, "Graham was reading Chinese philosophy, his latest passion, and watching me with increasing curiosity. Over and above kicking booze and drugs, the changes in me were so obvious—no temper tantrums, fewer arguments, my stridency ebbing out. So finally Graham began to ask questions. Only then was I given permission to unlock the zipper on my mouth."

Whereupon the born-again experience of the Galloping Gourmet became front-page news across the nation.

Here then, is the capsuled advice of these friends of mine who once were married to skeptics, but now know the joy of a home unified in Christ:

1. Claim for your situation that great promise, I Corinthians 7:14*, and know that it has always been God's

*"For the unbelieving husband is consecrated through his wife, and the unbelieving wife is consecrated through her husband."

plan to save the entire family: Jeremiah 31:1.**

2. Put a golden zipper on your mouth.
3. You are to get out of the way, so that Christ can work. This means no criticism of your married partner. Love him (her) with the love of Jesus. In prayer, ask Him to show you ways to give your husband (wife) joy—and He will. Thus Christ will become good news to your home rather than a divisive factor.
4. Be patient. Tiny tree seedlings and woodland ferns growing in the crevice of a craggy rock have been known to split it. Not even a rocklike skeptic can finally withstand the generous, joyous love of Jesus.

**"I will be the God of all the families . . . and they shall be My people."

On my 4100 mile walk from Guatemala to Pennsylvania, the most memorable words I heard were ...

GOOD MORNING, GOD

Eddie Fischer

The sun was hot. It seemed to burn right through my T-shirt. I'd been walking through Mexico for ten days and nights. I had blisters on my feet and had nearly worn through my second pair of shoes. My knapsack weighed a ton. Bordered by parched yellow weeds and shimmering in the noonday heat, the road stretched endlessly ahead.

I was discouraged and lonely.

When I had embarked on my "Walk for Water," my spirits had been high. I had left on Easter Sunday morning from the village of Concepción Las Lomas, Guatemala. In an effort to raise $300,000 for installation of a desperately needed irrigation and drinking water system for the impoverished Indians of Guatemala's Rabinal Valley, I was walking 4100 miles to Newtown Square, Pennsylvania, my hometown. My journey was to take me through Guatemala and Mexico, to Brownsville, Texas, where I planned to meet my older brother, Mark. From there, we'd travel across America, spending extra time in major cities for walk-a-thons, speaking engagements, and other fund-raising events. I wanted to be home by October. Home—never had it seemed farther away . . .

I'd been in Guatemala for nearly a year. Originally, I'd planned to stay, with Mark, for only six weeks, as part of a disaster relief mission. On February 4, 1976, a devastating earthquake had ripped across the tiny Central American country. Though we didn't arrive until that summer, the horror and shock of the tragedy still showed on the faces of the villagers. I had never seen such poverty and suffering in my life. People were wearing rags and living in makeshift shacks with flimsy walls of cornstalks tied together in bunches. Beans and tortillas, once a day, made up their meager diet. Bleary-eyed with dysentery, the men were compelled to walk the ten-mile distance to work and back, rather than pay a five-cent bus fare. By summer's end, we were fluent in Spanish. Mark made plans for returning home, but I sold my plane ticket. I had decided to stay.

Water, for drinking and irrigation, remained the villagers' primary need in the 180-square-mile Rabinal Valley. But installation of a permanent and effective system was just too expensive. Day after day, I watched the women, with their solemn faces and hungry children, as they carried their heavy earthen jars to wells and rivers, filled them with the muddy water and, staggering under the weight, walked painfully back. I couldn't seem to shake their image. Sometimes it kept me awake at night. And that's when I thought of the Walk. One big walk, I reasoned, might take care of all those little ones.

The first part of my journey had been easy. Throughout Guatemala, I had been joined by friends and well-wishers. If someone wasn't with me, they were meeting me along the way with food and drink or the name of a person to ask for when I reached the next town and needed a place to sleep . . .

But now, in Mexico, I was very much alone. Texas was 30 days and 1000 miles away. The stretch that I was traveling had a bad reputation for murderers, bandits and thieves. But far more than these dangers, I feared the loneliness—loneliness that already threatened to undermine my confidence and sap my strength.

I believed that God was with me, but He sure seemed far away. I tried praying, but my attempts seemed futile. "Hail Mary, full of grace . . ." Over and over, I repeated the passage, memorized since childhood. That, and the Lord's Prayer. But it wasn't long before the words sounded flat, empty. That's pretty much how I felt, too. And the farther I walked down that lonely Mexican road, with nothing but birds and dust for company, the more I began to lose faith—in myself and in the Walk.

The harsh cry of a crow caused me to look up. The sun, now, was high overhead. I was halfway between Mexico's Pacific and Gulf coasts. I was also hungry and thirsty, and glad to be approaching the village of Jesus Carranza. Just outside of town, a ramshackle wood-frame farmhouse seemed to beckon.

I knocked on the weatherbeaten door, bleached white by the sun. A leather-skinned man with twinkly black eyes answered. He asked me in for lunch—cold sodas and fruit. His name, I learned, was Manuel. Before we ate, he bowed his head and said a funny little prayer. Nothing fancy—kind of like he was talking to a friend. I couldn't hear exactly what he said. Then he poured me a soda.

"*¿Hace calor? eh!*" (Hot, eh?) he said.

"Yeah."

"Lonely?" he asked.

"Little bit."

"Not too bad when you've got God, though . . . Right?"

I looked at him. But he had left his seat and was over in a corner, rummaging around for something. He came back with a pair of shoes. Brand-new, too. The price tag was still attached.

"Here," he said. "Try these."

I pulled off my sneakers and slipped on the sturdy brown shoes. They fit perfectly. Manuel grinned. Like rays of sunshine, a thousand tiny lines exploded around his eyes. He saw me to the door. He would take no money.

The next few hours on the road passed unusually quickly. I was touched by this man who, living all alone and owning so little, had offered me—a total stranger—one of his most valuable possessions. The shoes were new. They would have lasted him at least a year, and yet he had taken such obvious and genuine pleasure in giving them. I thought of his funny little prayer. I wished that I had been able to understand the words.

The sound of a sputtering engine interrupted my thoughts. I turned around to see an old, beat-up Volkswagen chugging down the road. Manuel was at the wheel.

"*Senor!*"

He pulled over to the grass and greeted me.

"Here, " he said. "Take these." Into my hands he placed

two cool bottles of soda. Before I could say thank you, he was gone.

About three hours later, nearing dinnertime, I heard a familiar chugging. This time Manuel carried half a dozen fresh beef sandwiches and a basket brimming with fruit. Again, he murmured his prayer. I leaned close, but still couldn't catch the words. We ate by a nearby river and watched in contented silence as the waters slowly changed from a sparkling green, to pink, to rose, to purple. A full moon lit the road like a floodlight and I decided to keep on walking. I felt happy somehow—excited, but I couldn't put my finger on it.

"*Adios, senor.*" I thanked Manuel as he hopped in his car and headed home.

The time seemed to fly as I walked briskly toward the Gulf coast. It wasn't till about midnight that I began to tire—and worry about where I'd spend the night. The nearest town was hours away. I almost regretted my impulsive decision to keep on walking. And then, as if to drown out any gloomy thought, I heard again the cheerful chugging.

"*Senor!*" Manuel insisted that I return with him to spend the night at his house.

It was still dark, about six a.m., when the sound of stirrings in the little house woke me. Manuel was an early riser. He called me to the dining table. He bowed his head. This time, I caught part of his prayer, "*Buenos dias, Dios,*" he said. (Good morning, God.) *How strange,* I thought. *How casual.* But I had to admit there was something nice about it.

We had a small breakfast. Manuel took my knapsack and stuffed it with oranges and bread. He drove me to the very spot where he had picked me up just hours earlier.

"And now, *senor,*" he said, "I say good-bye to you."

We embraced like brothers. The little Volkswagen headed back to town. Again, I was alone. But this time it didn't bother me. I was alone, but I wasn't lonely. I was excited. I felt full of great expectations for the coming day, for the Walk, for my life.

The sky was pale yellow with the early morning sunlight. The breeze that tickled my face was cool, alive. I had to share my happiness with someone. I couldn't keep it in.

"Good morning, God!" The greeting spilled out unexpectedly. I almost wanted to pick up the words and put them back in my mouth. What kind of talk was that? But it happened again.

"Good Morning, God! Good Morning!" I started laughing. It was as though I had discovered a new friend. This must be the way that Manuel had been praying. And it was so easy to do! Suddenly, everything made sense. Though I had known God personally and thrilled in His power and love, I had never really known how to talk to Him. My prayers, until now, had been like carbon-copy form letters, like inter-office memos. No wonder I had been lonely. The freedom of our new one-to-one communication was intoxicating.

For the remainder of my walk through Mexico, it's been reported that I traveled alone. But I know better. God was with me all the way, and we had a lot of good conversations.

When Mark met me at the Texas border, I must have looked pretty ragged. I was sunburned, had lost some weight, and was about due for another pair of shoes. After a lot of hootin' and hollerin' and slapping each other on the back, there was a silence—kind of uneasy. It was the silence bred from long separation. It would take awhile, we knew, to get reacquainted, to catch up on each other's lives.

"Hot, eh?" said Mark.

"Yeah."

"Been lonely?" he asked.

"Not a bit!"

Mark looked at me quizzically. My answer had surprised him.

"It's not bad," I explained slowly, "when you've got God . . . Right?"

Mark grinned. "Come on," he said, motioning toward the waiting van. "Come on in and tell me about it."

Four months of hard work faced us, but I knew we'd make it. With a Road Manager like ours, how could we lose?

Editor's note: October 8, 1977, Eddie Fischer arrived victorious in Philadelphia, Pennsylvania, on his 22nd birthday. With the aid of individuals and groups he met along the way, he had raised a large part of the amount he was seeking. In March, 1978, he returned to Guatemala to assist with the village-by-village installation of the Rabinal Valley's new water system. Eddie brought along a five-ton capacity truck and a mobile medical unit to assist in the project—equipment contributed by private donors.

YOUR SPIRITUAL WORKSHOP

ARE YOUR DREAMS BIG ENOUGH?

A five-way test to measure and evaluate your goals in life.

Deep in your heart is there an unfulfilled dream? Perhaps you feel guilty about it—you think somehow that the dream is selfish. But you're not really sure.

This Spiritual Workshop will explore the subject of dreams—those deep desires in all of us which move some people to great achievement, and others to frustration, even tragedy. Here is a series of tests to help discover whether or not our dreams are right for us; whether they are self-centered or a part of what God wants for us.

How To Begin

Make a list of your deepest desires. Be specific and thorough. If you want a certain job, indicate the exact kind of job you think you want. If you want a new house, try to put down the kind of house, the location, etc. If you want a trip to Europe, list the countries you want to see—and why.

If you want a college education, what college and what courses? What capacities do you desire in yourself? For example, would you like the ability to speak well in public? Or greater concentration? Or more ability to make friends? Do you wish for better health?

What sort of ideas do you want? What spiritual graces

would you like to ask God for? What gifts? What kind of insights from Him?

Do not be afraid of being this specific, for remember that you are going to submit this list to a series of checks to amend, change, and correct. Don't show your list to anyone, though; this is between you and your God.

ve Tests

Having made your list as complete as you can, now you are ready to begin applying God's tests to see whether or not your desires are true "soul's sincere desires."

FIRST TEST: *Are the desires which you have put down true to your own nature?*

One way of getting at this question is to trace your steps back to childhood. What were your sincerest ambitions then? Put these down exactly as you remember them, no matter how silly they may seem now.

Here, for example, are the childhood ambitions of one woman:

To be a beautiful lady with plenty of perfume.

To be a great writer.

To be a great musician.

In analyzing these little-girl dreams 18 years later, the woman found that "the beautiful lady" and the "plenty of perfume" represented a normal desire for beauty, for fragrance and expressed an innate femininity. At the heart of the "great writer" was the love of ideas, a soul-satisfaction in trying to get those ideas on paper as well as possible. The woman did, in actual fact, become a writer. The "great musician" desire was at base the need for self-expression, but her musical ability turned out to be mediocre.

The point is—if you are frail and uncoordinated, don't dream of great athletic accomplishments. What a waste it would have been for a great scientist like Thomas Edison to have dreamed of becoming a novelist. What if Shakespeare had spent his life trying to be a painter?

SECOND TEST: *Is it an honest dream?*

Ask yourself if your dream is an attempt to imitate anyone else. Or to please someone else? (Parents, for example, sometimes try to force *their* dreams upon their children.)

Is there any backwash of envy, pride, ("I'll show them!") or jealousy in your dreams? To the extent that this is so, then these are not honest dreams.

Have you thought through what really would happen to you if your dreams were granted tomorrow?

One man who dreamed of being elected to a political office had his dream come true, only to discover that, by nature, he totally disliked the pressures it brought to his daily life. A sensitive introvert, he was miserable in the achievement of his dream.

Am I honestly willing to pay the price to realize my dream?

A girl dreams of becoming an opera singer. Is she willing to pay the price: dedication to her music, almost total concentration of time and energy in practice, practice, practice; the letting go of a myriad of other pleasures?

Think through carefully the unglamorous aspects of your dreams; the toil, the added responsibilities, the pressures.

Go over your list of dreams and rigorously apply the "honesty test" to each one. Remove some items from the list or add others.

THIRD TEST: *Is it in line with basic justice?*

Go over each dream on your list and ask yourself:

Do these dreams meet the test of absolute justice to my fellow men?

Will it take something that belongs to another?

Will I encroach on anyone else's privileges, property, or personality, in asking this of God?

Am I overlooking any debt (not just money!) which I owe another?

FOURTH TEST: *Is it pure?*

Ask yourself if you are trying to use anyone else as a means to the end you want?

For example, as a means to better yourself at someone else's degradation or expense?

Would anyone else have to lower his ideals in order for your dream to come true?

Be honest with yourself and with God here. Amend your list accordingly.

FIFTH TEST: *The Test of God's Greatness.*

If your prayers appear to go unanswered, it may be not because you are asking for too much, but because "your God is too small." Very often our vision is limited and our requests petty and lacking in beauty. So here is a joyous test to apply:

Do your dreams meet the test of God's beauty and harmony?

God's work in nature as in man's nature always is beautiful. A snowflake is beautiful. A maple leaf is beautiful, and also it is true to its own pattern and design.

Do not be afraid to ask for beauty in your life, only be sure it is real beauty.

Are your dreams *big enough* to have God's blessing?

A woman prayed for help for her partially-deaf child in learning to read. As it turned out, God's answer was not only help for this child, but through her for all the deaf children in that particular school district.

In other words, lift your eyes from yourself to take a long look at God's big horizons. Where do your small dreams fit into God's dreams for all His children?

nclusion

You have before you your "soul's sincere desires"—sifted, tested—undoubtedly a somewhat different list from the one with which you began. So now we suggest that you do something that may make no sense to you—we ask you to relinquish your dreams into God's hands. Here is a prayer you may want to use:

Lord, I know that You love me and want my life to be creative, happy and of meaning to others. Here is a list of my heart's desires. To the best of my knowledge, I believe they can be Your dreams for me as well as my own. So I leave them with You now, realizing that You can accomplish nothing through me without work, discipline and prayer on my part. Thank You, Lord, for helping me to see that it is not wrong to dream big—that I go wrong only when I dream without You.

With this act of relinquishment, do not worry about your dreams or even pray about them again for the next few weeks. For by this act, you are planting your dreams in the soil of the Kingdom of God. And remember—do not keep digging up the seeds you have planted—or they will die. You can have absolute faith that where tulips have been planted, tulips will come up. We do not have to plead that four plus four equals eight . . . or for the tides to come in.

Keep your list. What joy it will be in the future to go back over it and recall how and when God fulfilled this dream, and that one!

The Unlimited Power of Prayer

LORD, GIVE ME GRATI-TUDE

Chapter 6

Every person, regardless of circumstances, has one blessing in common. It is the blessing of God's love for His own. We scold a child who forgets to say "thank you" for some trifle received. Yet, do we say "thank you" for God's great gift—life itself?

The Bible tells us, "In every thing give thanks." (I Thessalonians 5:18) A difficult exercise, you might say, when your health is fragile, or you're lonely, or hungry. Read these stories. The people who speak have learned to count their blessings. In doing so, they discovered the key to a happy and meaningful life. They can help you find the key to unlock your heart and fill it with gratitude.

"Thank you." Two words we can pray every day, for all our days to come.

"If you can increase your sense of gratitude," says this distinguished American, "you will become a happier person."

THE TWO MAGIC WORDS

James Farley

Not long ago in my mail I received a request from a college student in Pennsylvania, a young man who said he was writing a thesis on government. He knew of my background in politics, and asked me to fill out a questionnaire.

There were at least 40 questions, and some of them called for detailed and complex answers. I was quite busy but, believing that any interest in government should be encouraged, I sat down with my secretary and dictated a long reply. It took most of one afternoon, but I finally sent it off with the little glow of satisfaction that comes from completing an arduous and voluntary task.

I looked forward to receiving from this young man some acknowledgment as to whether I had helped him or not. But I have yet to hear from him to this day.

I told myself that it was a matter of no great consequence and to put it out of my mind, forget it. But obviously, since I am writing about it now, I didn't forget it. I didn't forget it because I was disappointed.

The truth is, ingratitude hurts everyone. It also hurts the person who fails to show appreciation because he may make an enemy where he could have kept a friend.

Simply feeling gratitude isn't enough; it has to be demonstrated, one way or another. Perhaps the boy in Pennsylvania *was* appreciative but if so his appreciation is wasted because he never told me. Two words—*thank you*—could have made all the difference.

Furthermore, the incident made me examine myself. When someone's performance hurts or displeases you, it is a good idea to ask yourself whether traces of those unpleasant characteristics may not exist in *you*. So I asked myself, how much do most of us appreciate the countless little daily acts of courtesy or kindness on the part of other people that make our lives smoother and more comfortable? How grateful are we, really, for the privilege of living in a country where it is possible for most of us to take freedom and justice and security for granted? How much thankfulness do most of us feel for the marvelous gift of life itself, and how adequately do we express this to the Giver?

The honest answer to each of these questions was painfully clear. Not enough. Not nearly enough.

And so I have decided to make a New Year's resolution to try to change my attitude from a passive to a more active one where gratitude is concerned.

. . . To thank the people who make my world run smoothly—waitresses, elevator operators, taxi drivers, barbers, anyone—not just with a casual word or an impersonal tip, but with some expression of genuine interest in them as fellow human beings.

. . . To make myself more aware of the miraculous privileges involved in simply being an American, and to show my thankfulness by working without thought of reward (yes, even answering unsolicited questionnaires!) to make the best country in the world even better.

. . . To remind myself every day of the infinitely precious value of every minute of existence, and to show my gratitude to God not only with prayers of thanksgiving but by living as close as possible to the way He wants me to live.

A basic rule in showing appreciation, I have found, is this: *do it now*. Do it while your sense of gratitude is fresh and strong. If you put it off, it becomes all too easy to forget it. When Christ healed the ten lepers, only one came back to thank Him, and He commented a bit sadly on this frailty of human nature.* If you feel a flash of thankfulness, act on it before the impulse dies away.

If you do train yourself to act, you will discover that gratitude is by no means a simple thing. I believe, myself,

*Luke 17 : 12-19

that there are several stages or degrees. The first—and most familiar—is the spontaneous feeling of thankfulness for benefits received.

Children have this strong sense of gratitude. A few years ago, out in Iowa, a teacher asked her fourth grade pupils to write a prayer of thanks "for the small blessings which make your life happy and good." The 29 papers that were handed in gave thanks for such things as "the sound of laughter—erasers that make mistakes disappear—the smell of chocolate cake in the oven—colored leaves that swirl and fall in the autumn—big, red, garden tomatoes—my sister's smile on Christmas morning—and for God's care."

A second stage of gratitude is thankfulness, not just for the pleasures and benefits of life, but for its hazards and hardships as well. It takes some insight and maturity to realize that troubles and difficulties have values, but they do. All of us have heard of handicapped people who struggled so fiercely to overcome their handicap that ultimately they became champions. The Pilgrims thanked God for their first harvest, but they might well have thanked Him also for the difficulties that they met and overcame, because it was on this anvil of pain and suffering that they forged the character of a new nation.

The third stage of gratitude is what the poet E.A. Robinson had in mind when he wrote that there are two kinds of thankfulness, "the sudden kind we feel for what we take, the larger kind we feel for what we give." When you begin to feel gratitude for the opportunity to be of service, to help others, to make the world a better place, then you are getting close to the self-forgetfulness that the Bible tells us is the secret of true happiness.

If you can increase your sense of gratitude and your willingness to express it throughout the coming year, you will make the people around you happier, and you will become a happier person yourself. There is a great magic in those two words—*thank you*.

It is impossible to be grateful and embittered at the same time for gratitude must have an object, and if one is grateful for life, then one must be grateful to the Giver of life, the Giver of all things.

"Gratitude," says an old quotation, "is the fairest blossom

which springs from the soul; and the heart knoweth none more fragrant." This I will remember as I try to keep my resolution this year and in all the years God gives me.

A HOUSEWIFE'S PRAYER

Let me delight in the little things
In the morning dew
In the thrush that sings
In the green pine tree
In the dainty violet nodding to me.

Let me speak simply of common things
Of a clean, starched shirt
Of twin wedding rings
Of a child asleep in his own small bed
Of a fluffy cloud floating overhead.

Let me be grateful for everyday things
For the food at my table
For the joy music brings
For a star at my window winking at me
For a cooling swim in a salty sea.

When I cry aloud from the world's harsh stings
Let me think of my treasures of little things.

Let my spirit soar; let my heart take wings.
Joy and peace fill my storehouse of everyday things.

Phyllis Weichenthal

That was all I wanted, but there was something wrong with my prayer.

LORD, LET ME GO HOME

Ricardo Montalban

As I hung up the phone on our kitchen wall, I turned to see my wife Georgiana's smiling face. Her eyes were shining with excitement.

"You got the part?" she asked.

"Yes," I said slowly—still not quite believing the news myself. The role was in a new Broadway musical, *Jamaica*. It couldn't have happened at a better time.

It was 1957, and with a wife and four small children to support, I badly needed work. Our past few years in Hollywood had been pretty lean; my career had been one of ups and downs. But this, we understood, was the nature of an actor's life—to live from job to job in a state of constant uncertainty. Fortunately, Georgiana and I shared a firm faith in God and in the power of prayer that had never failed to see us through the roughest times. When I needed work, we prayed—with confidence and expecting an answer. That's the way I'd been taught as a youngster.

Still, landing the role in *Jamaica* was more than I'd hoped for. The part was, first of all, challenging; I was the only white actor in an all-black cast and would be playing the part of a Jamaican. The job promised to be steady; advance ticket sales for the show, at Broadway's Imperial Theater, indicated it was going to be a hit. Best of all, the work wouldn't take me away from my family; the contract included our all-expenses-paid move from California to New York.

It seemed too good to be true.

We arrived in New York with great expectations and

weren't disappointed. The play opened to good reviews and was booked for a year's run. As a family, we enjoyed the excitement of big city living and new acquaintances. At the theater, deep friendships developed among the *Jamaica* cast and crew. One of my dearest companions was my dresser, Charlie Blackstone.

Charlie was a quiet man, immaculately groomed, with a cheerful nature and quick grin that endeared him to everyone he met. He took his work seriously. From out of nowhere, it seemed, Charlie's efficient hands were always there when I needed them—adjusting a crooked belt buckle, sewing a button, delicately retouching a spot of makeup melted by hot stage lights. Rarely did Charlie speak about himself or his past, and I never asked him any questions; ours was a relationship based on a kind of silent understanding. We just felt comfortable in each other's company and never felt we had to say very much.

Charlie loved boxing, and we often spent intermissions watching the fights on television in my dressing room. Saturday nights were special. That's when Charlie and I went to midnight mass at St. Malachy's, also known as the Actors' Chapel because of its late-hour services and theater-district location on West 49th Street.

I grew to love that old church, with its cozy atmosphere and worn wooden pews. Charlie and I always sat in the same place. It was there it seemed I could best focus my thoughts and get close to God. I often thought how I would miss St. Malachy's when it came time to return to California.

Our year in New York had nearly passed and Georgiana and I were busy planning our trip home when, unexpectedly, I learned that the play was being held over. A new school year was starting, so Georgiana and the children went on to California without me. I took a temporary apartment with another actor, planning to join my family as soon as the play closed. At first our separation didn't bother me; I didn't expect it to last more than a few weeks.

But as weeks dragged on into months and *Jamaica* kept playing to sell-out audiences, it became apparent that I was stuck in New York indefinitely. I should have been happy for the show's success, but with each passing day I grew more and more miserable with homesickness. My family means everything to me. I missed them terribly. No matter what I tried to divert myself—books, television, shopping, museums, shows—nothing held my interest. All I wanted was to be home with my family. Phone calls and letters only made me feel worse; they were poor substitutes for the real thing.

Every day started and ended with the same prayer.

"Lord, let me go home," I'd say. "Let me be with my family soon."

But the show went on. The job that had been a dream come true had turned into a nightmare. With each closing curtain, I felt my throat tighten, my frustration turning into anger. It just didn't seem fair.

Finally, after one Saturday night performance, I thought I would explode. Storming into my dressing room, I slammed the door behind me.

"I am so sick of this," I hissed through clenched teeth. "Sick of it!"

Charlie Blackstone was sitting on a folding chair in the far corner of the room watching television. He looked up at me with troubled eyes, but said nothing. He had been waiting for me to go to mass.

We walked to St. Malachy's in silence. The midnight sky was inky black, the stars cold and brittle. A bitter wind sounded a mournful cry as it whipped around the church.

Charlie and I entered the chapel and slipped into our pew. The wooden seat was hard. The cement floor was cold on my knees. Whatever charm the church had held for me before was gone. I didn't want to be there. I didn't care who knew.

"Lord," I muttered, "I want to go home. I miss my family. I'm sick of this play. Please. . ." I hesitated. "Please make it end!"

The chapel seemed unusually quiet.

I glanced over at Charlie. His head was bowed and he was smiling, ever so faintly. His voice was low, but I caught the words. What I heard made my heart sink.

Charlie was *thanking* the Lord for his work—for the very thing I was praying would end. And Charlie, I knew, wasn't the only one. All around the city there were many others—actors, actresses, stagehands, musicians—who needed their jobs and felt the same way.

My face grew hot with shame. I felt torn apart, confused, guilty. I still wanted to go home—but certainly not at the expense of anyone else. For the first time in my life, I didn't know what—or how—to pray.

Charlie, I noticed, had fallen silent. He remained that way for a few moments, then raised his head. His expression was one of absolute peace. With eyes still closed, he began to say the Lord's Prayer.

"Our Father," he began.

His words were soothing. They seemed to whisper in my ear, finding their way into my own thoughts.

"Our Father," I repeated—and stopped.

Here, in these two small words, in this age-old prayer, was the answer to my problem!

Jesus, in teaching us how to pray, had made it clear that we were to speak not only for ourselves, but for *all* members of His family: not to my Father, but to *our* Father—not just for me, Ricardo, but for all those around me. This wonderful sense of sharing each others' burdens in prayer was further revealed as I continued . . . "Give *us* day by day *our* daily bread . . . Forgive *us our* sins . . . Lead *us* not into temptation . . . Deliver *us* from evil . . ." (Luke 11: 2-4)

In the past, my prayers had always been self-centered. There was a real freedom in thinking of others that I'd never before experienced. It was exhilarating.

Before we left the church, I simply asked the Lord for patience in understanding His will for me for the remainder of my stay in New York City. I didn't have to tell Him how badly I wanted to go home; I'd been telling Him for weeks.

I wish I could say my situation changed—it didn't. The play continued for five more months. But something far more important did happen. *I* changed. My anger was gone. And, gradually, the stabbing pains of homesickness that had made life intolerable melted away. What remained was a sweet sort of ache that was almost pleasant in the way it served as a constant reminder that there were loved ones at home waiting for me. Besides, I recognized now that I had another family, my theater family, to appreciate and love for however long we were to be together.

It was some time ago that I received word that Charlie Blackstone had passed away. It's been over 20 years since our night together at St. Malachy's. Since then, there have been many more times when I've called upon the Lord for guidance—times of trouble and confusion and despair that we all must endure. But now, thanks to Charlie, it's with the needs of others in mind—as well as my own.

It was easy to talk to the Lord by myself, but when others listened I stumbled for words.

THANKSGIVING PRAYERS

Jean Bell Mosley

It was Thanksgiving. Outside, snow swirled. Wind rattled the loose shutters. Icicles fringed the barn. Inside was an oasis of warmth, cheer and love. The big kitchen table was set with the best rose-sprigged china. The spoon holder and sugar bowl reflected light from the fireplace. The kitchen range kept the teakettle singing and the potatoes boiling.

When the meal was ready and we were all seated around the table laden with food from our own garden, fields and orchard, Grandpa offered the first prayer. It was full of praise for our Maker and for His loving care and watchfulness over us, and the gift of another harvest reflected in the food before us.

And while he prayed, I, at ten the youngest of the three-generation-under-one-roof family, thought of the summer corn fields and potato patch and bean rows I had helped keep free of weeds. It was not so much the work and the resulting food that I remembered, as the little side issues that moved in and out of the pleasant hours like a bright shuttle weaving time together. There was the day when the three little killdeer, long-legged, pert-tailed, full of new life, new voice, ran ahead of me down the long bean rows. They stopped, looked around, ran again. I had to laugh at their freshness, their surprise at life. They were so clean, so neat, each feather in measured place, their cries tiny replicas of their mother's. One, in its haste to keep up, stepped on a clod and turned a sort of somersault. "They didn't have to be there, Lord," I whispered as Grandpa prayed. "But they were and I remember and I thank."

It was easy for me to talk to the Lord when it was just the two of us. When others listened I stumbled for words, fearful I'd say the wrong thing in the wrong way. Spoken thanks for three little killdeer running down a long, monotonous bean row, laid alongside the fulfilled promise of seedtime and harvest, night and day, summer and winter, might seem frivolous.

Grandma was the next in line to offer her Thanksgiving prayer. Through custom I knew we would go in chronological order. After Grandma would be Daddy, Mama, my two sisters and I.

Among other things, Daddy was thankful that our cattle, from which we received a good portion of our income, had been healthy and that good pastures had been provided.

"Yes, Lord," I whispered. "Good pastures. There were millet and timothy. But, Lord, there were also those little clumps of daisies which didn't have to be there, weren't sown by us, not good hay, but so pretty, just like scattered white embroidery on a big green background. Lord, You put them there, didn't You? And I noticed them. Mama and Grandma fix up the house when company is coming. They wash curtains, polish lamps, make fresh bread. Company comes and sometimes they leave and don't even notice. Same as You fix up the world with little daisies and killdeer and pretty rocks and shiny trees. And I'm going to notice them, Lord. All my life I'm going to notice them—Your furniture, Your pretties that You fixed up for us while we're here."

A log in the fireplace broke in two. Mama was praying and her thanks turned toward the warmth of our home and the provision of fuel from our woods.

". . . and, Lord," I continued, "thank You for the light the fire makes, too. When I saw it on the sugar bowl, dancing, it seemed to make the painted roses open up bigger. We could get by without the light made by fires, but I'm glad for it. And moonlight and starlight don't make things grow, but it is so pretty, Lord. And about the flowers opening, they all do it differently. The morning glory untwists. The zinnias sprout stiff petals in a circle. The trumpet vine unfolds like paper folded over the end of a bottle. They could have all been alike."

Now Lillian was praying, thanking the Lord for the sun, the rain and the robins.

"Oh, yes, Lord," I whispered again. "Birdsong. It could have been squeaky and shrill, or no song at all. Oh, my, no birdsong! Lord, I thank You for the birdsong and the cricket and our old red rooster who wakes us up."

"Dear Lord," Lou began, and it was getting close to me. What had I said in former years? Couldn't I just say that again, whatever it was, or maybe say, "Yes, Lord, for all these things I, too, give You thanks."

"I thank You for the Pilgrims," Lou continued. "They could have given up. They were cold and hungry, but they didn't give up for they wanted to worship You in their own way. Amen."

"Dear Father," I began, hesitated, began again. "Our Father." The words were shaky. Another log in the fireplace broke. The teakettle simmered a contented little song. I thought of Lou's last words, "worship You in their own way."

"Dear Lord, thank You for the things we don't have to have. Amen."

There was silence. It stretched. Even the teakettle seemed to stop, shocked. Had I said the wrong thing? They were all looking at me in ill-concealed surprise, or was it disapproval?

"I mean there are so many things we don't have to have, but . . . "

"Never mind, Jeanie," Mama interrupted. "You don't have to explain your prayers to us. The One you're talking to understands what you mean."

Thank You, God, for that, too! I added silently.

*A relationship based on pity,
blossomed into one bound by love.*

THANK YOU, PHILIP

Johnny Bench
Catcher, Cincinnati Reds

If you had told me five years ago that a little boy was going to come into my life, steal my heart and turn me into a person capable of giving and receiving deep love, I'd have scoffed at the idea. I was a 25-year-old major-league baseball player for the Cincinnati Reds with only one goal—to become the best catcher in the history of baseball.

That was before I met Philip. He was a sad-looking kid, I remember thinking, when he showed up at an autographing session I was doing in 1973 as part of a product-promotion tour at a Dayton, Ohio, department store. It was November, so there weren't many suntans in that group that stood waiting for me to write my name on shopping bags, sweat shirts, ball gloves, even sales receipts, but Philip's complexion was as white as a flour bag. Also he was skinnier than a stray dog and he seemed to have no hair. Sue Lilly, an employee of the department store, who was helping me work the crowd, whispered that his name was Philip Buckingham, that he had leukemia and that chemotherapy treatment had left him bald.

"Come 'ere, Pardner," I said with an enthusiasm I didn't feel. It took little encouragement. Running as fast as his four-year-old legs would go, Philip jumped onto my lap and threw his arms around my neck. For an instant I started to pull back, then caught myself.

"I love the Reds, and Johnny Bench best of all," he announced with a beaming smile.

"Attaboy!" I answered, pulling his oversized Cincinnati

baseball cap over his eyes. Then I gave him my autograph and sent him on his way. "Good luck to you, Philip."

"You better win a pennant next year," he called back. I wondered if he would even be around the next year. Regardless, I was glad that was over. It made me nervous to be around sick people, and I'd had enough talk about cancer to last a lifetime. Late in the 1972 baseball season, I had developed some pain in my back. Doctors diagnosed it as a lung lesion, a tumor that would have to be removed. Could it be malignant? Not likely, I was told. Even so, I was enormously troubled, and I let few people know about the operation. Fortunately for me, the growth was benign, but the emotional shock waves were still vibrating when this four-year-old leukemia sufferer came along. I was happy to get him out of sight as quickly as possible. The trouble was, I couldn't get him out of my mind.

Later, I commented to Sue Lilly about "that poor kid." She told me how poor. The hospital expenses had been so astronomical that the Buckinghams were afraid of losing their home. Furthermore, they were without a car and Philip had to be taken by bus to the hospital for treatments. On the long bus ride he would often become sick from the chemotherapy and the public ordeal had further embarrassed and upset his parents.

For the month following our meeting, Philip's exuberant hug and brave grin had haunted me. It was such a heart-rending case. I wanted to do something, knew instinctively that I *should* do something, yet I was scared of getting involved.

Still, this feeling that I was obligated to do something for Philip gnawed at me, and after a month of vacillation I called the department store in mid-December and asked for Sue Lilly. Under the guise of business, I eventually got to the point. "By the way, Sue," I asked, "what do you hear about that little kid . . . what's his name . . . Philip . . . the one with leukemia?"

She told me that she had talked with Philip's mother and that he seemed to be doing fairly well. But the best news was that through a local newspaper story, money had been raised to help the family. "Some of us from the store are going to visit the Buckinghams the day before Christmas to take them a few things. Would you like to come along?"

I groped for an excuse. "Well, I've got this trip . . . I really can't because . . . I . . . I . . . I'd love to," I finally heard myself saying.

On the afternoon of December 24, Sue, myself and some friends knocked on the door of the Buckinghams' modest frame home. Philip's greeting nearly bowled me over. "Johnny! Johnny! Johnny!" he yelled, jumping onto my back.

Out came the toys we'd brought along for Philip and his older brother and sister. There were beanbags, a model airport, building blocks, and a sack of groceries my mother had provided.

While Philip was overjoyed with the gifts, he paid more attention to me personally. Grabbing my hand, he pulled me down on the floor and together we began building a fort out of blocks.

Suddenly Philip looked up at me and asked point-blank, "Did you *really* want to come, Johnny?"

"Sure I did," I said, but his question startled me. Had he sensed a hesitancy about my coming, somehow knowing that I'd almost chickened out? I was ashamed to think I'd had reservations about reaching out to this little boy. Me, a guy who has so much.

Just as we were about to go, someone asked Philip, "Don't you think Santa Claus should give your mommy and daddy something?"

"Santa"—a friend of Sue Lilly's—pulled out a set of keys belonging to a used car Sue had arranged to buy for the Buckinghams, and an envelope containing a check to keep them from being evicted. Tears of gratitude filled their eyes.

I don't think I've ever had a better Christmas. I was glad I could brighten Philip's day, but more than that, I sensed that I, too, had received something. Just what it was, I didn't know then, but something significant had happened to me.

When it was time to go to Florida with the Reds for spring training in February, I called to tell Philip good-bye. "Don't forget to win the pennant," he reminded me. "We'll sure try," I told him.

Philip, I discovered while in Florida, could talk all day on the phone, and while he was surely feeling pain, he refused to let on. He was a very brave boy, and I found myself rooting for him as much as he was rooting for me. I didn't hit too well during spring training, but when I'd call from time to time, he'd tell me to keep trying. "You, too," I'd answer.

Just before the '74 season began I asked Philip, "How'd you like me to dedicate my first home run to you?"

"Wouldja?" he shouted so loudly through the receiver that he nearly popped my eardrum.

In April, Sue Lilly helped arrange Philip's first visit to Riverfront Stadium, home of the Reds. It was a dream-come-true for the little guy because the only baseball games he'd seen had been on TV. Even though we were beaten by the Dodgers that night, you'd never have known it from the way Philip carried on. When I met him in the locker room afterward, his eyes were full of excitement and his smile was as wide as home plate.

"Hey, Phil," I asked when we left the ball park, "would you like to take a ride in my car?" He war-whooped his answer. After the ride he gave me a big hug. This time I squeezed back. "Thank you, Johnny," he said. "Thank *you*, Philip, for being my buddy." A relationship that had begun on pity had blossomed into one held together by love. That was the truth. I really loved the gutsy little guy.

As the year went by, the news from Dayton became more and more important to me. "Treatments are continuing . . ." his mother Melissa would report. "Philip is holding his own . . . he asks about you every day." One morning on the telephone Melissa told me something Philip had said to her that startled me.

"Mommy," he had said, "Baby Jesus came to visit me last night and soon I'm going to live in Heaven with Him." That's a pretty big thought for a boy not yet five, but Philip had experienced a lot in his brief life, so maybe it wasn't so surprising. Philip's childlike faith was impressive and it started rubbing off on me. Never big on prayer before, I found myself praying for him—all that summer—in airplanes, during batting practice, in the shower—everywhere.

When another Christmas came around—1974—again I was drawn to Dayton. Though Philip looked better—golden hair had grown on his head—I knew the doctors had increased his drug dosage. For the second year in a row Sue Lilly and the gang rounded up presents for the Buckingham family, including a Bible that we all signed and gave to Melissa and her husband Carl.

When we got ready to leave, Philip followed me outside to

my car. Reaching into the glove compartment, I pulled out one last present for him—a little china Cincinnati Reds doll, emblazoned with No. 5, my uniform number.

"Can you use this, Phil?" I asked.

"You bet," he said, grabbing it from me and running back to the house.

Several weeks later I received a telephone call from Melissa Buckingham.

"I knew you'd want to know right away, Johnny," she said. "Philip died just a few hours ago."

"Thank you," I said, struggling for something to say and at the same time fighting back tears.

"Johnny," Melissa went on, "when Philip went into the hospital for the final time, he was clutching that little china doll you gave him. He wouldn't let go of it. . . . We want to bury it with him."

As she spoke, Philip's words, "Soon I'll be living in Heaven with Baby Jesus," flashed through my mind and now the tears really started running down my face. Words couldn't express the deep loss I felt, and even today it's hard to explain what Philip meant to me. How could a skinny little kid with big blue eyes and a half-nelson hug turn me into such a softy?

But Philip showed me something very important: that we should be open to everyone we meet, no matter who they are. Because I was open to Philip, his love flowed through me, making me vulnerable and more caring and breaking down my fear of letting real feelings come out.

Thank God for that little boy who truly opened my eyes as well as my heart.

A famous actor gratefully remembers his father's gift of listening.

A TIME FOR SILENCE

Lorne Greene

Three years before I was given the television role of the father in *Bonanza*, my father died. But in another sense he lives every time Ben Cartwright walks before the TV cameras. The way the role was originally conceived, for example, Cartwright was an aloof, unfriendly sort of person who greeted strangers with a rifle. I remember one early line I had to speak.

"We don't care for strangers around here, Mister. Git off the Ponderosa—and don't come back!"

Well, I said it, but my heart wasn't in it, and gradually I began to play Ben Cartwright more like the father I knew best. His way of greeting strangers was to invite them home to dinner. There were only three of us in our family, Dad, Mother and me, but our house in Ottawa, Canada, always seemed to be full of people. My most typical childhood memory is of creeping halfway down the stairs after my bedtime to listen to the company talking in the living room—and wondering in the morning who had found me asleep and carried me back to bed.

The people Dad, who made his living as a shoemaker, invited home most often were actors, artists, musicians, anyone connected with the world of beauty and make-believe that had been closed to him as a child and young man. Dad's family had been poor. He'd gone to work early, apprenticed to a leather worker at 15, and Dad's friends filled in a part of life he'd missed.

Dad was a huge man. He wasn't unusually tall, but he was

tremendously broad across the chest and shoulders. And like so many big men, he was exceptionally gentle.

He had one special quality which I have come to think of as the essence of his fatherhood. It's such a simple thing, on the surface. He knew that there is a time for silence.

I remember the day I discovered this quality in my father. It was my eighth birthday, and Mother and Dad had given me a watch—a gift so far beyond my wildest dream that I had to keep taking it from my pocket to be sure it was real. At bedtime Dad warned me about winding it.

"It's wound tight now. Tomorrow, when it's run down some, I'll show you exactly how to do it."

Of course, I promised not to wind the watch and went to sleep in a fever of impatience for the morning.

Several times that night I woke up: Would daylight never come? At last I drew the watch from safekeeping under my pillow, stared into its phosphorescent face and came to the incredulous conclusion that it was not yet three o'clock.

Surely it was later than that! My watch must be losing time! It was as though my dearest friend lay dying in my arms. Dad had said not to wind it, but wasn't it almost murder to let it run down?

And so after a regrettably brief struggle, I wound the watch. After every few twists I held it to my ear but the watch ran no faster. Desperate now, I wound and wound until finally I fell asleep. . . .

Early next morning Dad came into my room. "Well Lorne! What time is it?" Dad picked up the watch, his eyes still shining with the pleasure that giving the gift had brought him. Then he frowned. "Five minutes past three?" he said. He held it to his ear, then tried the stem. "Lorne, did you wind this watch?"

I must have felt much like Adam in the garden, with the taste of apple still in his mouth. "No, Dad, I didn't wind it."

I looked up at Dad and there in his eyes I saw some deep communion broken. For a full 10 seconds he watched me without speaking and then he left the room.

He didn't speak of the matter, then or ever, and he had the broken mainspring on the watch repaired, but his silence demolished me. I sobbed for hours. I hated myself—whereas a lecture might have let me twist things around and hate him—and I never forgot it.

I was 15 before I tried deception on my father again—and this time I went in for it in a big way. It happened that Mother went to New York for two weeks to visit her sister, leaving Dad and me alone in the house. The more I thought about that house, standing empty and peaceful all through the day while Dad was at the shoeshop, the more delightfully it contrasted with the restraints of school. I took out a sheet of Mother's note paper, experimented with her signature until I was satisfied, then signed an illness excuse and began to enjoy a few days of leisure.

One morning I picked up my pile of books as usual, and left the house. Dad always left for his shop at 8:30, but I was taking no chances: I waited until 9:30 before going home. I let myself in, gloating at my own cleverness, and slammed the front door behind me.

"Who's there?" Dad's deep voice boomed through the hall.

He stepped out of the bathroom, a towel around his shoulders, and my cleverness deserted me. Staring into his eyes the only thing I could think of was:

"I—uh—came back for an umbrella."

Both of us instinctively glanced out the window. As luck would have it there was not a cloud in the sky. In the immense silence proceeding from my father I went through the wretched pantomime of taking an umbrella from the closet. I was halfway out the door when he spoke.

"Aren't you forgetting your rubbers?"

Miserably, I crept back for those, too.

"Lorne," Dad said, "let's you and me have lunch together today."

Now ordinarily this was a great treat, to meet him at a restaurant downtown during the school lunch hour, and I tried to sound hearty as I accepted.

I knew what that lunch date was for: It was a chance for me to tell him anything that might be on my mind. But somehow when I got there the words stuck in my throat. Dad didn't press me on the subject of my behavior; he maintained that powerful silence of his which said so much more than words. After the meal, he said simply, "I'll walk you back to school."

We walked up the high school steps, down the hall, into the principal's office, and there, of course, it all came out: the illegal absences, the forged note, everything. That principal bawled me out for half an hour. He threatened and harangued and banged the desk and said a great many things, all of which were probably very well put and doubtlessly true. And five minutes after we left his office I couldn't have told you one of them. All the while Dad said nothing at all. He simply sat looking at me. And whereas I cannot tell you a thing the one man said, the well-timed silence of the other has haunted me ever since.

I remember once during my first semester at college when I faced a decision about the future. I was enrolled in the chemical engineering course at Queen's University in Kingston, Ontario, about 100 miles from home. I'd been intrigued by chemistry for years, but I had another love, too, perhaps born on the hall stairs one night as Dad's guests talked in the living room. I wanted to be an actor. Not professionally, perhaps, but as a hobby. One reason I'd chosen Queen's University was because of the Drama Guild there.

But as soon as I started classes I made a jolting discovery: Being a scientist was going to take all of my time! There were lectures in the morning, labs all afternoon, and written assignments for the evening. Only people in non-lab could go out for the Drama Guild.

Suddenly I wanted very much to be talking this all over with Dad. I put through a phone call and raced the three-minute limit to get it all said.

"Isn't this a coincidence!" Dad's voice interrupted me. "I'll be passing right through Kingston tomorrow on my way to Toronto. Why don't I stop by the school and you can tell me more?"

Today, of course, I know he didn't have to go to Toronto any more than he had to go to the moon. He closed his shop and made that 100-mile trip because there was a boy with something on his mind who needed a good listener.

At the time I only knew that we sat all that September afternoon on the shore of Lake Ontario while I poured out my thoughts, my hopes, my dreams for the future and that by the time I had finished I had chosen a lifetime in the theater.

What he thought about my plans, whether he would have been prouder of an engineer in the family than an actor, or whether he cherished completely different dreams for me, I never knew.

I was talking with a friend not long ago about Dad's gift of creative silence. My friend, Joe Reisman, is a song writer, and suddenly he picked up a piece of paper and started jotting down some of the things I'd said. Here's what he wrote:

You can talk to the man.
He's got time. He'll understand.
He's got shoulders big enough to cry on.
Tell all your troubles, and take your time.
He's in no hurry. He doesn't mind.
It matters not how bad you've been:
You can talk to the man.

Now I'd been talking about Dad. But by the time Joe had set the words to music and we'd made a record of them, the word "Man" had become capitalized, and the record was about God the Father of us all.

But that's a natural progression, when you come to think about it. Doesn't what we know of the Father in heaven start with a father here on earth? We believe in His love because we've known human love. We believe that He listens to our prayers because another father has listened to our words.

PRAYER FOR SMALL BLESSINGS

Lord, give me a heart that often sings,
And finds great joy in little things;
The song of a bird, the smell of a rose;
A gentle breeze that playfully blows;
A savory meal with loved ones dear;
The sound of a church bell sweet and clear;
A mother's love, a child's caress;
These are the things that truly bless.
Mildred Kirkland

One of America's best-loved writers reminds us of the freedoms we too often take for granted.

PRAYER FOR THE 4TH OF JULY

Marjorie Holmes

Thank You, God. First and foremost that I'm a woman. What's more, an American woman—that luckiest of all possible beings. For nowhere else in the whole wide world could I be so respected, so cherished, so privileged (some people call it downright spoiled) and yet so free.

Thank You that I can vote or run for office (and win, too). That I can marry or not, have children or not, work or not, and it's nobody's business but my own; there's nobody really to stop me but me.

Thank You that, although discrimination dies hard (men have run Your world so long, God, and forgive me, but You made men proud and slow to change), no doors are really closed to me. I can be a doctor—surgeon, dentist, vet. I can be a lawyer, I can be a judge. I can dance, swim, act—be an artist, drive a truck, umpire a baseball game. I can work in forests or harvest fields as well as offices if it suits me.

But, dear Lord, how I thank You that my government doesn't *make* me do any of these things. I can stay home and be a wife and mother if I please. I can be my own boss as I cook and sew and chase the kids and clean. (And while I'm at it, thank You for the marvelous conveniences that make keeping house in America easier than anyplace else on earth.)

Thank You, God, for the prosperity and plenty of this

incredible country. The abundance of our resources—coal and oil and water and grain, and human energy and skill. For You know how hard we've worked to get where we are. Unlike the skeptical hireling of the parable, we didn't just bury the gifts You gave us, but plowed and sowed and sweat and made them bear fruit. And then, with arms and hearts overflowing, we rushed to the whole world's aid.

Thank You that we inherited not only our forefathers' and mothers' achievements, but their generosity, their willingness to share. That never in all our history have we turned our back on another nation in need.

Thank You, God, that my children were born in this remarkable land. *Born free*. Daughters as well as sons, just as free as I am to do with their lives what they will.

Oh, help us truly to value that freedom, God, and guard it well. Don't let us take it for granted. Don't let us become weak, soft, vulnerable. So afraid of being considered old-fashioned, so eager to be sophisticated, modern, that we play into the hands of those who would take it away.

Don't let us discount it, downgrade it. And dear God, make us just as quick to praise our country's virtues and triumphs and blessings as we are to criticize. For who can do his best—man, woman, child or nation—if no credit is ever forthcoming? No appreciation—only blame?

Help us to stop criticizing *ourselves* so much, God. Restrain our own breast beating. Help us to remember that no nation since the beginning of time has ever had even half the freedom and advantages we enjoy.

Light in us fervent new fires of patriotism, Lord.

Patriotism. A word of passionate honor in almost every country except the one that deserves it so much! Make us proud to be American patriots once again. Willing to shout our heritage from the housetops. Let us thrill once more to the sight of our star-spangled banner. May it fly from every flagpole, be honored in every schoolroom. Let us and our children pledge our allegiance to it wherever Americans gather, and sing the words of its anthem with love and thanksgiving.

Oh, Lord, dear Lord, remind us: We are so *lucky* to be Americans. And I'm so lucky to be an American woman.

A noted writer depicts the kind of wisdom one must have if he is to be a truly grateful person.

THE WAY OF ACCEPTANCE

Arthur Gordon

A few years ago some friends of ours were given the heart-breaking news that their teen-age son was going blind, that nothing could be done. Everyone was torn with pity for them, but they remained calm and uncomplaining. One night as we left their house, deeply moved by their fortitude, I tried to express my admiration.

I remember how the boy's father looked up at the stars. "Well," he said, "it seems to me that we have three choices. We can curse life for doing this to us and look for some way to express our grief and rage. Or we can grit our teeth and endure it. Or we can accept it. The first alternative is useless. The second is sterile and exhausting. The third is the only way."

The way of acceptance . . . how often that path is rejected by people who refuse to admit limitations, hide behind denials and excuses, try to shift the blame for failures, react to trouble with resentment and bitterness. And how often, conversely, when someone makes the first painful move toward repairing a damaged relationship or even a broken life, that move involves acceptance of some reality, that has to be faced before the rebuilding can begin.

It's a law that seems to run like a shining thread through the whole vast tapestry of living. Take alcoholism, for instance, that grim and mysterious disease: Where does recovery begin? It begins with acceptance of the unacceptable, with the uncompromising four words with which members of Alcoholics Anonymous introduce themselves at meetings: "I am an alcoholic." Or take a failing marriage: Any marriage counselor will tell you that no reconciliation succeeds unless it involves acceptance of the other partner, faults and all—and acceptance, too, of the fact that the blame for the trouble must be shared.

Difficult? It's hideously difficult! But in terms of courage and cheerfulness and ultimate happiness the rewards can be beyond measure. I knew a man once, an Episcopal minister, who through some hereditary affliction was very deaf and almost blind. He went right on preaching, visiting the sick, listening to people with his hearing-aid, laughing uproariously at jokes and having a marvelous time.

I remember going with him at Christmas time to buy some trifle in a crowded drugstore. On the back of the entrance door was a mirror, so placed that as we turned to leave my friend's reflection came forward to meet him. Thinking that someone else was approaching, he stepped aside. So did the image. He moved forward and once more met himself. Again he retreated.

By now an uneasy hush had fallen on the spectators. No one quite knew what to say or do. But the third time my companion realized he was facing a mirror. "Why," he cried, "it's only me!" He made a grand bow. "Good to see you, old boy! Merry Christmas!" The whole store exploded in delighted laughter, and I heard someone murmur: "That man really has what it takes." But what "it" was, surely, was the gift of acceptance, acceptance of limitations that in turn brought the power to transcend them.

Is there any way to be receptive to this gift of grace, to learn to rebound from the inevitable slings and arrows that wound the ego and try the soul? One way is to face your difficulty, your problem, your loss, look at it unflinchingly, and then add two unconquerable words: *and yet*. This is the situation, you have to say to yourself, and yet . . . All this has happened to me, and yet . . . The words are unconquerable because they shift the focus from what has been lost to what remains and what can still be gained.

Some people confuse acceptance with apathy, but there's all the difference in the world. Apathy fails to distinguish between what can and what cannot be helped; acceptance makes that distinction. Apathy paralyzes the will-to-action; acceptance frees it by relieving it of impossible burdens. Former President Eisenhower's mother was a deeply religious woman. When he was a boy, she would say to him, "Ike, the Lord deals the cards; the way you play them is up to you." There's acceptance in that philosophy, and without a hint of apathy. There was no apathy, either, in the acceptance of our friends whose boy lost his sight. They helped him learn Braille. They convinced him that a life could be useful and happy even though it had to be lived in darkness. He's halfway through college, now, doing splendidly, and his attitude seems to be cheerful: "My handicap's blindness; what's yours?"

What acceptance really does in such cases is liberate people by breaking the chains of self-pity. Once you accept the blow, the disappointment, then you're free . . . free to go on to new endeavors that may turn out magnificently.

I remember being given a glimpse of this truth quite early in life. It was during my first year at college. Home for a brief visit, I was faced with the unpleasant necessity of telling my parents that my brave plans for working my way through college were not succeeding—at all.

The field I had chosen involved selling. Students ran the campus concessions for such things as dry cleaning and laundry, and freshmen could compete for positions in these organizations by selling service contracts. I waited until my last night at home. Then I told my parents that I had done my best, but that I was not going to be among the successful candidates. My father asked why.

Nothing is so indelible as the memory of failure. I remember how the coal fire muttered in the grate and the tawny light flickered on the shadowy bookcases. "Because," I said slowly, "I'm a terrible salesman, that's why. I get self-conscious. I get discouraged. Other people do the job much better. I'm in the wrong pew, that's all."

On the mantel, the old clock ticked. I waited for the remonstrance, the exhortation, the you-can-do-it-if-you-really-try lecture. But there was just silence. Finally my father laughed gently. "Well," he said, "that's fine. It's just as important to learn what you can't do as what you can. Now let's forget about that and talk about getting you into the right pew!"

Accept . . . forget . . . move on: Some great Americans

have ordered their lives along those lines. Abraham Lincoln once told a visitor that in the fiery crucible of the Civil War he did the best he could, regardless of criticism, and would do it to the end. "If the end brings me out all right," he added, "what is said against me won't amount to anything. If the end brings me out wrong, ten angels swearing I was right would make no difference." Acceptance . . . acceptance of the iron rule that results matter more than intentions. On President Truman's desk was a wry little sign: "The buck stops here." Again acceptance . . . acceptance of the frightful responsibility, the awful loneliness of the presidency.

Just as acceptance has its rewards, so non-acceptance has its penalties. We knew a couple once who had three children. The oldest was a girl, sweet-tempered, but very slow. It was clear that there was a degree of mental retardation, but the parents could not bring themselves to accept this. They tried to pretend that the child could do anything a normal child could do. They put her in schools where she could not keep up. They begged for performance that she could not give. They tried to rearrange the whole world to fit her limitations, meanwhile neglecting the emotional needs of their other children. They meant well; they thought they were doing right. But their lack of acceptance made life a burden for all of them.

Perhaps in the long run the beginning of wisdom lies here, in the simple admission that things are not always the way we would like them to be, that we ourselves are not so good or so kind or so hard-working or so unselfish as we would like to believe. And yet, we can say . . . *and yet* . . . with each sun that rises there is a new day, a new challenge, a new opportunity for doing better.

"O Lord," goes one variation of the old prayer, "grant me the strength to change things that need changing, the courage to accept things that cannot be changed, and the wisdom to know the difference."

People have called it the prayer of acceptance. They are right.

A wise housewife tells how to double the pleasure of giving . . . and receiving.

THE SECOND THANK YOU

Phyllis Amy Wohlfarth

For my birthday last year I fixed a celebration dinner and after dessert my children brought forth their presents. All were wrapped in a sun-burst of mismatched colors.

My husband Fred's gift was a gold lapel pin, but other than a quick, small thank you to him, I didn't have a chance to tell him how lovely it was.

The children were anxious for me to open their gifts and their voices buffeted me from all sides of the table. "Open this one, Mama," John shouted. "No, I'm the oldest," Janet announced, "she's going to open mine first."

So, putting aside the small pin box, I quickly gathered the children's gifts in front of me, shut my eyes and chose the first box to open. Slightly mollified, the children quieted down as I quickly slipped the wrapping from first one and then another, assuring each that his was a gift that I truly needed.

I'm ashamed to say it wasn't until the next Sunday that I thought to thank Fred again for his pretty pin. Dressing for church, I fastened it to the shoulder of my suit. It looked lovely against the smooth Italian knit. I smiled at Fred, "Thank you, Darling. It was very thoughtful."

His face had a sudden wistful look. "I'm sure glad! I didn't think you really liked it. . . ." Then, hesitatingly, he added, "My grandmother used to wear it to church. I've always admired it. I remember so clearly watching her pin it on, when we kids lived with her. I found it recently in a box of old things of hers in the attic. I thought of you at once."

As I rushed across the room to hug him, tears filled my eyes. I'd never have known how important the little gold pin was or how deeply Fred cared if I hadn't said that second thank you.

The first thank you on receipt of a gift is often perfunctory, but it is the second one, rendered after the gift has been savored, appreciated and put to use, that is the deeper expression of gratitude. I hope never to forget this second thank you.

A PRAYER FOR WORTHINESS

Almighty One, a single day in
My simple, average life must seem
A tiny grain
Among the sands of Your forever.
Help me, Lord, to make this
Little dot of time—
My today—
Something more than just
A particle of dust:
Let it be a speck of gold
Shimmering with a glint
Of Your greatness. Amen.

Terry Tucker Francis

Cancer had left me not handicapped, but uniquely qualified for a highly specialized service.

THE WAY BACK

Doris Knight

Her medical chart said that she was in her mid-30s, but framed by the four white corners of an overstuffed pillow and the high collar of a lacy pink bedjacket, her small face looked more like that of a lost and frightened little girl.

"Mind if I open the blinds?" I asked.

"Whatever," she responded listlessly.

I reached to pull the slender cord and the tiny hospital room was filled with the gray, wet light of a rainy day.

"My name is Doris Knight," I smiled, pulling up a chair. "Your doctor suggested that I stop by for a visit."

Still, she stared straight ahead.

"You see," I continued, "eight years ago, I had breast cancer, too, and the same kind of operation that you just had. Your doctor thought we might talk about it."

"I'd rather not," she said in a low voice.

And then, slowly, she turned to face me, eyes filled with fear and desperation. For a moment, I became lost in their bleak and empty blueness. Looking beyond her, I felt my mind spin back to a cold and drizzly Sunday morning in October, 1970 . . . .

Nestled in an easy chair by our warm and crackling fireplace, I was trying to find the strength to tackle an endless list of long-overdue thank-you notes. I'd been home from the hospital for three weeks, but it was the first time I'd been left alone.

My husband, John, was at church. Our 27-year-old son,

Steve, was a continent away, stationed at San Diego's U.S. Naval Air Station. My sister, who had flown in from out of state to be with me, had returned home to her family yesterday. And two days had passed since I'd heard from any of my friends—loyal neighbors, church members, and co-workers. Loneliness, until now held at bay, swiftly moved in to envelop me.

Equally disheartening was my extreme discomfort, weakness, and inability to do the simplest chores. Just getting into and out of my clothes had become a task of staggering proportions. Back zippers and hooks were impossible. I had spent the entire morning getting dressed.

And, I was depressed. Gone, now, were the blessed sedatives and pain killers that had made life bearable for the past few weeks. And gone with them was the spunky trooper, the incredibly cheerful optimist whose post-operative good humor had elicited choruses of "Gosh, isn't she wonderful," from friends and family. In her place was a 53-year-old scared and hurting woman.

How I longed for someone to talk to. Lurking in the darkest part of my soul were deep-seated fears too painful, too horrifying, for me to even admit. I knew I needed more than the expert medical counsel provided by my doctors. I needed more than the well-intentioned pep talks proffered by my friends. I even needed more than the unspoken love and compassion that showed in the eyes of my husband. What I needed was someone to *talk* to—a woman, perhaps, who had been through this whole ugly ordeal herself and who could understand firsthand what I was going through.

Reaching for a pen, I brushed against the corner of a slim volume of inspirational verse, a gift from a friend, that had been balanced on the arm of the chair. It clattered to the floor. Without thinking, I bent to pick it up. I moved too quickly. Searing pain, like nothing I'd ever felt before, pierced my chest.

"Why?" I sobbed. "Why?"

All the fears I had been trying to repress were unleashed at once with savage fury. A barrage of words, nightmarish and taunting, swirled behind my closed eyes. *Breast cancer . . . malignancy . . . mastectomy . . . prosthesis . . .*

I shuddered and pulled my robe more tightly around me, trying not to notice my oddly concave right side. I knew the pain was temporary; that the jolt I had just suffered was merely damaged nerve endings in the slow process of mending. I knew that with time and exercise I'd be able to resume near-normal use of my affected side. The doctors had said so. But the ugly scar would be with me forever.

Where, I wondered, *was God? How could He have let this happen to me?*

Never had I felt so helpless. I was especially worried about my career. After working for the telephone company for nearly half my life, a few months ago I had finally found my niche as staff editor for one of the company's state-wide magazines. It was rewarding, challenging and exciting work. But it was also a job that required strength, stamina—and self-confidence. I felt no longer qualified.

More than anything else, I was worried about my husband. John, who had been a tower of strength, had a severe health problem of his own. A victim of worsening emphysema, he soon would be facing early retirement and be needing me more than ever. In those fast approaching days, how would I, a crippled half-shell of a woman, ever be able to give him the love and support—emotional and physical—that he deserved?

If only I had someone to talk to. Surely other women who had survived breast cancer had suffered similar problems. I wondered how they coped. I wondered what they knew that I didn't.

Again, I reached down to pick up the fallen book. This time I moved slowly, deliberately, bending from the waist. The book had landed face-up. Picking it up, my eyes were drawn to two short lines of verse.

"This body is my house—it is not I.
Triumphant in this faith, I live and die."

The author was unknown, but the words seemed to have been written expressly for me. I reread the passage out loud. It had a strangely calming and soothing effect. Gradually, it occurred to me that perhaps this was God's way of talking to me. Perhaps this was His way of reassuring me that He had never deserted me; that He would continue to stay by my side. I recalled how, in the past, whenever He had seemingly closed one door in my life, He had always opened another. *Why,* I tried to cheer myself, *should this time be different?*

With this in mind, I resolved to stop worrying—at least for

the moment—and concentrate all my energy on getting better. After all, I reasoned, I should be thankful. I had survived.

Settling back in the deep, soft chair, I closed my eyes. Listening to the falling rain, the crackle and pop of burning embers, the steady, rhythmic ticking of the old clock in the hall, I slept.

Two months later, I was strong enough to return to my job. I worked hard. Most evenings I came home too exhausted to worry about anything more complicated than slipping into something loose and comfortable, fixing a simple supper for John and myself, and going to bed.

As time went on, the ragged scar healed, leveled out, and all but disappeared. I was fitted with a standard prosthesis and, to the casual observer, my appearance was absolutely normal. Still, a part of me died inside whenever I saw the curious eyes of those who knew about my operation travel to my chest. It was even worse when encountering someone who was obviously doing everything humanly possible *not* to look. It wasn't until some time later that I realized what a wide variety of highly sophisticated, natural-looking breast forms were available. I splurged on one of the more expensive ones. It was worth it. Before long, I was comfortable and confident wearing it all day long, and my self-image improved considerably.

It would be misleading to imply that every day thereafter was sunshine and roses. There were bad moments—undressing before a mirror with a too-critical eye, or waking in terror in the middle of the night when dark panic threatened like a storm cloud and unreasonable fears swept through me like a cold wind. John, however, was always there—there to hold me close and whisper words of reassurance and encouragement. Together, we prayed for continued strength; together we thanked the Lord for getting us this far.

One spring day, I received a letter from the American Cancer Society. "Mrs. Knight," it read, "your name is on our list as having recently undergone a mastectomy. Would you be interested in helping to organize a local Reach to Recovery chapter in your community for women who have undergone similar surgery?"

Through enclosed brochures, I learned that the Reach to Recovery Progam was founded in 1953 by Mrs. Terese Lasser, herself a mastectomy patient, and today has active chapters nationwide. The Program depends on trained volunteers, all former mastectomy patients, who call upon new patients and help them adjust to their various psychological, physical and cosmetic needs.

The planning meeting was scheduled to take place at Valdosta's Mental Health Office, 7 p.m., on a Wednesday night. Aching and tired from a full day at the office, I almost didn't attend.

It was a good thing I did. It was an evening of discoveries; most notably that my struggle with cancer had left me not handicapped, not less of a person—but uniquely qualified for a highly specialized service . . .

My gaze returned from the hospital window to the despondent young woman lying on the bed next to me. Her breakfast tray, I noticed, was untouched.

"I understand how you feel," I said softly. "Would it be all right if I just sat with you for a while?"

"If you like." She looked away and busied herself folding and refolding a green cloth napkin.

"I'm just so darn weak," she murmured. "I can't find the strength to do anything."

"Yes, I know."

"And I'm so sore, it hurts me to even move. Especially my elbow—here, where I've been leaning on it."

Ah, I thought. *Just the break I'd been waiting for.* I reached in my bag for a doughnut-shaped piece of foam rubber.

"Here," I said, "rest your elbow in this."

Accepting the soft cushion gratefully, she smiled. For the first time since our meeting, the veil of fear that had clouded her pretty blue eyes lifted.

"I really do understand how you're feeling," I repeated. "But there's no reason why, with time and effort, you can't be just as useful, productive, whole and happy a person as you were before your operation. I know how unbelievable that may sound at the moment, but it's true. And that's why I want you to feel free to talk."

From then on, our visit was easy. Question followed question, and soon we were engaged in lively conversation. Together we worked on the prescribed simple therapeutic exercises. She followed with interest as I walked my fingers up the wall and grinned ironically when I told her we referred to that one as "Climbing the Wall." Before we knew it, 45 minutes had flown by and it was time for me to leave.

"Now remember," I said, playfully wagging my finger. "Next time we meet, I want to hear you've been climbing the walls!"

She actually laughed out loud.

And in that sound was sheer joy and relief—for both of us. Her laughter seemed to travel back in time to soothe my own pain of eight years ago when I, like she, had so desperately needed someone to talk to. In a sudden flash of insight, I better understood the wonder of God's working in our lives; how He, in His own time and ultimate wisdom, can use the most hopeless and tragic human conditions for eventual good.

It had stopped raining and yellow sunlight streamed in through the open blinds. As I gathered my bag and coat, I couldn't recall when I'd ever been happier.

POSTURES BEFORE GOD

Let us learn how to
kneel *before the Lord for strength;*
stand *before Him to praise His name;*
sit *before Him for His loving counsel.*

Source unknown

YOUR SPIRITUAL WORKSHOP

WHAT THANKSGIVING CAN DO FOR YOU

A three-step program designed to heighten your appreciation of life.

If we could extend the mood of thanksgiving to the entire year, would we be a happier, more out-going people? Better friends and neighbors? Would we develop a stronger faith? Grow closer to God? This Spiritual Workshop is presented in the belief that the answer to all the above questions is YES.

In the pages that follow are three specific suggestions as to *what you can do* to increase your flow of thanksgiving. We suggest that you undertake this workshop as an experiment and continue it to Thanksgiving Day. Then evaluate any difference it has made in your life.

Guideposts editors believe that the person who has developed a natural and instinctive thankfulness has made a crucial breakthrough in his search for a oneness with his fellowman and God.

. Every Day, Surprise Someone With A "Thank You."

Surprise is the key here and rules out the thanks anyone could expect from you in the conventional course of things. There is a children's book used in many nursery schools which shows a little boy visiting a farm to thank the cow for the milk he had for breakfast. Then he goes to the hen house to thank the chickens for his eggs; he thanks a sheep for his warm bathrobe and so forth. The idea, of course, is to help children become aware of the bigger world on which their small daily rounds depend.

Most adults would balk at thanking animals whose gifts are unintentional, but all of us could use thanks as a door to awareness of much that we take for granted. We have various services delivered to our homes without ever considering a word to show our appreciation. How long has it been since you thanked the mailman, milkman, or newspaper boy for their reliability or punctualness? Is there a certain radio program or newspaper column that's always part of breakfast? These people don't know unless you tell them the part they play in your life. If you receive over-ripe fruit do you complain to your grocer? Do you likewise tell him if it was especially delicious?

Opportunities to surprise people with thanks present themselves all day long. In his book *Try Giving Yourself Away* David Dunn suggests "second thanks" as a way of adding surprise even to conventional thank you situations. Whenever, for example, he receives a book, he thanks the giver at once. Then when he finishes it—perhaps many months later—he writes again, mentioning specific ways in which the book has been helpful to him. He has found he can apply this technique to any kind of gift.

Most of the time you will never know what effect your thanks have on the recipient—though you can be sure that occasionally they will be more important than you dream.

The story is told of a housewife who came across an old geography book while cleaning in her attic. As she leafed through its dusty pages, the woman remembered the spinster teacher who had taught the course, telling stimulating stories which painted indelible pictures of far away places in the minds of her young students. The housewife, who loved to visit new lands, loved to read about the people and customs of other countries, realized that the seed had been planted by this teacher. Taking the book to her desk, she wrote a note thanking the teacher for "doing more than teaching geography." A short time later, an answer came to the housewife. The teacher, since retired, wrote in scrawling letters, telltale of her age, "You are the first student in all my years of teaching who ever said thank you."

Though response to your efforts is unpredictable, the effect on your own life is certain. You will be training yourself day by day in seeking out the good and praiseworthy around you, rather than the more attention-catching evil and annoying things.

These results will not come about overnight, but they will come with persistence. The important thing is not to let a single day slip by without surprising someone with a thank you.

Every Day, Thank God For Something You Have Never Until Now Thanked Him For.

Thankfulness toward other people is, of course, both a preparation for and an indication of our thankfulness to God. It is probably easier to develop a sense of gratitude to other human beings just because their goodness to us is of necessity limited and specific. But from God "all blessings flow"—and in that "all" we run the risk of losing sight of the individual instances around which human emotion centers.

It is good to start any prayer of thanksgiving to God with some statement of overall indebtedness: As the Book of Common Prayer states it, "For our creation, preservation, and all the blessings of this life." But also try to add each day some different, perhaps very tiny blessing for which you are grateful.

The day will probably suggest its own specific. The gift of sight on an autumn morning, apples at cider time, warm clothes as days grow colder. The discipline of thanking God for a different blessing each day doubtless could be continued for a lifetime without repeating.

One family took turns around the dinner table, a different child returning thanks each evening. When the four-year-old's turn came his grace was, "Thank You, God, for wallpaper." The mother wrote Guideposts that she has enjoyed wallpaper more ever since.

Your thanks always will not be confined to little things, of course. There will be days when a Christian is overwhelmed by the magnitude of Christ's sacrifice for him and can thank God for nothing less.

One of the saddest stories in the Gospels is Christ's healing of the 10 lepers. On their way to the priests' house where Jesus had sent them, they discovered what had happened.

One of them, St. Luke records, *finding himself cured, turned back praising God aloud. He threw himself down at Jesus' feet and thanked him. . . .*

*At this Jesus said: 'Were not all 10 cleansed? The other nine, where are they?'**

All 10 had been recipients of a miracle, but in only one was the thanksgiving faculty so developed that at the moment of great elation he knew both where credit was due and how to express it.

3. Every Day, Thank God For Something About Which You Now Are Not Happy.

This is both the hardest exercise in thanksgiving and the one that comes closest to the heart of the spiritual life. To the oppressed Ephesians an imprisoned Paul wrote, *In the Name of our Lord Jesus Christ give thanks every day for everything to our God and Father.***

Clearly, this kind of thanksgiving goes deeper than simple thanks rendered for good received. We commonly think of thanksgiving as following an action of God's. But what if it also works the other way? What if an attitude of thanksgiving for *everything* that comes to us is a first step in getting our hearts and minds in line with God's purposes and making us open to His goodness that flows through everything?

Someone has called thanking God for seemingly bad events and circumstances the first step of faith in *action.* If you can stand before a financial setback, a disappointment, even death itself, and thank God for what in His hands these circumstances will become, you are acting out your conviction that He can bring good when you yourself do not see it.

The story of Joseph is certainly one of the best illustrations of this. He could not understand his brothers selling him into slavery or why he should be cast into prison, but Joseph was faithful unto God and in retrospect he told his

---

*St. Luke 17: 12-19 New English Bible

**Romans 8:28 New English Bible

brothers, *You thought evil against me, but God meant it unto good.* What seemed to be a terrible injustice did, in fact, become a great blessing in Joseph's life. If *All things work together for good to them that love God*, we can in confidence give thanks for *all* things.

During this experiment between now and Thanksgiving keep a day-by-day record of the new ways you have discovered to show appreciation to both man and God. Review your experiences often. They might suggest follow-up actions.

In particular, record the unwelcome circumstances for which you have, in faith, given thanks. Leave space next to these for insights as they come. One month or one year, or even one lifetime may not be long enough to watch God bring to completion each event with which you have trusted Him, but the practice of thanksgiving will bring about increased faith.

The Unlimited Power of Prayer

LORD, GIVE ME COMPASSION

Chapter 7

Sometimes it is so very difficult to feel concern for others—to even see a need—when you are overwhelmed by your own problems. So, we ask you, pray for compassion. Ask God to open your heart to those around you.

The gifts of loving are God-given. He will grant them to you. The people in these stories did not have special gifts. They are just like you. But they asked God to use them so that His love could be shared with others.

St. Francis prayed, *"Lord, make me an instrument of your peace."* Pray for compassion so that you, too, can be God's instrument of peace.

The doctors gave the little girl practically no hope. But the Sisters insisted, "Give her to us!"

AN ANGEL NAMED MARIA

Elizabeth Sherrill

"There was a baby born here two weeks ago that no one knows what to do with," the doctor said into the telephone.

He went on to explain that the infant was a vegetable: a hydrocephalic without sight or hearing or any human potential. The mother had disappeared from the hospital after seeing it and the state had no provision for handicapped children under the age of six.

"It will never live that long," the doctor's voice continued hastily. "At the outside it might live six months. Meanwhile there is the problem of care. . . . "

"Bring us the baby," answered the voice at the other end of the line. It belonged to Sister Marie Patrice, the nun in charge of the day-nursery which the Sisters of Mercy ran for working mothers in the Charlotte, North Carolina, area.

Sister Patrice was at the cottage door when a car pulled into the driveway that afternoon. The doctor carried a bundle in, then pulled aside the hospital blanket for the nun to see. For a moment she could make no sense of the two shapes before her. Then she realized that one was an enormous head; the other, where a back should have been, a tumor the size of the head. Stumps hung where there should have been legs and feet: Only the little arms and hands were properly formed.

Sister Patrice stretched out her arms. "Give her to us," she said.

And so another baby joined the nursery—a baby for whom nobody called when the day was over. A "vegetable" was the last thing she made the Sisters think of, for she cried constantly as though in pain. Whenever they picked her up, however, the crying stopped. So the Sisters began carrying her about with them while they looked after the other babies and while they ate and went to chapel and even while they slept.

Six months came and went. The baby they had baptized "Maria" grew so heavy that the nuns had to pass her more often from one pair of arms to another. But she would not startle at a noise, nor blink when a hand was passed before her eyes. Never once in all those months had she given a hint of awareness.

And then one day as Sister Patrice rocked her in the nursery playroom, the unbelievable happened.

"She smiled!" the Sister cried. "Maria smiled at me!"

Sister Patrice was the only one that day to see the smile. But a few days later another nun saw it, and then another, until the whole convent glowed with Maria's smile.

After that, the weeks and months sped by as the Sisters discovered first one talent, then another, in the baby that had no potential. They plunked the nursery piano and discovered that Maria had hearing. They placed her hands on the light switch just inside the cottage door and discovered that she had the muscle control to turn it on and off herself.

She was playing this favorite game one winter afternoon when she was almost two, making the room bright and then dark again while one of the Sisters held her up to the switch, when suddenly she turned to stare at the bulb burning in the ceiling. Her lips parted.

"Light!" said Maria.

As a first word it could not have been better chosen. For it seemed to the Sisters that with it came light from God about this child, that the next step to be taken in faith was removal of the tumor that dwarfed the little body on which it grew.

The surgeon they consulted was dubious. Without the tumor, he reasoned, all the excess fluid might settle in the head, distending it still further and hastening the inevitable death.

But the Sisters had glimpsed the hope that is stronger

than reason. The tumor was removed and the very reverse of the doctor's fear occurred. Instead of gaining fluid, the head began to drain. Over a period of two years it shrank nine inches until, as Maria herself grew, it looked very nearly normal. They were wonderful years. The Sisters bought a tiny wheelchair that Maria herself could roll with her strong arms and hands. They made a swing for her and a play table and a special seat in the chapel.

Most important, to Maria, they bought her shoes. As other children dream of being ballerinas, Maria dreamed of wearing shoes. She would never walk, but the Sisters understood that shoes are for more than mere transportation. And so they took her back to the surgeon, and he shaped a place on the unformed legs for shoes to go.

But meanwhile great changes had come to the little cottage on the convent grounds. As word got around that the Sisters were sheltering a defective child, another such infant was brought to them. Then another, and another. These children took more time than normal babies. Some, like Maria, had to be held constantly. Others went into spasms when touched. Some had to be tube fed, some needed oxygen.

The Sisters worked around the clock and still the babies kept coming, from all over the state and far beyond: the mongoloid, the microcephalic, the palsied. And to the Sisters, God's light had grown blindingly clear. There were other nurseries around Charlotte for normal children. For these injured ones, there was nowhere else.

I went to visit Holy Angels Nursery wondering how a home that held only deformed babies would affect me. A curly-haired little girl met me at the door, the ruffles of her starched blue dress concealing the arms of a wheelchair. "I'm very pleased to meet you," she said politely, "do you like my shoes?"

Of course it was Maria. Her shoes were white, with little bells on them and lace around the top, and I told her truthfully that they were gorgeous. Maria and Sister Patrice led me through the sunny new home built with gifts from Protestants, Jews and Catholics all over the country. And as we walked from room to room, misgiving gave way to a feeling I could not name. Baby blue cribs with new toys in them lined walls hung with Mother Goose scenes. Every baby girl wore a pretty dress, every boy a crisp romper, no two alike. Volunteers from a nearby girls' school crooned to babies in rocking chairs around the room. It was like stepping into the private nursery of a treasured only child—multiplied by dozens.

I believe they were each an only child to Sister Patrice as she recounted the life and death struggle waged over each crib. "We were so worried about Johnny last week, but penicillin is helping." "I did 80 miles an hour getting Ellen to the hospital Thursday. The police gave me two motorcycles, and the convulsion was halted in time." "The doctors don't give George another month. But—" squeezing the tiny hand, "we're going to fool them, aren't we, George?"

On we went, crib after crib—67 of them— and in each one, Sister's favorite child. I saw Jewish babies, Protestants, Catholics, Negroes and whites, children of architects and mill hands, doctors and migrant workers. The only thing I didn't see was a secondhand toy or a threadbare blanket. "Most of them can't see, you know," said the Sister. "That's why it's up to us to be sure they have only pretty things."

We reached the last room and I realized what it was I had been feeling. In each crib Sister Patrice had made me see a person, an individual unique in all creation, a human soul of infinite worth. When I told her so she beamed.

"Oh, yes!" she said. "And do you know what the greatest moment of all is? When this person leaps free at last from his poor, hurt body!"

She had been at the cribside each time a baby died, she said. "God tells me when He is taking one of them. And then this little person stands suddenly free, whole and straight, more beautiful than you dreamed. It's only an instant, you know, for these babies fly straight to the heart of God."

I stared at the Sister, at the bottles of blood plasma behind her, the oxygen tents, the rows of drugs. I hardly knew how to phrase the question that was in my mind.

"Why struggle then to keep them here as long as we can?" she asked for me. She ran her hand through the gold-brown curls that make a halo of Maria's head.

"God has all the bright angels of heaven for His joy," she said gently. "We struggling servants of His here below—we need angels too."

Papa wasn't concerned about the stolen money. His heart reached out to the man who, in one foolish moment, was ruining his life.

PAPA AND THE BANK ROBBER

Louise DeGroot

I wonder sometimes if we really know what it means to be a good neighbor today. Every time I get irritated at what a family does down the street, I scold myself and think back through the years to that incredible experience when my father risked his life to save a neighbor—who was a thief.

We then lived in Red Wing, Minnesota, and my father was a lawyer. I recall so vividly his iron-gray hair, deep blue eyes, wide square shoulders—and the way he always kissed me when saying hello or good-bye. He was strong, loved people and his favorite saying was, "A man's most priceless possession is his good reputation." He fought for this principle in court many times—often for no fee.

Across the street from us lived the Edwardses in a house somewhat nicer than ours. They had three children, as our parents did, and Mrs. Edwards dressed them beautifully.

Mr. Edwards traveled a lot and worked hard and people said the family lived beyond its means, something that was frowned on in those days. But our parents, who neither gossiped nor permitted us to listen to gossip, called the Edwardses "nice people who do the best they can."

Then late one winter day the unbelievable happened.

Papa was looking out the window of his law office at the snow and ice that had blanketed the town. Then, down the street, he saw Mr. Edwards suddenly dart from the bank and break into a run. Papa, curious, closed his office and joined the crowd that had begun milling around the bank.

Don Edwards had robbed the bank. Armed and desperate, he'd escaped with thousands of dollars before anyone could stop him.

The crowd began to mutter. Edwards had stolen the town's money. Bank deposits were not insured then, and for many the robbery could spell ruin if the bank failed.

But Papa wasn't concerned about the stolen money. His heart reached out instead to Don Edwards, who in one foolish moment was ruining his life. Sick to his soul, Papa walked as fast as he could the snowy mile to our kitchen door.

Mama couldn't believe the news about Mr. Edwards—nor could she believe what Papa proposed to do next. "Go after him?" she gasped. "Philamon Ballou Green, you'll do no such thing. The man has lost his reason and he has a gun. Besides, you'll never find him."

Papa's voice sounded calm and natural, but his blue eyes glowed when he turned to Mama. "Poor Edwards has made a terrible mistake," he said. "I must try to help him."

Then he patted Mama, kissed me and went to the barn to hitch up the sleigh. With a crack of the whip he was off.

It was quite obvious to Papa that Edwards had fled by horsedrawn sleigh in but one direction—across the frozen river. You'd have to see the great Mississippi River locked in its northern cold to imagine what Papa faced. As he started out across the ice floor, cruel, cutting winds whipped at Papa and the horses. For just an instant, Papa must have asked himself, "Why am I doing this?"

As the sleigh cut across the ice, however, he needed all his strength and determination. For he wasn't sure that strong ice covered *all* the river's width. And what about the tiny islands with their growth of stubby trees and bushes? Frozen roots might trip a horse, and stiff branches could impale a man. Even barring encounters with obstacles, or a plunge into icy waters, how long could the horses survive the frightful cold?

As he did all his life, Papa put aside his fears and trusted in his God.

"Only three miles," Papa repeated half to himself, half to God. "Only three miles across the river, Lord, or maybe four. Protect the horses, Lord,and lead us to Don Edwards."

Directly across the broad part of the river was a small

town. There was a hotel there. Papa reasoned that Edwards would head for the hotel that night, then resume his flight later.

Papa reasoned right, but Don Edwards never reached the town. After what must have seemed like hours, Papa's horses suddenly stopped in their tracks. The light of the moon shone on the figure of a man directly ahead. He was standing upright near the river bank, exhausted, unable to climb over the brink. His sleigh was nowhere to be seen.

Papa never told me what happened at this point, but from a fact here and a word there, it isn't hard to figure it out. My father drove up to Edwards and looked into the face of a man in wild despair. "We're going home, Edwards," he said quietly.

"No, no," the nearly frozen man mumbled. He fumbled for his gun with desperate, pawing hands.

Papa took him firmly by the arm and propelled him into the sleigh. Then my father swung himself in beside Edwards, cracked the whip and headed the horses home.

While the horses stumbled onward, feeling their own way, Papa threw an arm around the fugitive who was huddled beside him, now trembling with terror and cold. Perhaps it was Papa's body heat, perhaps the ardor of his continuous spoken prayers, which revived and calmed Edwards. Miraculously, men and horses arrived home safely.

Our town greeted news of Papa's journey with wildest adulation.

But Papa wasn't interested in playing the hero role. He was concerned only about the human beings involved: Edwards, his wife and three children. First, the stolen money was returned. Then Edwards faced court action and was sentenced to a two-year jail term.

When his neighbor had served his time, Papa helped him get a job so that he could pay off his debts. The family stayed together and eventually regained a respected place in the community. No one ever dared look down on Edwards—at least not with Papa around. And I'm sure Edwards would have given his life for my father, he was so grateful.

As a lawyer, Papa saw much of the seamy side of life. But up to the day of his death, he never stopped looking for God in every single person he met.

As he boarded the plane he had only one thought in mind: sleep. But God had another flight plan for him.

THE VACANT SEAT

Don Mott

"Good morning, sir, it is 4:30 a.m.," the cheery voice of the hotel operator broke into my dreams. As I stumbled to my feet I think I had never been so sleepy:This speaking tour meant a different town each day, long distances between.

At the airport I was the first person aboard the plane. As I dropped into a seat next to the window I repeated almost mechanically the prayer I always say when traveling, "Lord, if there is anybody on this plane You want me to talk to, let him take the seat beside me."

The other window seats filled up rapidly, then the aisle seats. The one next to me remained empty. At last the plane door was closed, the steps rolled away and we were bumping over the ground to the runway. With a sigh of gratitude I let my seat back as far as it would go, fastened my seat belt, and shut my eyes.

"Lord," I said, "I'm going to sleep from here to Chicago." But God had another flight plan.

It was at that moment that I felt someone sit down beside me. I opened my eyes. It was the stewardess, buckling into a belt for take-off. I was about to close my eyes again when I saw that she looked quite upset.

"What's the matter?" I whispered.

She gave me a startled look. "My goodness, does it show?"

Reluctantly I let my seat straighten up. "I'm afraid it does," I said.

The young woman didn't speak again until we were airborne. At last she said, "The man I was going with has dropped me. I think he ran off with another woman."

"Well," I said, "why don't you thank the Lord and get yourself a good man?"

For the first time she looked straight at me. "I want to talk to you," she said. "But first I have to get the tea and coffee orders."

When she sat down again after serving us, she had apparently looked up my name because she said, "Mr. Mott, what does a girl do when she's going to become a mother and she's unmarried?"

"You tell me," I said.

"I had an operation." Her voice was very small. "But I know now it was wrong. I feel like a murderer and have considered killing myself. That's why I'm going to a psychiatrist."

I was trying to choose words to say to her when all at once I realized that they had already been chosen for me.

"Here in my briefcase I have a copy of a prayer that a man prayed who was guilty of the same two sins that are haunting you," I told her. "This man had committed adultery and he had committed murder. And yet as a result of this prayer, God forgave him. He cleaned him inside and out and made him as innocent as the day he was born."

She said, "I sure would like to read that prayer."

I opened my briefcase, took out my Bible and for the rest of the flight she and I studied the 51st Psalm, David's prayer. I explained to her that if she would confess her sins to God, hiding nothing, but just surrendering everything, He would give her in place of her old life, the life of His Son Jesus Christ.

At last she asked me, "When will all this happen?"

"Before we get to Chicago if you ask Him."

"I don't know how to ask," she said. "Will you help me?"

And there, before the plane descended over Chicago, we bowed our heads and she prayed, repeating after me words that I believe she meant from her heart.

"Oh God, I have sinned. I confess my sin. I pray that You will forgive me. Thank you that Jesus died on the cross for sinners like me. I now accept Him as my Saviour. Come into my heart, Lord Jesus, and make me a new creature."

There were tears of joy glistening in her eyes as she stood

up. I followed her with my eyes as she walked back to her hostess station. And as I did I noticed every seat on that entire plane—with the single exception of the one beside me—was occupied.

The plane came to a stop. The aisle filled with people and coats and briefcases, but I sat still. I was remembering that I had been the very first one aboard, that every one of these people had had to decide against taking this seat.

I was reflecting what a serious transaction prayer is, even such a sleepy, half-grudging prayer as mine had been this morning. I was thinking that when we ask God to use us, we mustn't afterwards be surprised when He does.

Lord, make me an instrument of your peace
Where there is hatred . . . let me sow love.
Where there is injury . . . pardon.
Where there is doubt . . . faith.
Where there is despair . . . hope.
Where there is darkness, light.
Where there is sadness . . . joy.

Oh Divine Master, grant that I may not so much seek
To be consoled . . . as to console,
To be understood . . . as to understand,
To be loved . . . as to love,
FOR
It is in giving . . . that we receive,
It is in pardoning, that we are pardoned,
It is in dying . . . that we are born to eternal life.

St. Francis

I was the counselor, but he taught me a very special lesson that summer.

ALL BECAUSE OF MARK

Jeff Japinga

"Hey, Uncle Jeff! Aren't we supposed to be getting ready for the service now?"

The 12-year-old's voice was shrill. It interrupted my first peaceful moment all week. I was lying on the beach by a quiet shore of Lake Michigan. I wished the kid would just disappear. Why did I have to get stuck with him?

"No, Mark," I said, an exasperated look crossing my face. "I think we still have a half hour of free time left . . . Oh, come on, we'll go." I got up reluctantly.

People had always told me being a counselor at a Christian camp would be fun. You were outdoors all summer. You got paid to play games and swim. You had the opportunity to present Christ to junior high and high schoolers. It seemed like a crime to call it a job.

Now it just seemed like a crime against me.

This seventh week of summer started out being a special challenge. "Mark is going to be in your cabin this week," I was told Monday morning. I felt a tremor of uncertainty because I knew what a special person Mark was.

Mark had cancer.

It was supposed to be a secret. He wanted to be treated just like any other camper that week. It was difficult, of course. His face was puffed and his eyes nearly swollen shut—the effects of his disease. He used crutches to support his weakened knee joints.

The crutches gave us a chance to cover up the real situation. "Mark twisted his knee, and has to use crutches until it heals," I would explain, giving Mark a grin. "That's right," he'd say quickly, "but it will be better soon."

We almost began to believe it ourselves.

But Mark's problem created a conflict for me with the group. How much time and attention could I give him? He was a very special kind of guy, and deserved every moment I could spare. But what about the other 14 boys in the cabin? It really wouldn't be fair to neglect them. And there were 200 other campers that week who deserved some of my time.

It was simply impossible to do it all. Mark's weakened joints made running, jumping and many other activities impossible. He was not eager to participate, fearing more pain and injury, or just embarrassment. Most of the boys in the cabin agreed, saying Mark wasn't good enough. They didn't want our team to lose in competition. And I was caught in the middle, wanting Mark to participate as much as possible without risking injury to his fragile body and spirit.

And so it went. If I sat with Mark and played checkers, or watched the sailboats scamper across Lake Michigan, I became very uneasy. I wondered what the others were doing, picturing myself with them on the softball field or in the pool. But if I was with the rest of the boys, I couldn't enjoy myself. My thoughts would quickly swing back to Mark.

I wasn't looking forward to each day anymore that week. The morning wake-up horn sounded like a foghorn, warning of gloom ahead. The sparkling sunsets didn't hold the beautiful qualities they once had; they now served only as a countdown to the weekend.

"Lord, help me with my attitude," I would ask, feeling guilty. "Please don't let me get in the way of these kids. After all, it's their week, not mine." And for a while I felt better, until I was double-jumped by Mark in checkers or heard the joyous screams from the pool. I was angry with myself and my selfishness, and my personal anger and frustration began spilling over in the form of harsh words directed at the kids. I knew that if I didn't snap out of this soon, their whole vacation might be ruined.

The answer, I thought, would have been to tell everyone that Mark had cancer. Then all the boys would play checkers with him, and quit being angry if he couldn't run or play ball. And they would feel sorry for me, too, and get off my back.

But I couldn't do that. I had promised.

Mark was too tired to go to our special Thursday night consecration service, and another boy in the cabin was too stubborn. So there I sat inside that darkened cabin while my insides turned into a pressure cooker. I had been so proud of my faith when the summer began. I had thought I could handle any situation. And now, a problem I couldn't solve had rendered all those Bible verses and youth group discussions useless.

Finally, the service was over, the boys were back in the cabin and all was quiet. I sat in a folding chair under the tall pines outside our cabin, wondering what I could do to improve my attitude. One boy came out to ask me some questions about the service, and although I answered him as best I could, my heart wasn't in it.

Then I saw Mark. He hobbled out the door, not using his crutches. "Can I talk with you?" he asked solemnly.

"Sure," I answered, trying to figure out what was coming.

"You know," Mark said, "this has really been a great week for me. I just love the lake, and all the trees, the beach, but especially the people. I wish I didn't have to leave at the end of the week, but I suppose that's impossible."

He went on, telling me about his house, his family, his Sunday school, his grin widening with every word. How he had personally accepted Christ on Mother's Day, how being a Christian was really the most fun of all. Then came the zinger. "Are you going to be here next year when I come back? I really hope so. We've had so much fun this week . . . I like you a lot. You're a great counselor," he said.

I was stunned—remembering my bad mood all that week. "Of course, I'll be looking forward to it," I fumbled. Mark smiled even wider, then got up and started limping back to the cabin.

I sat there, numbly. Me, a great counselor? *Mark never complains about the pain*, I thought, *even though I'm sure it's pretty bad. He just talks about those sunsets, about nature, people, about God, about coming back . . . He simply loves life, and everything it brings him.* I, on the contrary, had spent my time resenting the small frustrations the week brought me. If I were a counselor, I was not one in the mold of Jesus, The Counselor.

I cried a few tears on that lonely August night. Tears for

Mark, that such a young and beautiful person had to bear such a tremendous burden. And tears for myself. I had been so rooted in my own petty concerns that I had missed the beauty of life and the presence of God . . . in Mark.

The summer was easy from that minute on. The workload seemed lighter, the campers friendlier, the counselors even better friends, my faith stronger. Mark and I shared the lake, the woods, the worship together during his final days at camp.

Mark didn't come back the next summer; he never will. He will never see the diamond glitter of another Lake Michigan sunset. But I will. And I will try to see them as Mark did, appreciating every moment—good or bad—for what it really is . . . God's wonderful creation.

The rest of my life will be richer, too. All because of a 12-year-old boy who didn't let his problems pinion his soaring spirit or break his gallant heart.

YOU PRAYED FOR ME

You did not know my need,
Or that my heart was sore, indeed.
And that I had a fear I could not quell
And so you prayed for me.
And as your prayer did soar
God did, in love, on me a blessing pour
The day you prayed for me.

Rosina Stallman

Some helpful hints on . . .

HOW TO HANDLE A MEAN PERSON

Norman Vincent Peale

The letter, signed "Heather," had no return address. From her handwriting, I judged Heather to be 11 or 12, and she was a friendly young lady because she had cut out a paper heart and pasted it on the envelope. But Heather had a problem; evidently someone was giving her a hard time. "Dr. Peale," she wrote plaintively, "how do you handle a mean person?"

Well, that's a question people of all ages ask me often. So here are some of the answers I usually give, and if Heather happens to read them here in Guideposts, I hope they may be of help to her.

First, if someone is being unkind to you, I think it's important to distinguish between a mean person and a person acting in a mean manner. Few people are fundamentally mean. But something can cause a person who is not fundamentally mean to display a mean streak.

Instead of reacting with anger or hurt feelings, it's much better to adopt a cool, dispassionate, analytical attitude. Study the person calmly. Ask yourself the reason why he or she is being mean.

Such an objective attitude on your part will begin to neutralize the hostility the other person is displaying. It will show that you care about him or her as a human being, that you're putting your own feelings and emotions last. This will create an atmosphere in which meanness is reduced.

I once worked with a most difficult man whose irascibility was a problem for all his associates. Everyone was aware of his ability, but none was spared his sarcasm and bitter tongue. He could be, and often was, extraordinarily mean. Although it was difficult, I tried to adopt the calm, dispassionate attitude I just mentioned. For a long time it seemed to do no good.

But finally long patience paid off. One day this man suddenly appeared at my office and announced that he wanted to talk. "All I want you to do is listen to me," he said. "I can't hold it inside of me any longer or I will explode." He talked for an hour or more about a domestic situation that was causing him great emotional pain. At the end he thanked me and went away. The matter was never mentioned again. But somehow there gradually came about in this man a quieter, more controlled attitude. One night several years later he lay down to sleep and never awakened. But later his secretary sent me a sealed handwritten note. It said simply, "Thanks for understanding and bearing with me. You helped me a lot." So try to remember that many outwardly mean people are made so by the relentless pressure of some secret pain.

Another thing to do if someone seems to be treating you badly is examine your own treatment of him. Have you said or done something to anger him? Have you been overly critical or judgmental? Have you withheld deserved praise?

I have known cases where people seemed mean because they were starved for recognition. Some years ago, for example, an American mining expert was asked to look into conditions in a coal mine in Britain where there was a lot of friction. While he was in the mine, a minor mishap occurred; a section of the roof of one of the tunnels caved in. No one was hurt. The foreman organized a crew of workmen and repaired the damage quickly. "That was an excellent repair job," the American said to the foreman. "You should really be proud of yourself and your men." The foreman looked at him for a really long time. Finally he said, "I've worked in this mine for forty years. Those are the first words of praise or appreciation I ever heard." No wonder the workers seemed surly and production in that mine was low!

Shyness can often be disguised as meanness, too. A sense of inferiority, a feeling of personal inadequacy, can cause an individual to retreat behind a personality barrier that people interpret as mean and harsh. Actually, such gruffness is a psychological protective device; such "mean" people are often troubled people who wear the mask of meanness in order to ward off more trouble.

Sometimes it's possible to get past that mask if you can just find some special path to a better relationship. I was once a reporter for a daily newspaper in a small city. My regular duties required a visit to a police sergeant for police blotter news. This man had a massive face overwritten by a perpetual scowl. When he sat at a desk, his huge body overflowed his chair. His voice was a fierce growl and his blue eyes were ice-cold. To a timid young reporter, he was terrifying. I was sure that he did not like me, and that was unfortunate, because there was no other source for police news at all.

Then one day I met a young couple who had an adorable little girl. They happened to tell me that she was the granddaughter of the tough old police sergeant, and that this child could twist the old boy around her little finger.

So that night when I called at the police station to be growled at by the ogre I said, "Sergeant, I met your daughter and her husband today, and little Jennie. Believe me, that little girl is a honey. I've never seen anyone sweeter."

He stared, then a big smile (first one I'd ever seen) spread across his face. The gruff voice was still there. But the sergeant and I were friends ever after. He wasn't so mean after all—once I found the key to his big, old loving heart.

The last suggestion I make to people who find themselves dealing with a mean person is simply this: pray for them. Ask God to help them resolve the problem that is pressuring them into what seems like meanness. I know it's not easy to pray for someone who is treating you badly. But that is what Jesus Christ Himself told us to do. "Bless them that curse you," He said, "and pray for them which despitefully use you." (Luke 6:28)

When you have to handle a mean person, that's the best and wisest solution of all.

Gideon. Such a strong name for a troubled child. He had so very far to go and needed so much help.

DON'T SMASH THE RUBBER ELEPHANTS

Marilyn Cram Donahue

Thus says the Lord God: "I myself will take a sprig from the lofty top of the cedar, and will set it out; I will break off from the topmost of its young twigs a tender one, and I myself will plant it upon a high and lofty mountain . . . that it may bring forth boughs and bear fruit, and become a noble cedar . . . "

(Ezekiel 17:22-23 RSV)

Gideon was late to class. He arrived without a word of apology, slamming the door behind him. Noisily, he took his seat in the front row, making a production of opening and closing his desk, dropping his spelling book and commenting in an undertone to anyone who wanted to listen. Never once, however, did he raise his eyes, even to acknowledge that there was a strange teacher in the front of the room.

I placed a work sheet on the corner of his desk, marked him tardy, and went on explaining the assignment. It had looked like the beginning of a good day. Substitute teachers learn to pick up positive or negative vibrations within the first ten minutes, and the feelings I received from these fifth graders had been good ones.

Even when Gideon put his head under the lift-up desk top and stayed there for some time, I didn't sense any trouble. I would give him a few more minutes to settle down, for he really wasn't disturbing anyone. The entire class seemed to have tuned him out. No one watched him. No one responded to his mutterings. I should have recognized the signals: Gideon was not part of their world.

I was beginning to lose patience when, after the fourth request, he finally emerged from his desk with a broken pencil in one dirty hand and a bunch of strange-looking objects in the other. At first I thought they were plastic animals until I saw the round holes in the bottoms. They were rubber erasers . . . the kind that make cheap prizes at Halloween carnivals. Each of the brightly colored erasers was shaped like a little elephant. Gideon lined them up on the desk: red, blue, green, yellow. Then he began to move them around, changing places and positions. The work sheet was forgotten, the broken pencil still unsharpened.

"Gideon," I said, "it's time to get to work." He glanced up at me and pulled the paper in front of him. Then he looked at the pencil and sighed. "Perhaps it will write better if you sharpen it," I suggested.

I caught the defiance in his eyes. And there was something else that should have made me walk with velvet slippers. It was a look of unutterable tiredness, the expression of a child who has gone without sleep. But other classroom duties called me, and I put it out of my mind.

When I looked in Gideon's direction again, the pencil was sharpened, but the paper was still untouched. He was rearranging his rubber elephants and muttering softly to himself. I held out my hand. "I'll keep those until you finish your work," I said.

Usually children hand over their playthings, a little grudgingly, but with no real ill will. They know they'll be returned at recess. Gideon just stared. I walked over to his desk and reached for an elephant.

"Don't touch that," he said. His voice was perfectly calm.

So was mine. "You're not doing your work," I explained. "Playthings are for playtime." I started to pick one up, but his hand was over mine like a flash, his fingernails digging into my skin.

"Leave it!" he screamed.

I couldn't have left it if I'd tried. His grip was fierce, and his hands were strong. There was a strange hush in the classroom. I felt sure that something like this must have happened before. Then I struck the spark that ignited the bomb. I reached out my free hand and put it on Gideon's shoulder.

I thought I heard him growl deep in his throat. Then he was on his feet. He pulled back his arm and swung at me, fist clenched, muscles straining.

I ducked in time and caught the blow on my shoulder. Even then, it was enough to unbalance me. He stood there trembling, cramming all four elephants into his torn pocket. "They're mine!" he shouted.

I pointed at the door. There was only one thing I was glad of at that moment. The principal's office was just across the yard, and I could make sure that Gideon went there. We walked rapidly across the blacktop. I reached once for his arm. "Don't touch me!" he shrilled. And I didn't.

The secretary nodded when she saw him coming. "He's hyperactive," she announced, as if that explained the problems of the world. "He always makes trouble for substitutes," she added. It didn't make me feel any better. I felt oddly defeated as I walked back across the yard and into a quiet, well-ordered class.

At the ten o'clock recess I sought out the principal. He was sorry about what had happened, he said. I was not to worry. He would give the boy work papers in his office. He wouldn't be bothering me again.

But he *was* bothering me. The whole thing bothered me. "I wish I'd known that Gideon gets upset so easily," I said. "I might have handled the situation better if I'd realized he reacts this way to substitutes."

He looked at me and shook his head. "Sometimes he reacts this way to his regular teacher. But you're right. Understanding helps. The thing is . . . we never know if he'll be here or not. He only comes to school when he feels like it." Gideon's mother, he told me, had been married seven times and was currently between husbands. Gideon and his two little sisters were pretty much on their own and were frequently locked out of the house for a day at a time. He took care of them as best he could, but he was only a child himself.

No wonder the boy mumbled, I thought.

"I really don't know how he copes as well as he does," he told me. "He has so much responsibility, and no one to turn to. He has practically nothing he can call his own."

I read his mind. "The little rubber elephants!" I exclaimed.

He nodded. "That's why he flew into such a rage. He thought you were going to smash them."

"*Smash* them?"

"That's what he said. He claims they're all he owns. He seems to live in fear that they'll be destroyed. Oh, yes . . . there's one other thing you should know, Mrs. Donahue. Gideon can't stand to be touched. All of us avoid putting our hands on him . . . it upsets him so."

He could say that again. I opened my mouth to say as much, then stopped. I knew the penalty for hitting a teacher; something had kept me from telling that part of the story. Instead I said something that surprised myself.

"If it's all right with you, I'd like Gideon to come back to class."

He looked at me, surprised. "It would probably be the best thing for him, if you're willing," he nodded.

Gideon arrived soon after recess, entering in the same noisy way. The elephants took their places on his desk. His pencil was broken again. I stood beside him and bent over, being careful to keep my distance. He stared straight ahead. He hadn't looked at me since that scene this morning.

"You're welcome in this class," I said, "but I want you to understand something. I'm not going to take your elephants. They can stay on your desk. But I want you to do your work in class and play with them later."

"They're mine!" was his answer. But he reached for his paper and began to write. I was amazed at his abilities. He whizzed through math with little effort, completed his unfinished morning's work, and was ready for P.E. with the rest of the class. I watched him on the ball field. He was good. With a little more nourishment and a pinch of self-confidence he might be *really* good.

Gideon. Such a strong name for a troubled child. Perhaps, I thought, the Biblical Gideon had once been like a tender twig. Perhaps the Gideon who ran across the field before me had that same chance of becoming a cedar. But he had so very far to go and needed so much help. I remembered how he'd touched those little rubber elephants and looked at them with shining eyes. They were his and no one else's. I wondered if he felt that they touched him back, for no one else could.

We all have known things that bring us comfort, I

thought. Our security blankets, we laughingly call them. We keep them until we need them no longer, then put them aside, when we find our own inner strengths.

"Lord, please touch Gideon," I prayed. "In Your infinite wisdom, find a way to reach past his fears and let him feel a hand of love. In the meantime, Lord, please don't let anyone smash his rubber elephants."

A strange prayer? Perhaps, but God knew what I meant.

Gideon was the last to leave the room that day. I was sure he wasn't too anxious to reach home. Besides, he had to collect his erasers, brush them off and examine them carefully.

"Are they all right?" I asked.

"Yep."

I took a chance. "Do you think you might ever use them?"

He stared at me in disbelief.

"Well, they'd do a good job, you know. They're much better than the little erasers that come on pencils. They'd be just right for wiping away mistakes. Of course, that would be up to you."

He hesitated, obviously trying to find the right words. Gideon was hyperactive, mistreated, hungry, dirty, and often scared. But he was not dense. "Mebbe some day. I dunno. But not today," he told me.

Without thinking, I smiled and put my hand on his shoulder. "Today didn't turn out so bad, did it?"

His face was dead serious. "I'm glad you didn't smash my rubber elephants," he said. Then he was gone. It was some minutes before I realized that I had touched him, and he hadn't cringed.

YOUR SPIRITUAL WORKSHOP

CREATIVE PRAYER FOR OTHERS

You don't have to quit what you are doing to say a prayer.

Do your prayers for other people seem rather feeble? Nine out of 10 people pray weakly, ineffectively, somewhat like a low-grade broadcasting station. By persistent training, however, you can make your prayer-life a radiant, creative force.

Any person can do this through a sense of imagination and discipline. The purpose of this Spiritual Workshop is to challenge you to try some prayer experiments. This prayer will not concern self, but the well-being of others.

Get Out Of Your Prayer Rut

First, be willing to discard or change old habits of prayer. For example, *the position of your body during prayer does not matter*. It is not essential to close or raise your eyes, to kneel or stand, to fold hands or lower head. Some positions are valuable if they relax your mind and body.

Use Those Fragments Of Idle Time

During the day every person wastes dozens of small time segments: in the bath, dressing, walking down stairs, riding or walking to a destination, in an elevator. Such moments can be filled with a prayer 10 seconds to a minute long, or "flash prayers."

When you climb into your automobile and remember that a friend is soon going into surgery, the thought may come, "Lord, be with Janet and guide the doctor's hand." Some people sit in a bus and look around at the other riders. They pick a face that seems discouraged and aim their prayer at the person, saying to themselves several times, "Jesus will help you."

Flashing hard and straight prayers at people in a bus while repeating, "Jesus . . . Jesus . . . Jesus . . ." will sometimes make those near you act as if they had been spoken to. When you do this, it seems that you are pushing these prayers from your breast and fingers, as well as from your brain—from your whole nervous system. After a while the bus, or car, or room, seems gently "excited" like the magnetic field around a magnet.

To skeptics who consider such prayer pointless, remember that if it raises the spirits of a few people on a bus, lifts the atmosphere in a roomful of tense people, or simply changes one person's thinking from negative to positive, then it is *real prayer at work*. And if enough people did it in and about our tense city areas, it might change the whole climate in a neighborhood.

Pray With Pencil And Paper At Hand

Find some time each day for meditation. When God sends a thought, write it down and keep it visible until it can be carried into action. Pray for individuals by name. The clearest thoughts are often written so tersely they snap like a whip. Be sure to record any results of your prayers. A notebook is recommended for this.

Pray While You Read

When reading a newspaper, pause for a second over the name of a world leader, or a man suffering hardship, and whisper, "Lord, this man may be hungry for Thee." If it becomes a habit you soon will be spreading thousands of secret blessings over the world.

Pray While Listening To Music

While sitting quietly listening to music, try this prayer,

"What do You have to say to me now, Lord? Think Your thoughts in my mind. Use me as Your channel to reach the person that needs You now." Believe then that He is using you to reach a son, a daughter, mother, father, a friend, a mate, or an enemy.

Pray While Walking

Walking and exercise can be a very definite aid to prayer. As you walk, talk to Him in the rhythm or cadence of your steps. It is exhilarating to stride into a crowd and "waft prayer" in all directions. This will help strengthen your soul, just as victims of paralysis strengthen their weak muscles by physical exercise.

Pray When Falling Asleep

When people have trouble sleeping at night, they waste endless hours. Try putting these sleepless hours to use. You can do this by simply turning those fragments of thought into prayers for the people who come to mind. For example, "Lord, help the President to realize his need for You . . ." "Lord, be with Jim. . . ."

One man discovered that his nightly prayers for friends and relatives were more effective when he had their photographs all about his room. In the darkness, he would single out one person and shine a flashlight on the picture as he prayed. To his astonishment he received letters from those close friends, written, he learned later, a few moments after his prayer for them.

Pray While You Work

One woman found a new way to pray one day while ironing. She got to thinking about how many lines there were—bus lines, telephone lines, clothes lines, fishing lines. Why not a prayer line? Result: she strung a short rope across one corner of her kitchen and hung cards on it with names of shut-ins, of the sick and the bereaved. As she irons, she prays for these people by name. When friends heard about this, she began to get regular calls, "Hang me on your prayer line, please."

A powerful story of intercessory prayer was told by an alcoholic who was taken to a hospital for psychopathics in

San Diego many years ago. He was placed in a room with three other patients who did nothing but scream. When night came, he prayed to be able to sleep, but the screams continued.

Then suddenly he began to pray for his three roommates, "May God give you peace," he said quietly over and over. The screams stopped. "Not only that," the alcoholic reported later, "it was as if something broke in me. Praying for them released my own tension. I was free."

As it happened, at the next examination the doctor smiled and pronounced him well enough to go home. He was truly a free man.

When you have a sense of creative spontaneity in your love for God and people, you will find that your prayers not only become a kind of adventure but also increase tenfold in power.